BRISSON · CHRISTMAS · CHANKHAMMA

SHELTERED

A PRE-APOCALYPTIC TALE

CO-CREATED AND ILLUSTRATED BY
JOHNNIE CHRISTMAS

CO-CREATED, WRITTEN AND LETTERED BY
ED BRISSON

COLORED BY
SHARI CHANKHAMMA

EDITED BY
PAUL ALLOR

IMAGE COMICS, INC.
Robert Kirkman - Chief Operating Officer
Erik Larsen - Chief Financial Officer
Todd McFarlane - President
Marc Silvestri - Chief Executive Officer
Jim Valentino - Vice-President

Eric Stephenson - Publisher
Ron Richards - Director of Business Development
Jennifer de Guzman - Director of Trade Book Sales
Kat Salazar - PR & Marketing Coordinator
Jeremy Sullivan - Digital Marketing Coordinator
Jamie Parreno - Online Marketing Coordinator
Emilio Bautista - Sales Assistant
Branwyn Bigglestone - Senior Accounts Manager
Emily Miller - Accounts Manager
Jaemie Dudas - Administrative Assistant
Tyler Shainline - Events Coordinator
David Brothers - Content Manager
Jonathan Chan - Production Manager
Drew Gill - Art Director
Meredith Wallace - Print Manager
Monica Garcia - Senior Production Artist
Vincent Kukua - Production Artist
Jenna Savage - Production Artist
Addison Duke - Production Artist
IMAGECOMICS.COM

DEDICATIONS

JOHNNIE

For Analia.

I'd like to give a giant, heartfelt "thank you" to my families: Christmas, Pereda, Kusmin, Pici, Karamanian, Johnson/Ogawa

I'd also like to acknowledge the immeasurable wisdom and support of Corrie Pond, Lisa Jackson, Thea Jardine, Lisa Alexander, Sarah Lipsett and Bunn Junior Leonard.

And thanks to Eric Stephenson and everyone at Image Comics.

ED

Thanks to everyone who's picked up this book, talked about it, recommended it and passed a copy to a friend. I'm doing what I've always wanted to do and wouldn't be here without readers like you.

Thanks to Janet for her unwavering support.

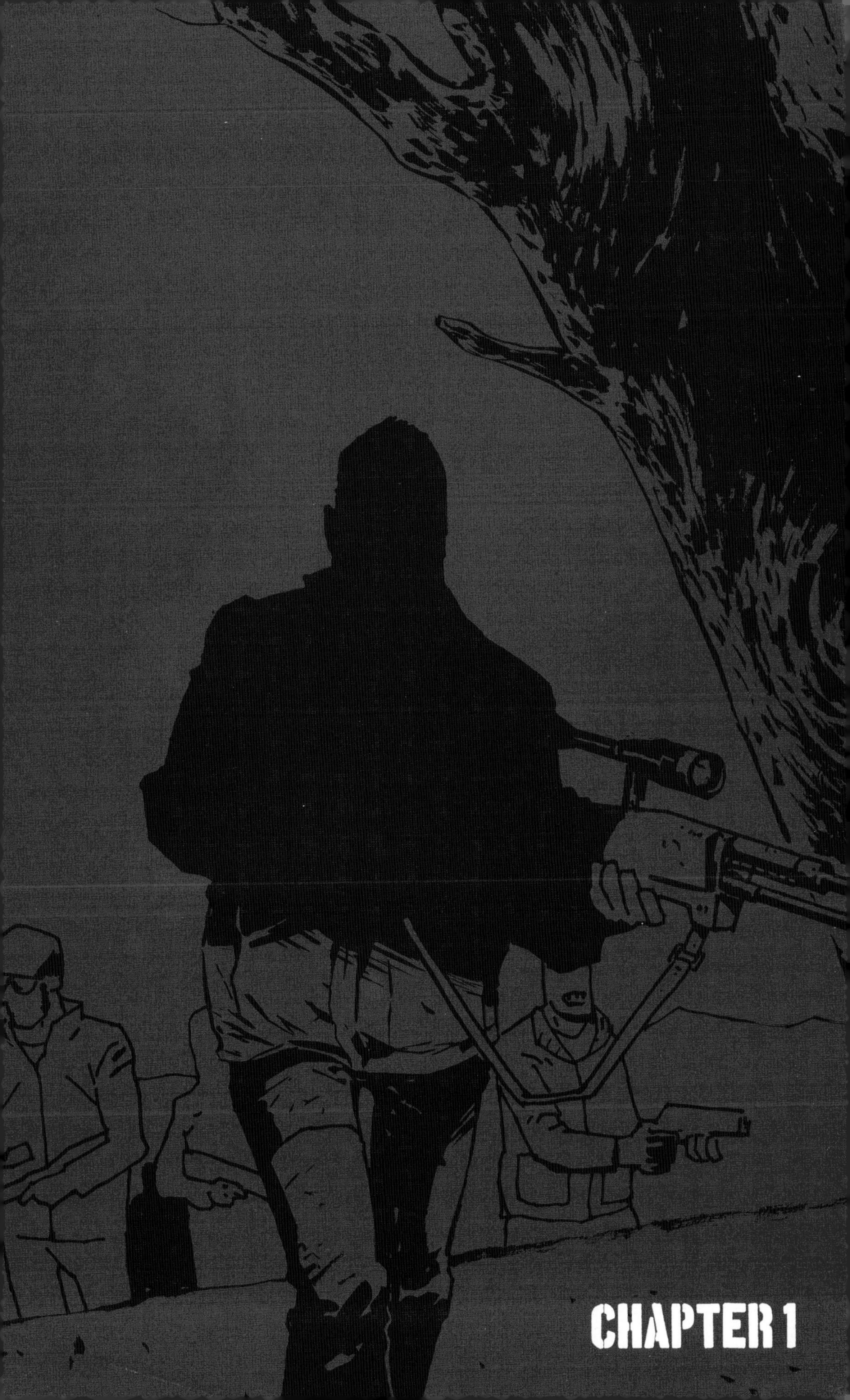
CHAPTER 1

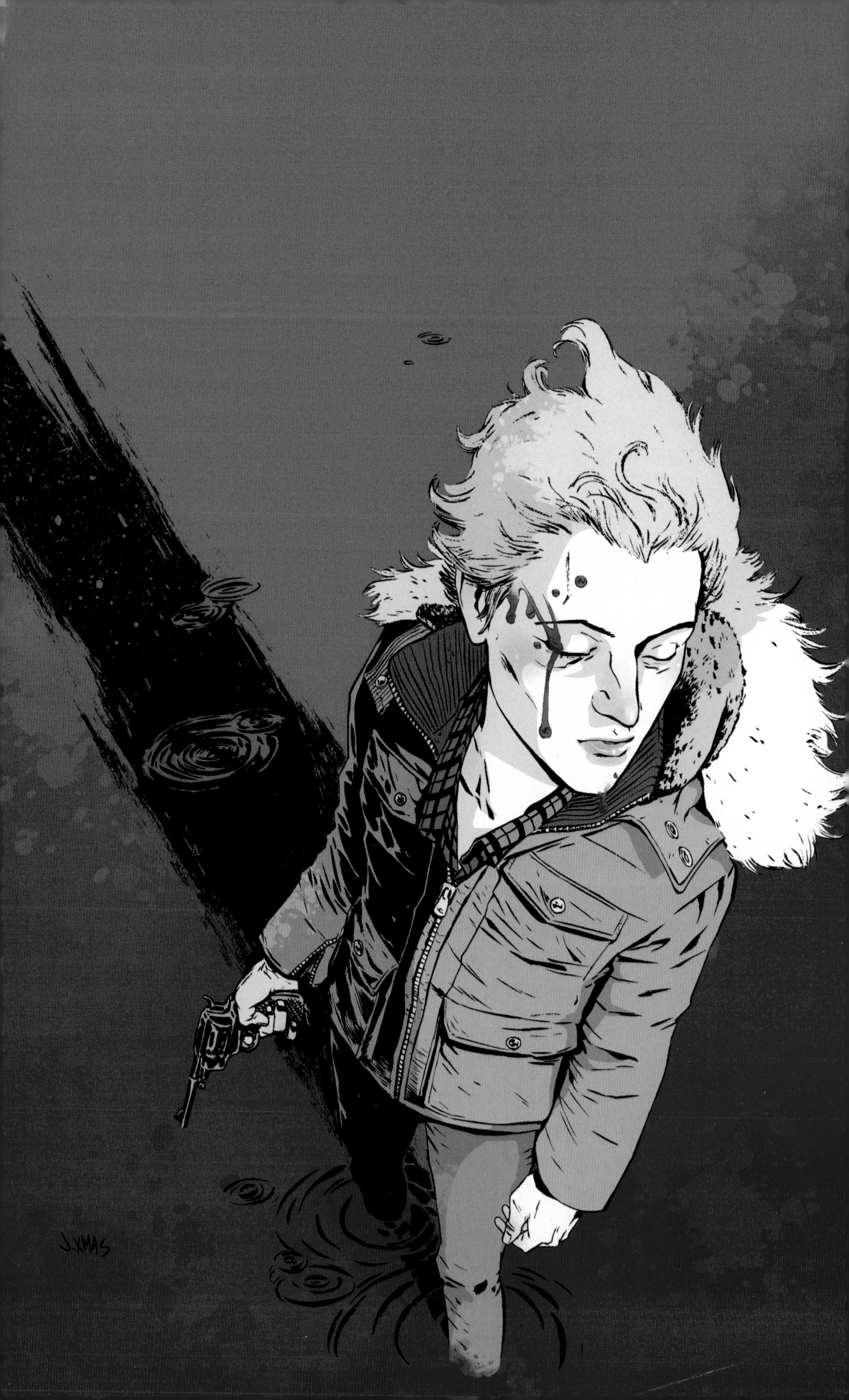
J.XMAS

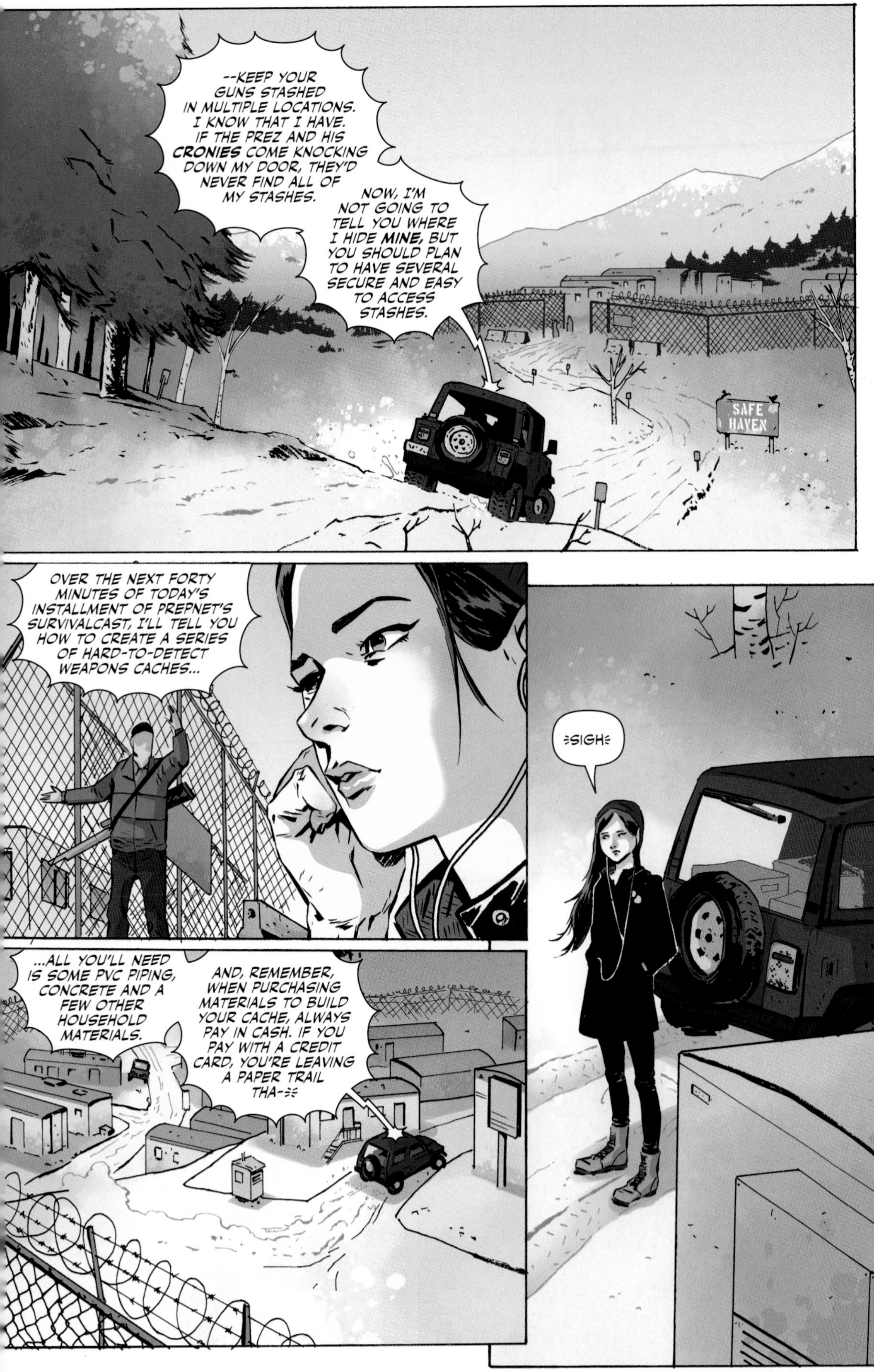
--KEEP YOUR GUNS STASHED IN MULTIPLE LOCATIONS. I KNOW THAT I HAVE. IF THE PREZ AND HIS CRONIES COME KNOCKING DOWN MY DOOR, THEY'D NEVER FIND ALL OF MY STASHES.
NOW, I'M NOT GOING TO TELL YOU WHERE I HIDE MINE, BUT YOU SHOULD PLAN TO HAVE SEVERAL SECURE AND EASY TO ACCESS STASHES.
SAFE HAVEN
OVER THE NEXT FORTY MINUTES OF TODAY'S INSTALLMENT OF PREPNET'S SURVIVALCAST, I'LL TELL YOU HOW TO CREATE A SERIES OF HARD-TO-DETECT WEAPONS CACHES...
SIGH
...ALL YOU'LL NEED IS SOME PVC PIPING, CONCRETE AND A FEW OTHER HOUSEHOLD MATERIALS.
AND, REMEMBER, WHEN PURCHASING MATERIALS TO BUILD YOUR CACHE, ALWAYS PAY IN CASH. IF YOU PAY WITH A CREDIT CARD, YOU'RE LEAVING A PAPER TRAIL THA-

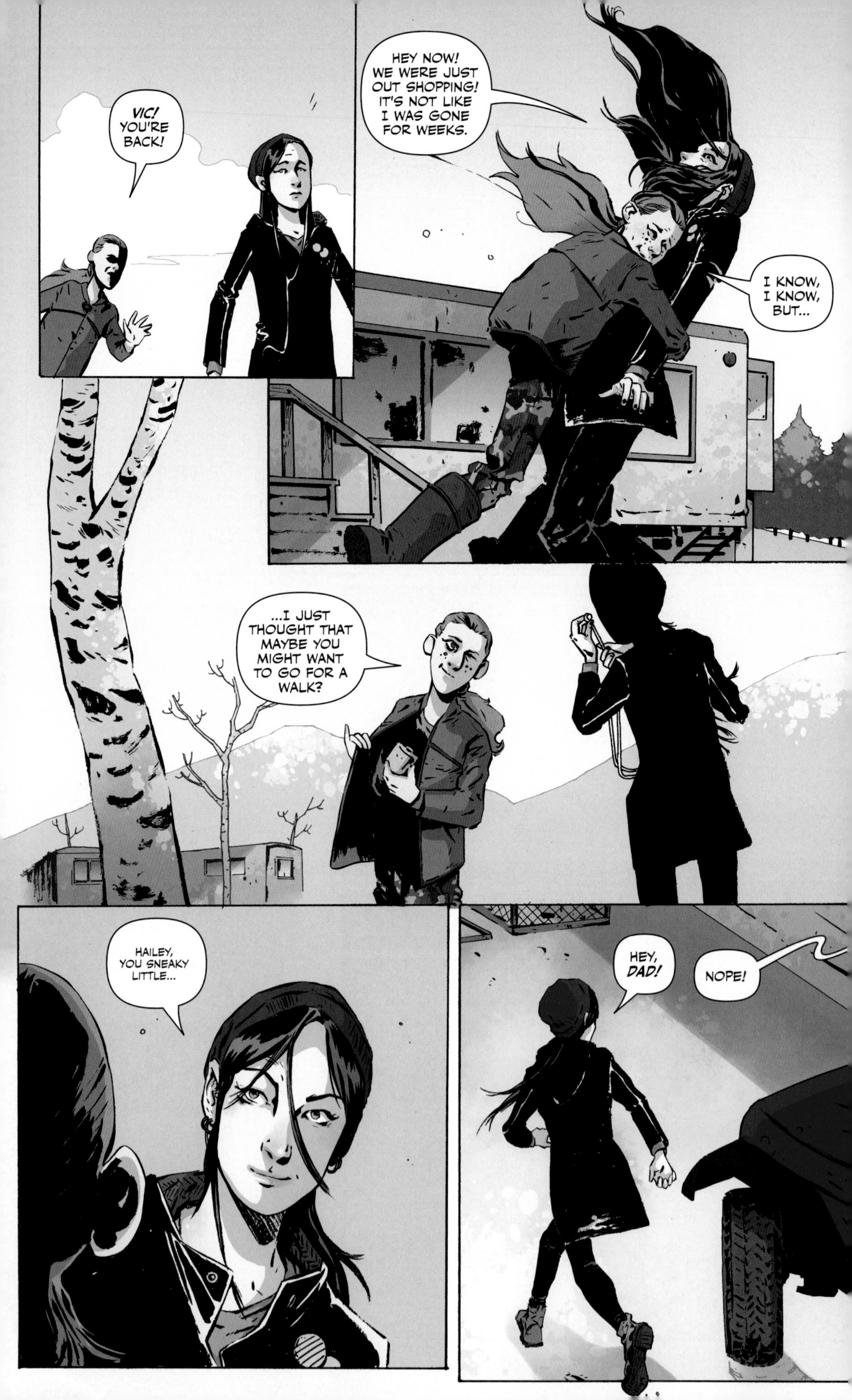
VIC! YOU'RE BACK!
HEY NOW! WE WERE JUST OUT SHOPPING! IT'S NOT LIKE I WAS GONE FOR WEEKS.
I KNOW, I KNOW, BUT...
...I JUST THOUGHT THAT MAYBE YOU MIGHT WANT TO GO FOR A WALK?
HAILEY, YOU SNEAKY LITTLE...
HEY, DAD!
NOPE!

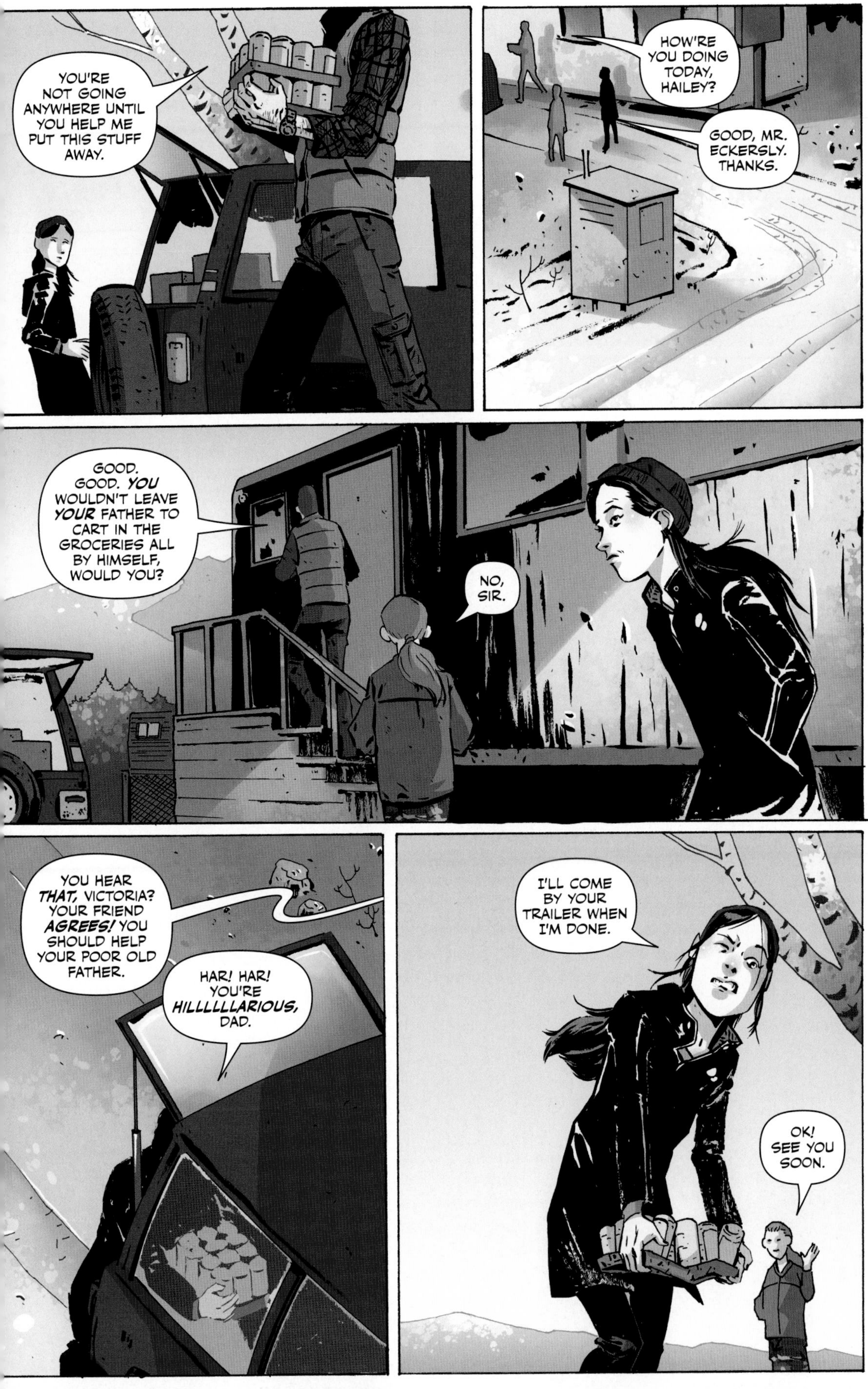
YOU'RE NOT GOING ANYWHERE UNTIL YOU HELP ME PUT THIS STUFF AWAY.
HOW'RE YOU DOING TODAY, HAILEY?
GOOD, MR. ECKERSLY. THANKS.
GOOD. GOOD. YOU WOULDN'T LEAVE YOUR FATHER TO CART IN THE GROCERIES ALL BY HIMSELF, WOULD YOU?
NO, SIR.
YOU HEAR THAT, VICTORIA? YOUR FRIEND AGREES! YOU SHOULD HELP YOUR POOR OLD FATHER.
HAR! HAR! YOU'RE HILLLLLLARIOUS, DAD.
I'LL COME BY YOUR TRAILER WHEN I'M DONE.
OK! SEE YOU SOON.

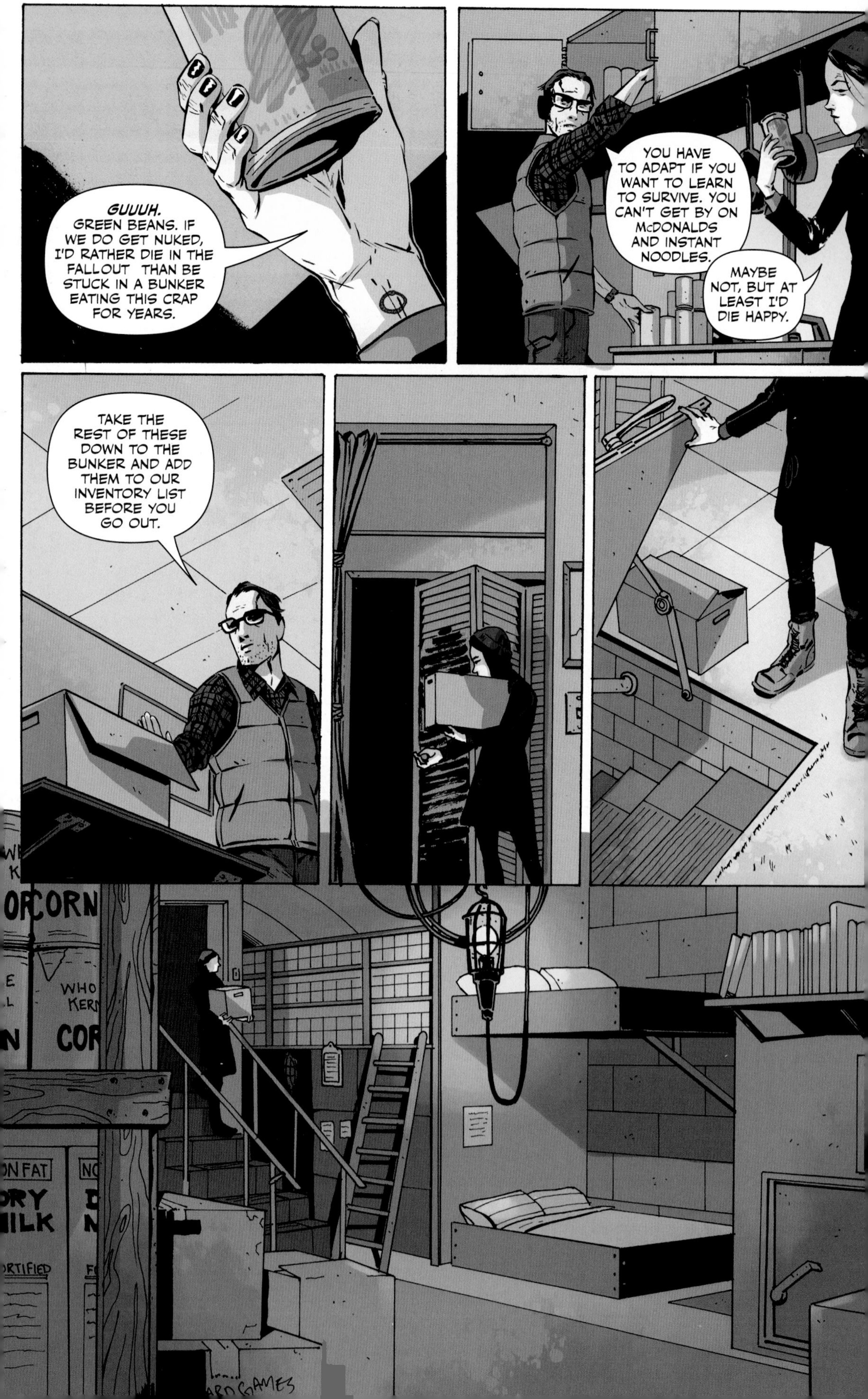
GUUUH. GREEN BEANS. IF WE DO GET NUKED, I'D RATHER DIE IN THE FALLOUT THAN BE STUCK IN A BUNKER EATING THIS CRAP FOR YEARS.
YOU HAVE TO ADAPT IF YOU WANT TO LEARN TO SURVIVE. YOU CAN'T GET BY ON McDONALDS AND INSTANT NOODLES.
MAYBE NOT, BUT AT LEAST I'D DIE HAPPY.
TAKE THE REST OF THESE DOWN TO THE BUNKER AND ADD THEM TO OUR INVENTORY LIST BEFORE YOU GO OUT.

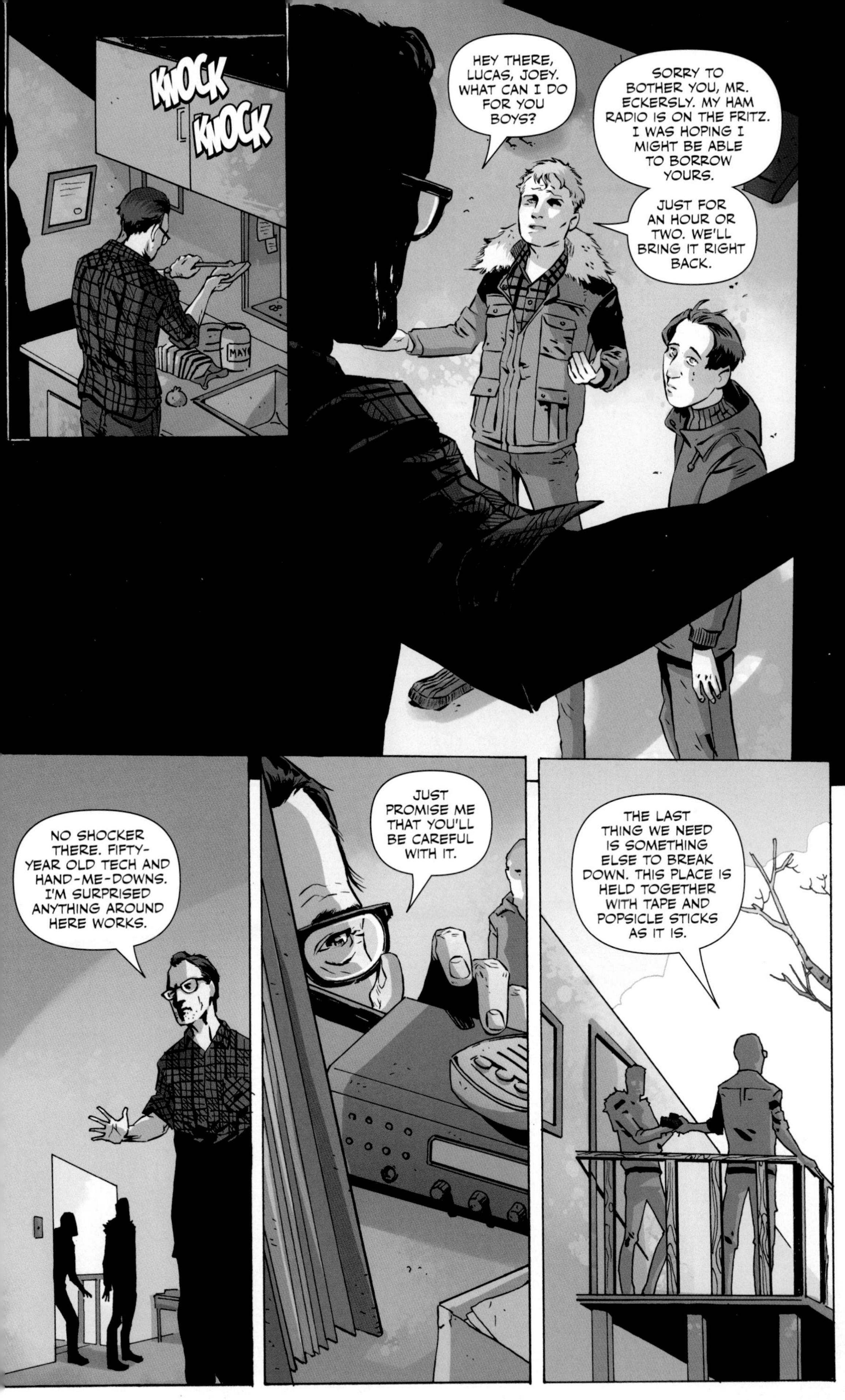
KNOCK
KNOCK
HEY THERE, LUCAS, JOEY. WHAT CAN I DO FOR YOU BOYS?
SORRY TO BOTHER YOU, MR. ECKERSLY. MY HAM RADIO IS ON THE FRITZ. I WAS HOPING I MIGHT BE ABLE TO BORROW YOURS.
JUST FOR AN HOUR OR TWO. WE'LL BRING IT RIGHT BACK.
NO SHOCKER THERE. FIFTY-YEAR OLD TECH AND HAND-ME-DOWNS. I'M SURPRISED ANYTHING AROUND HERE WORKS.
JUST PROMISE ME THAT YOU'LL BE CAREFUL WITH IT.
THE LAST THING WE NEED IS SOMETHING ELSE TO BREAK DOWN. THIS PLACE IS HELD TOGETHER WITH TAPE AND POPSICLE STICKS AS IT IS.

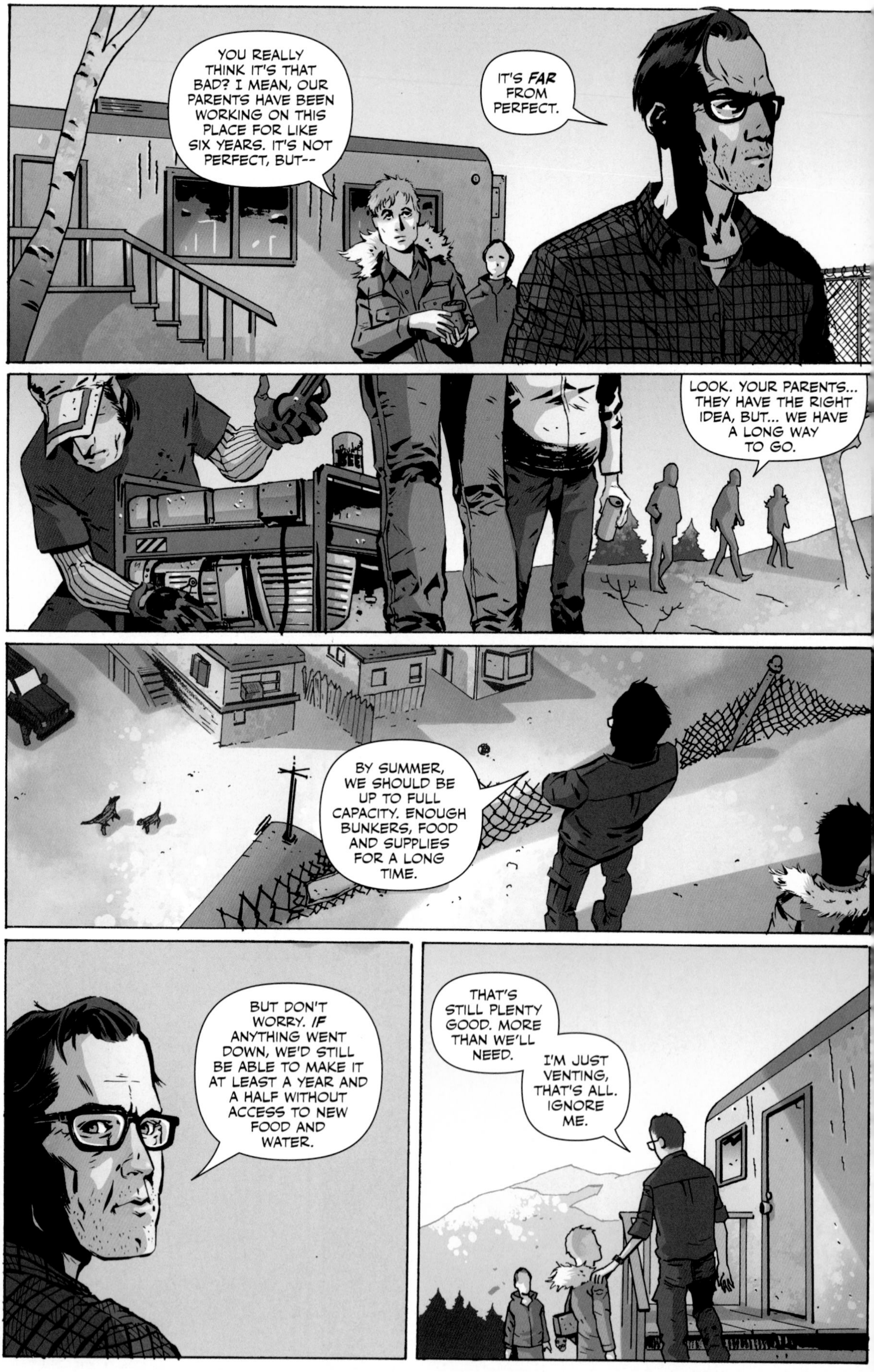
YOU REALLY THINK IT'S THAT BAD? I MEAN, OUR PARENTS HAVE BEEN WORKING ON THIS PLACE FOR LIKE SIX YEARS. IT'S NOT PERFECT, BUT--
IT'S *FAR* FROM PERFECT.
LOOK. YOUR PARENTS... THEY HAVE THE RIGHT IDEA, BUT... WE HAVE A LONG WAY TO GO.
BY SUMMER, WE SHOULD BE UP TO FULL CAPACITY. ENOUGH BUNKERS, FOOD AND SUPPLIES FOR A LONG TIME.
BUT DON'T WORRY. *IF* ANYTHING WENT DOWN, WE'D STILL BE ABLE TO MAKE IT AT LEAST A YEAR AND A HALF WITHOUT ACCESS TO NEW FOOD AND WATER.
THAT'S STILL PLENTY GOOD. MORE THAN WE'LL NEED.
I'M JUST VENTING, THAT'S ALL. IGNORE ME.

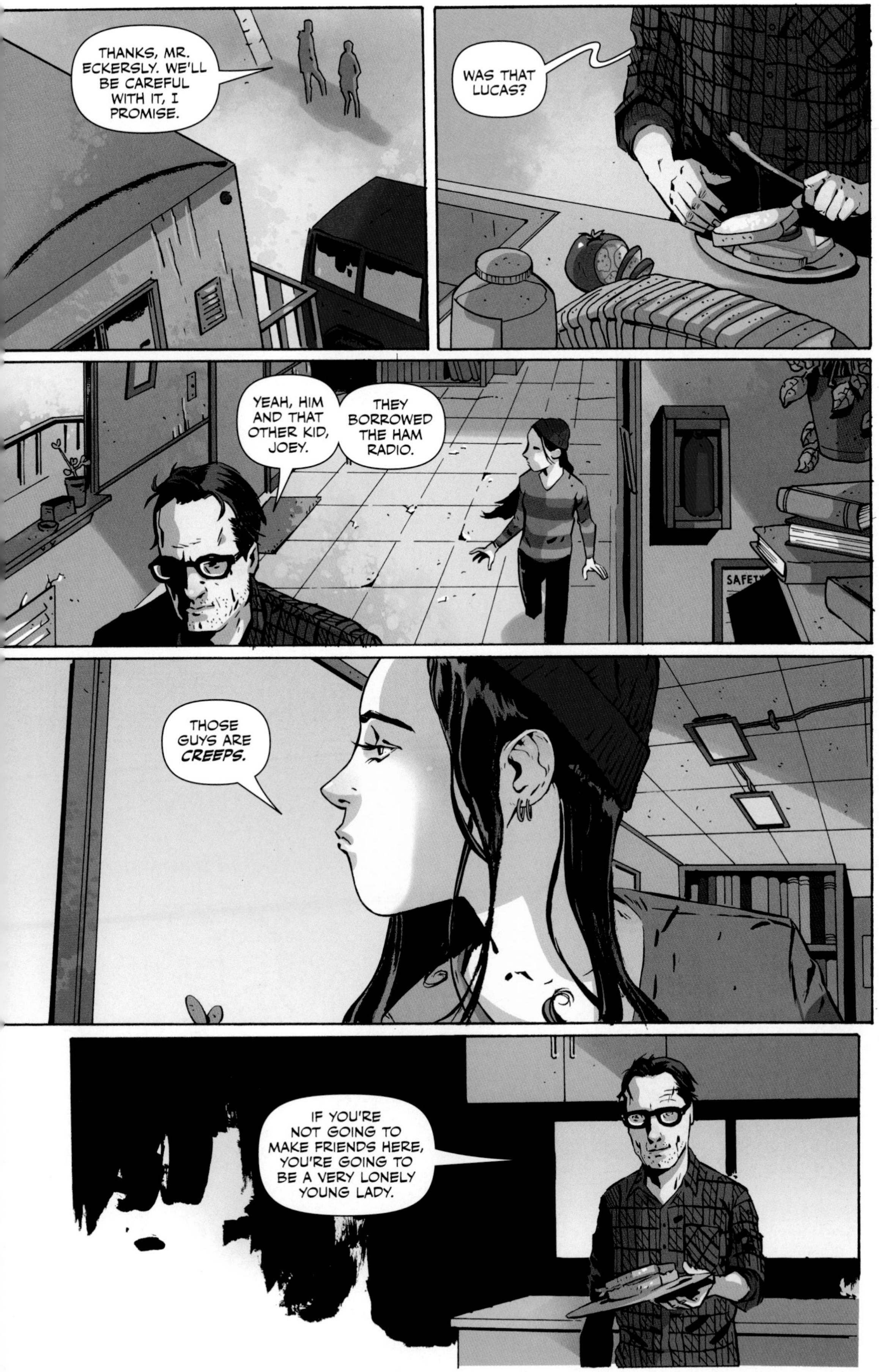
THANKS, MR. ECKERSLY. WE'LL BE CAREFUL WITH IT, I PROMISE.
WAS THAT LUCAS?
YEAH, HIM AND THAT OTHER KID, JOEY.
THEY BORROWED THE HAM RADIO.
SAFET
THOSE GUYS ARE *CREEPS.*
IF YOU'RE NOT GOING TO MAKE FRIENDS HERE, YOU'RE GOING TO BE A VERY LONELY YOUNG LADY.

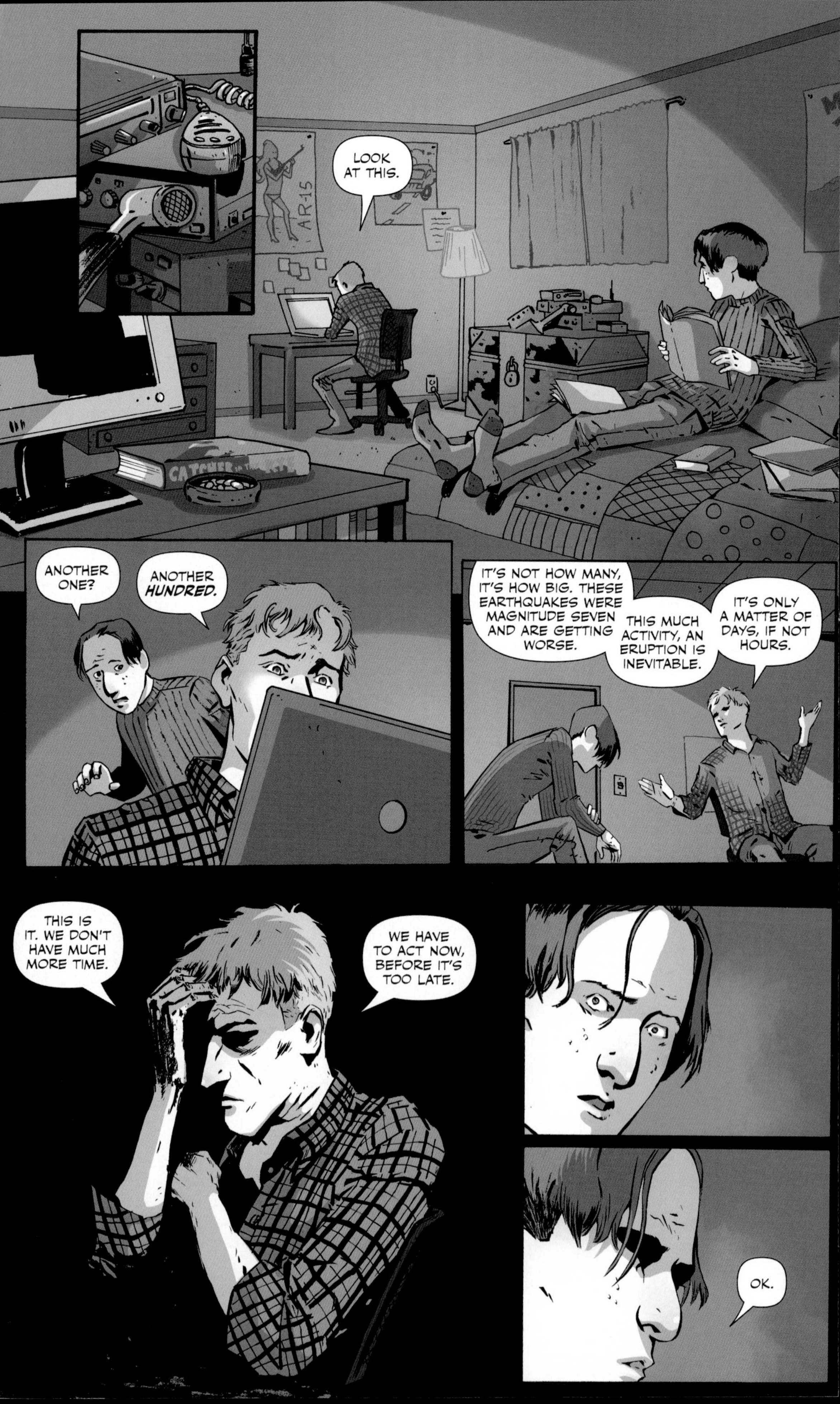

LOOK AT THIS.
AR-15
CATCHER
ANOTHER ONE?
ANOTHER *HUNDRED.*
IT'S NOT HOW MANY, IT'S HOW BIG. THESE EARTHQUAKES WERE MAGNITUDE SEVEN AND ARE GETTING WORSE.
THIS MUCH ACTIVITY, AN ERUPTION IS INEVITABLE.
IT'S ONLY A MATTER OF DAYS, IF NOT HOURS.
THIS IS IT. WE DON'T HAVE MUCH MORE TIME.
WE HAVE TO ACT NOW, BEFORE IT'S TOO LATE.
OK.

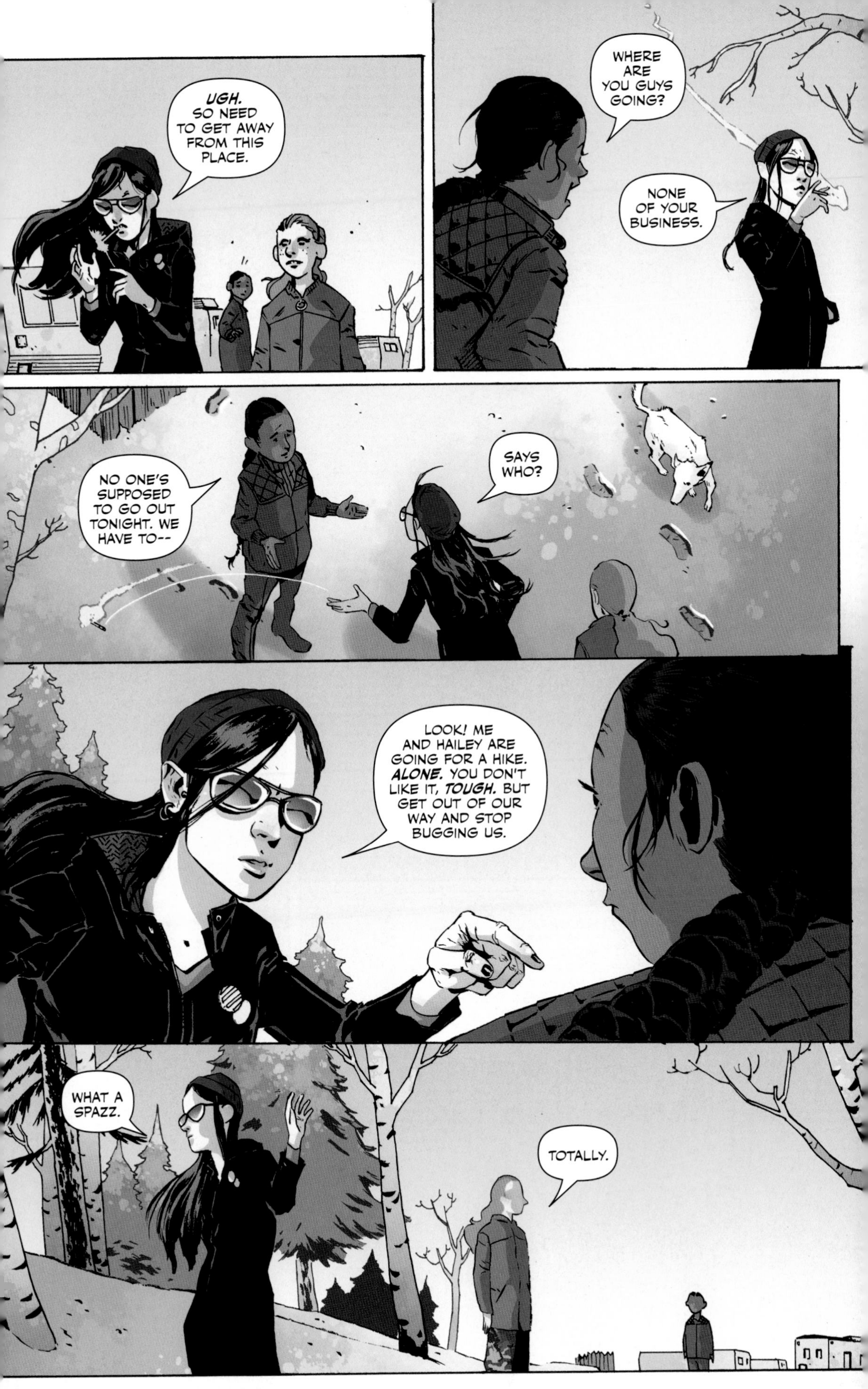

UGH. SO NEED TO GET AWAY FROM THIS PLACE.
WHERE ARE YOU GUYS GOING?
NONE OF YOUR BUSINESS.
NO ONE'S SUPPOSED TO GO OUT TONIGHT. WE HAVE TO--
SAYS WHO?
LOOK! ME AND HAILEY ARE GOING FOR A HIKE. ALONE. YOU DON'T LIKE IT, TOUGH. BUT GET OUT OF OUR WAY AND STOP BUGGING US.
WHAT A SPAZZ.
TOTALLY.

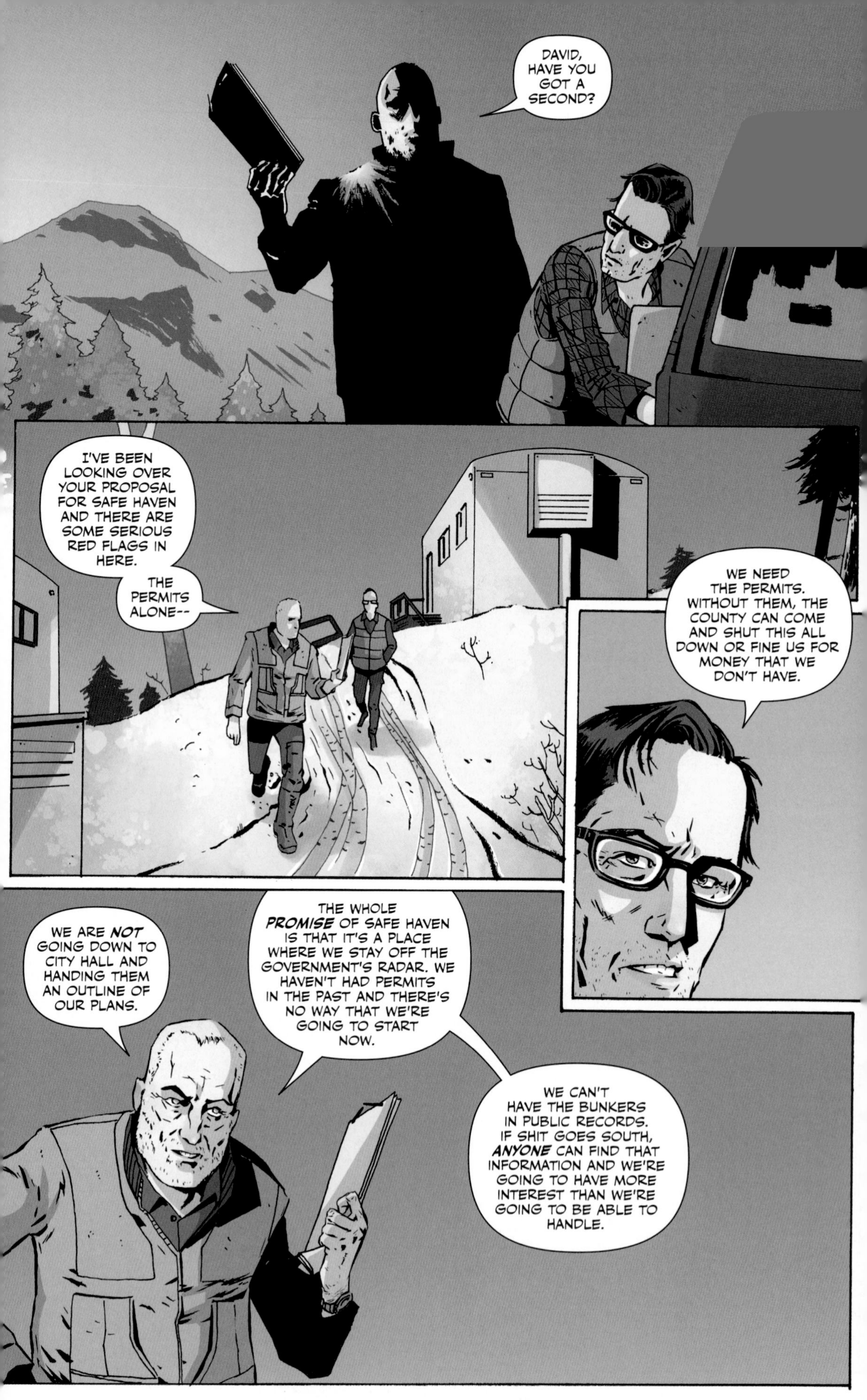

DAVID, HAVE YOU GOT A SECOND?
I'VE BEEN LOOKING OVER YOUR PROPOSAL FOR SAFE HAVEN AND THERE ARE SOME SERIOUS RED FLAGS IN HERE.
THE PERMITS ALONE--
WE NEED THE PERMITS. WITHOUT THEM, THE COUNTY CAN COME AND SHUT THIS ALL DOWN OR FINE US FOR MONEY THAT WE DON'T HAVE.
WE ARE *NOT* GOING DOWN TO CITY HALL AND HANDING THEM AN OUTLINE OF OUR PLANS.
THE WHOLE *PROMISE* OF SAFE HAVEN IS THAT IT'S A PLACE WHERE WE STAY OFF THE GOVERNMENT'S RADAR. WE HAVEN'T HAD PERMITS IN THE PAST AND THERE'S NO WAY THAT WE'RE GOING TO START NOW.
WE CAN'T HAVE THE BUNKERS IN PUBLIC RECORDS. IF SHIT GOES SOUTH, *ANYONE* CAN FIND THAT INFORMATION AND WE'RE GOING TO HAVE MORE INTEREST THAN WE'RE GOING TO BE ABLE TO HANDLE.

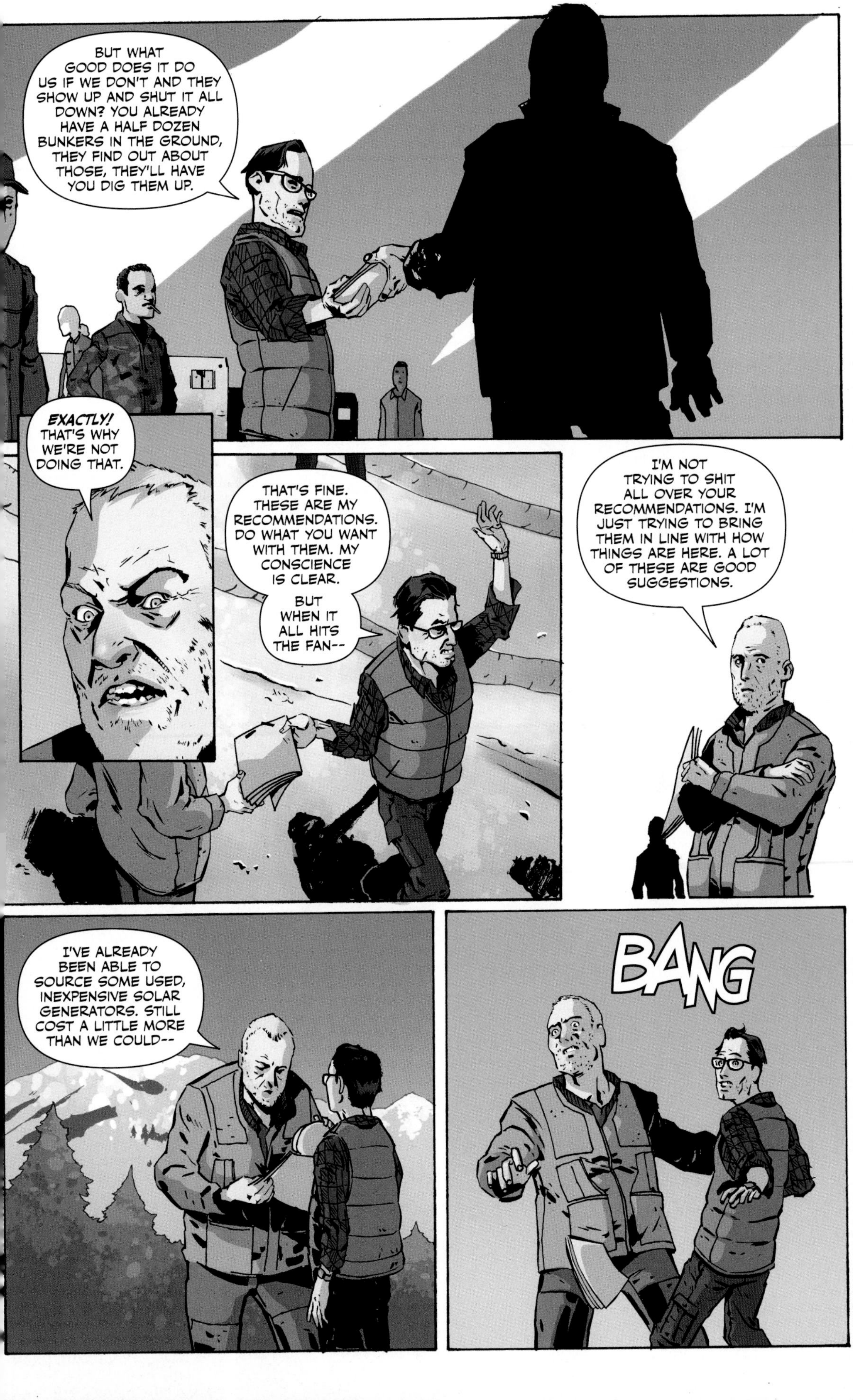
BUT WHAT GOOD DOES IT DO US IF WE DON'T AND THEY SHOW UP AND SHUT IT ALL DOWN? YOU ALREADY HAVE A HALF DOZEN BUNKERS IN THE GROUND, THEY FIND OUT ABOUT THOSE, THEY'LL HAVE YOU DIG THEM UP.
EXACTLY! THAT'S WHY WE'RE NOT DOING THAT.
THAT'S FINE. THESE ARE MY RECOMMENDATIONS. DO WHAT YOU WANT WITH THEM. MY CONSCIENCE IS CLEAR.
BUT WHEN IT ALL HITS THE FAN--
I'M NOT TRYING TO SHIT ALL OVER YOUR RECOMMENDATIONS. I'M JUST TRYING TO BRING THEM IN LINE WITH HOW THINGS ARE HERE. A LOT OF THESE ARE GOOD SUGGESTIONS.
I'VE ALREADY BEEN ABLE TO SOURCE SOME USED, INEXPENSIVE SOLAR GENERATORS. STILL COST A LITTLE MORE THAN WE COULD--
BANG

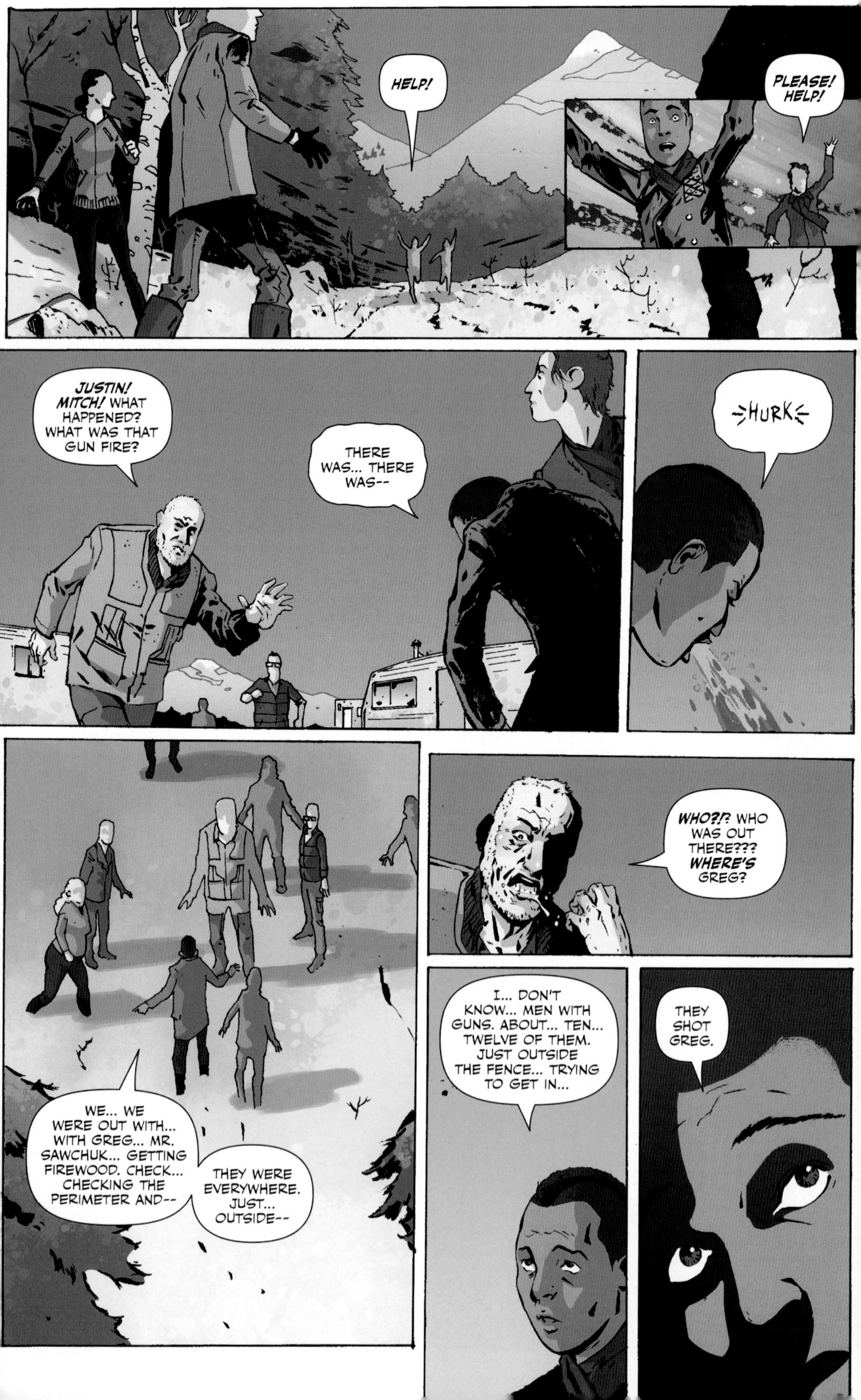
HELP!
PLEASE! HELP!
JUSTIN! MITCH! WHAT HAPPENED? WHAT WAS THAT GUN FIRE?
THERE WAS... THERE WAS--
HURK
WE... WE WERE OUT WITH... WITH GREG... MR. SAWCHUK... GETTING FIREWOOD. CHECK... CHECKING THE PERIMETER AND--
THEY WERE EVERYWHERE. JUST... OUTSIDE--
WHO?!? WHO WAS OUT THERE??? WHERE'S GREG?
I... DON'T KNOW... MEN WITH GUNS. ABOUT... TEN... TWELVE OF THEM. JUST OUTSIDE THE FENCE... TRYING TO GET IN...
THEY SHOT GREG.

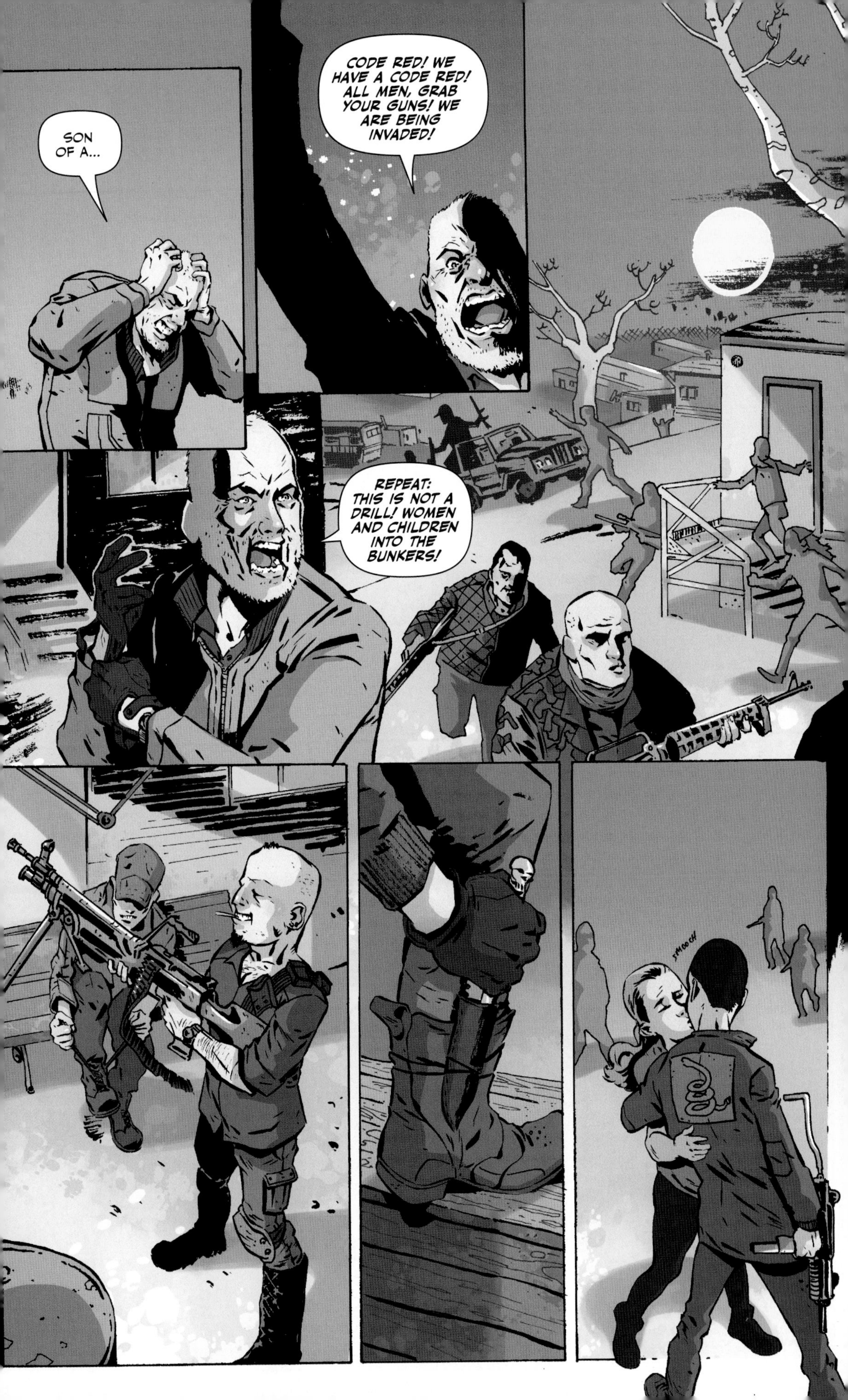
SON OF A...
CODE RED! WE HAVE A CODE RED! ALL MEN, GRAB YOUR GUNS! WE ARE BEING INVADED!
REPEAT: THIS IS NOT A DRILL! WOMEN AND CHILDREN INTO THE BUNKERS!
SMOOCH

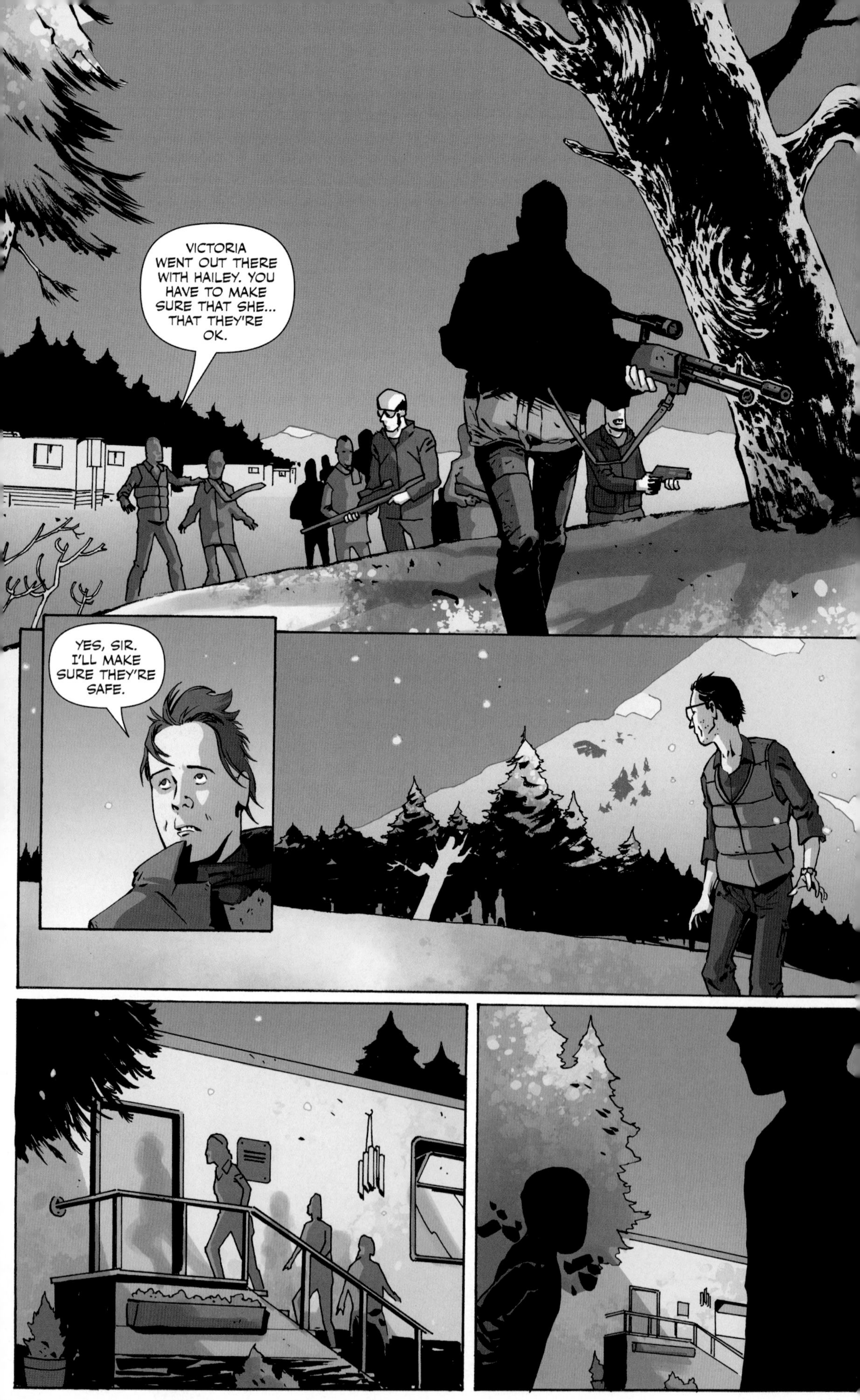
VICTORIA WENT OUT THERE WITH HAILEY. YOU HAVE TO MAKE SURE THAT SHE... THAT THEY'RE OK.
YES, SIR. I'LL MAKE SURE THEY'RE SAFE.

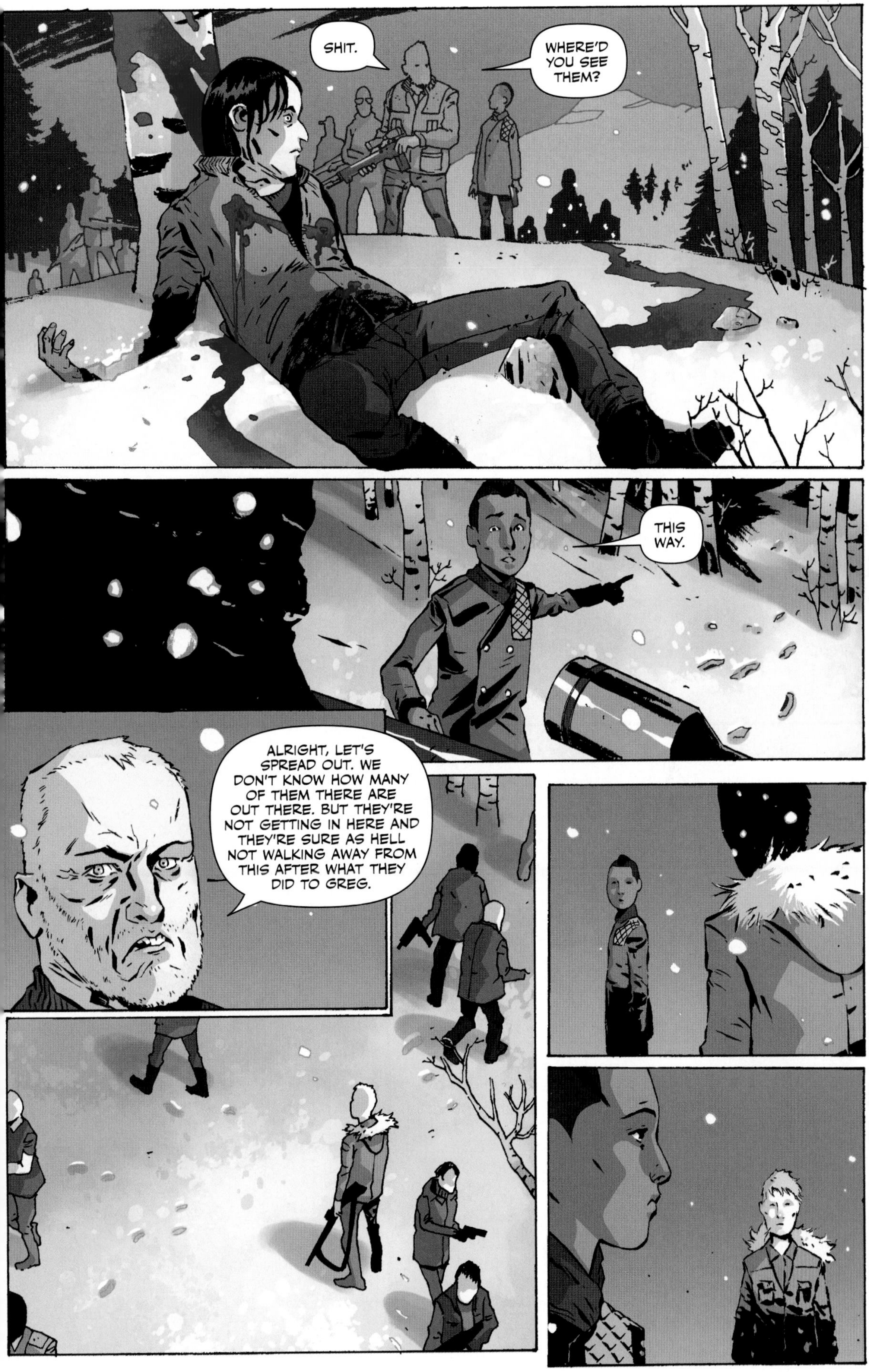
SHIT.
WHERE'D YOU SEE THEM?
THIS WAY.
ALRIGHT, LET'S SPREAD OUT. WE DON'T KNOW HOW MANY OF THEM THERE ARE OUT THERE. BUT THEY'RE NOT GETTING IN HERE AND THEY'RE SURE AS HELL NOT WALKING AWAY FROM THIS AFTER WHAT THEY DID TO GREG.

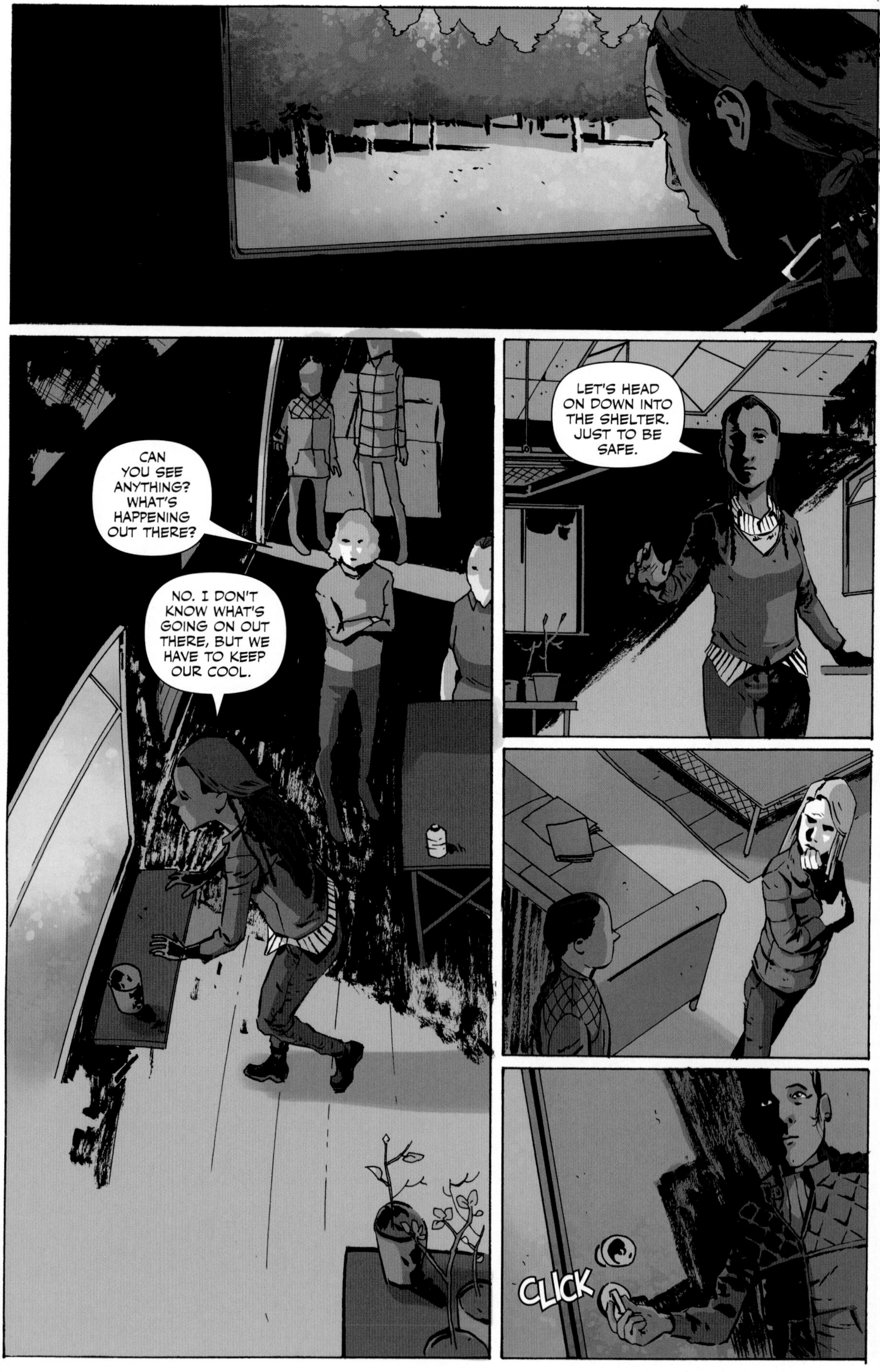
CAN YOU SEE ANYTHING? WHAT'S HAPPENING OUT THERE?
NO. I DON'T KNOW WHAT'S GOING ON OUT THERE, BUT WE HAVE TO KEEP OUR COOL.
LET'S HEAD ON DOWN INTO THE SHELTER. JUST TO BE SAFE.
CLICK

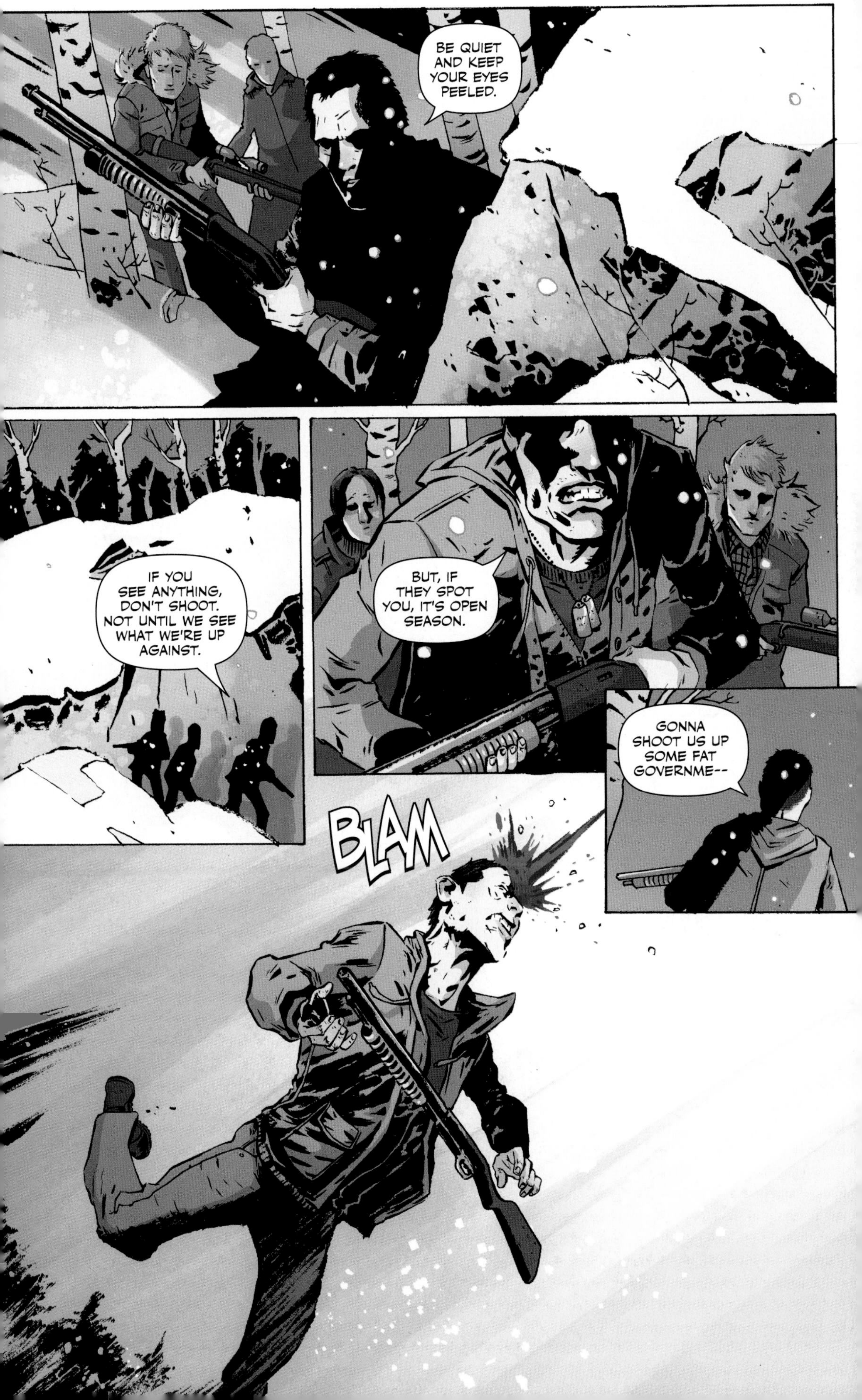

BE QUIET AND KEEP YOUR EYES PEELED.
IF YOU SEE ANYTHING, DON'T SHOOT. NOT UNTIL WE SEE WHAT WE'RE UP AGAINST.
BUT, IF THEY SPOT YOU, IT'S OPEN SEASON.
GONNA SHOOT US UP SOME FAT GOVERNME--
BLAM

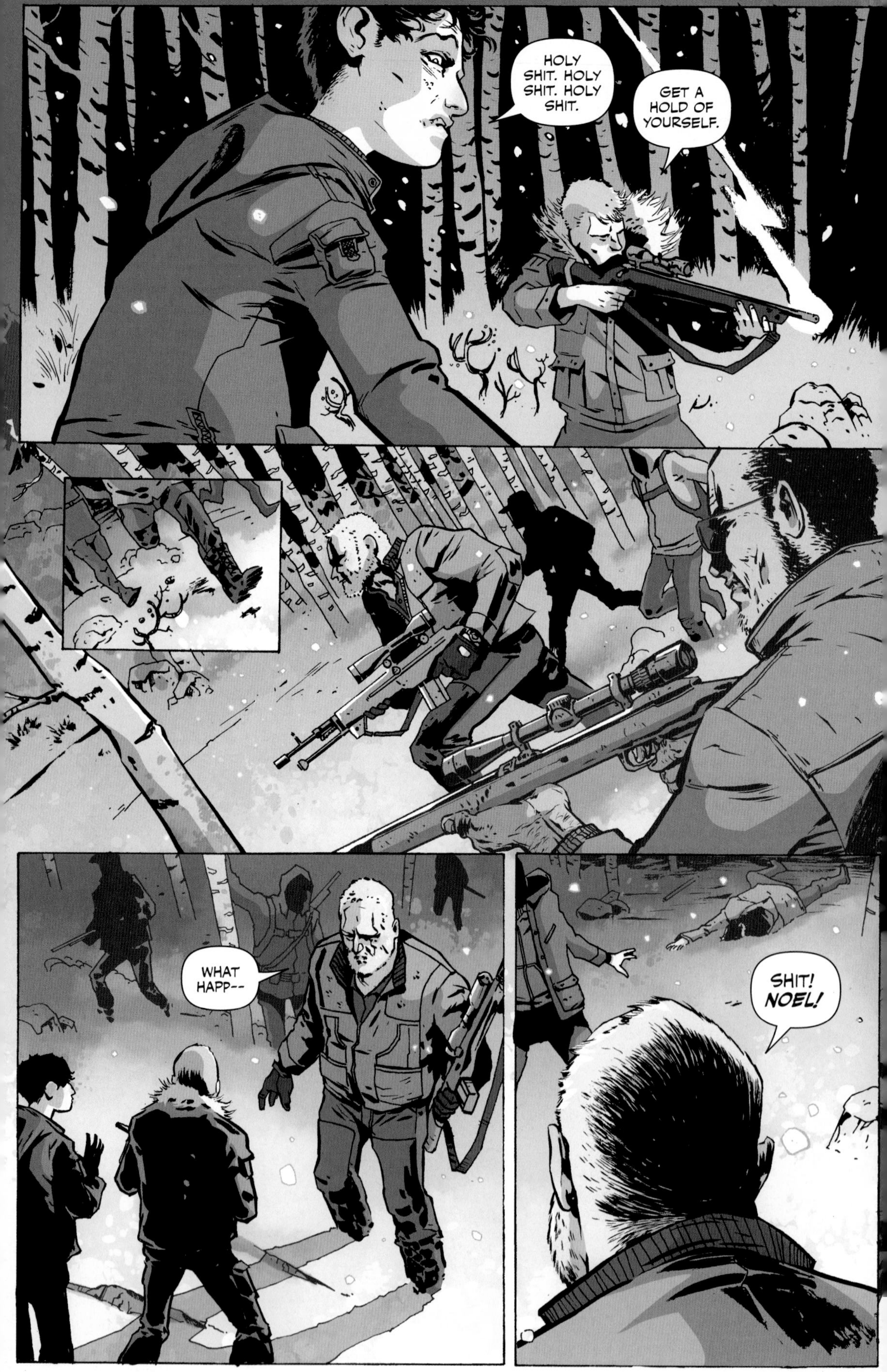
HOLY SHIT. HOLY SHIT. HOLY SHIT.
GET A HOLD OF YOURSELF.
WHAT HAPP--
SHIT! NOEL!

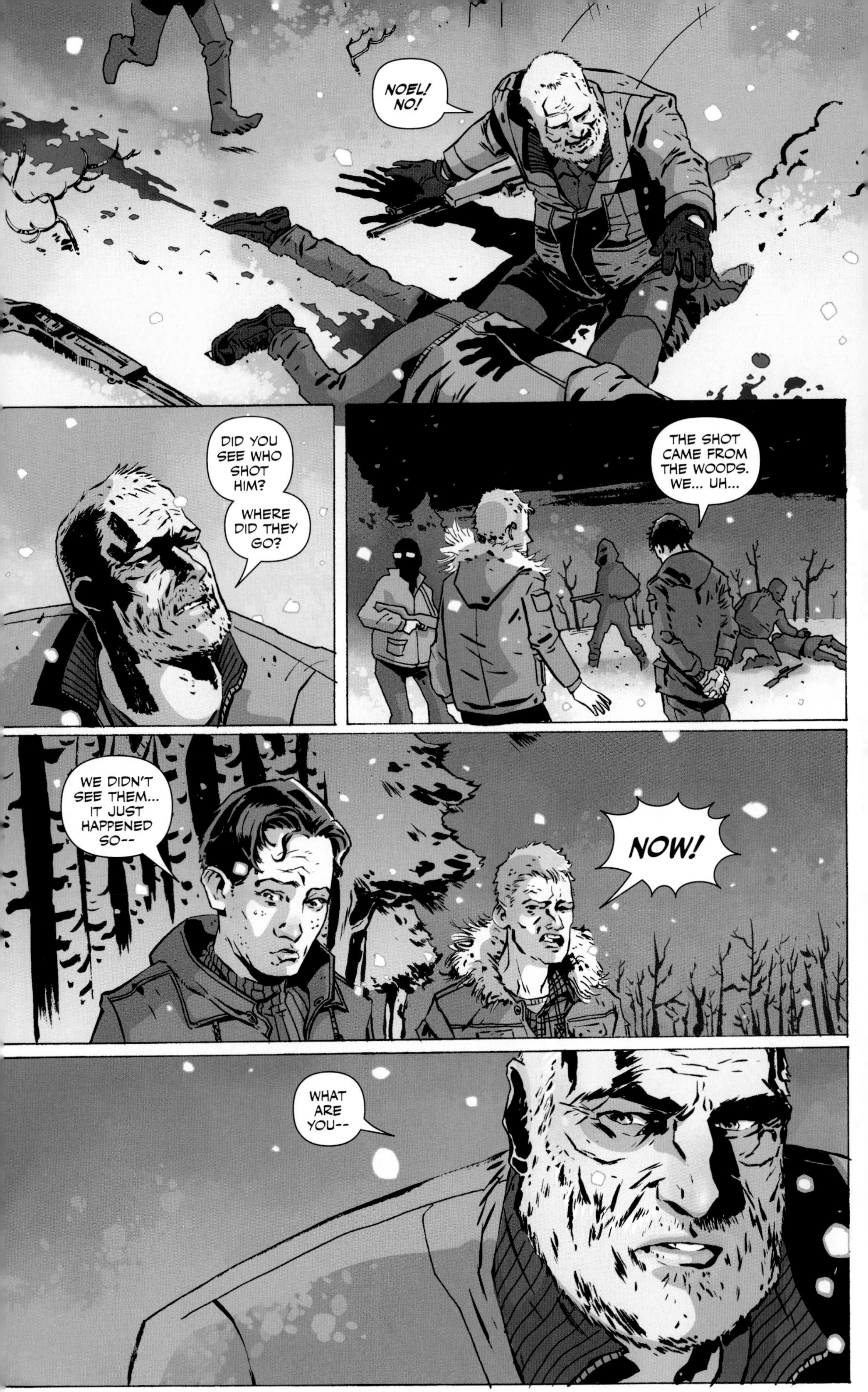
NOEL! NO!
DID YOU SEE WHO SHOT HIM?
WHERE DID THEY GO?
THE SHOT CAME FROM THE WOODS. WE... UH...
WE DIDN'T SEE THEM... IT JUST HAPPENED SO--
NOW!
WHAT ARE YOU--

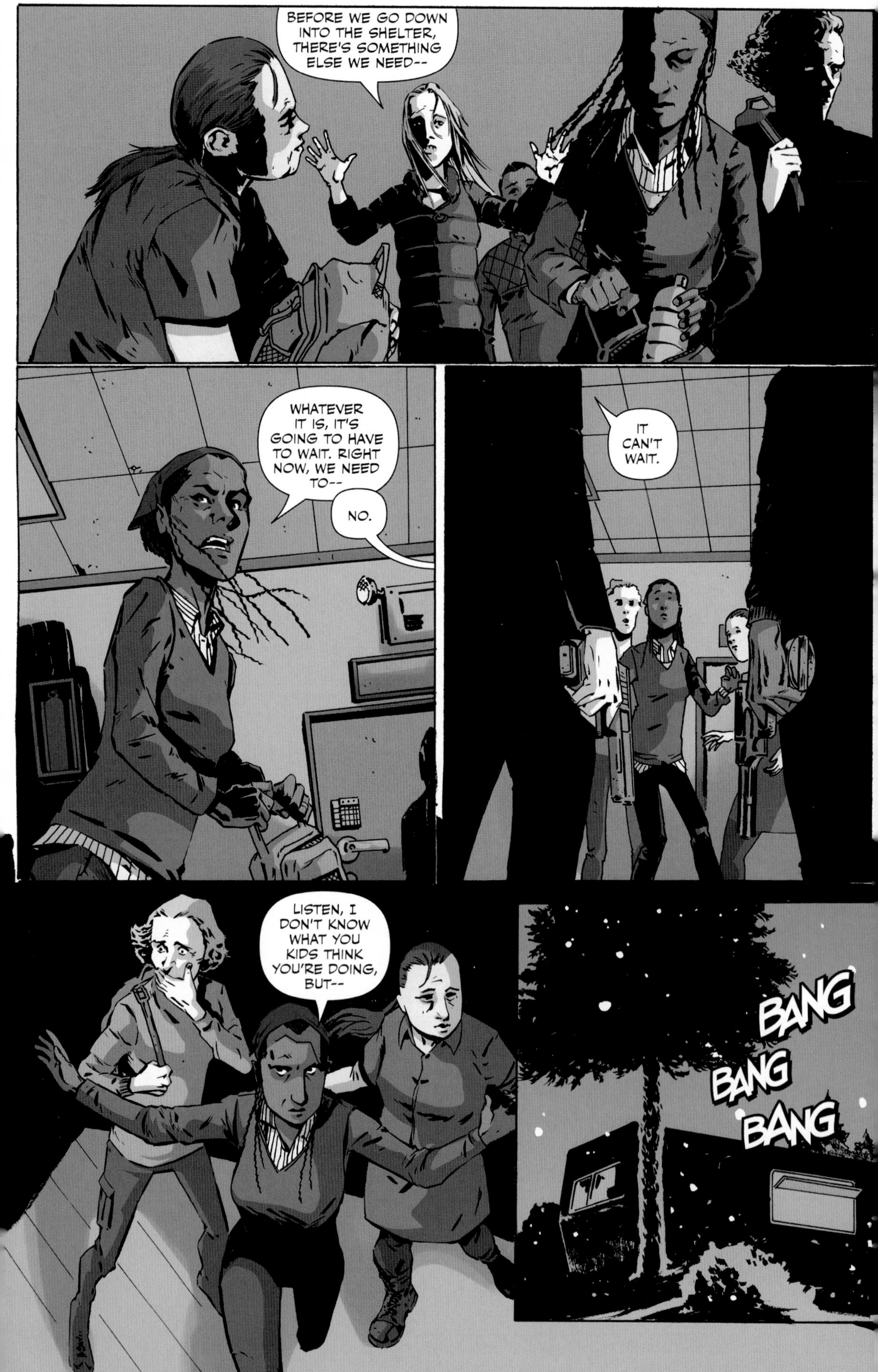
BEFORE WE GO DOWN INTO THE SHELTER, THERE'S SOMETHING ELSE WE NEED--
WHATEVER IT IS, IT'S GOING TO HAVE TO WAIT. RIGHT NOW, WE NEED TO--
NO.
IT CAN'T WAIT.
LISTEN, I DON'T KNOW WHAT YOU KIDS THINK YOU'RE DOING, BUT--
BANG
BANG
BANG

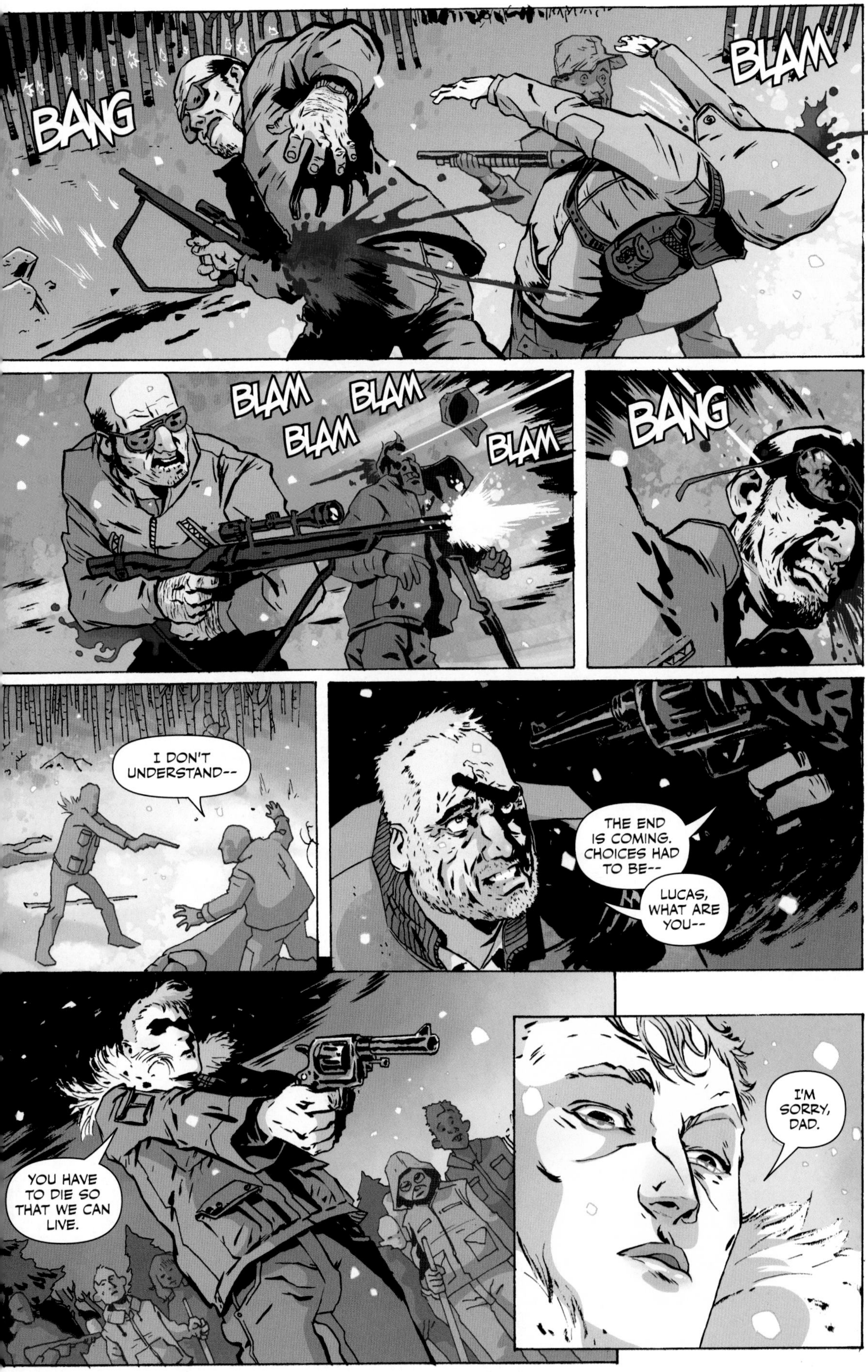
BANG
BLAM
BLAM
BLAM
BLAM
BLAM
BANG
I DON'T UNDERSTAND--
THE END IS COMING. CHOICES HAD TO BE--
LUCAS, WHAT ARE YOU--
YOU HAVE TO DIE SO THAT WE CAN LIVE.
I'M SORRY, DAD.

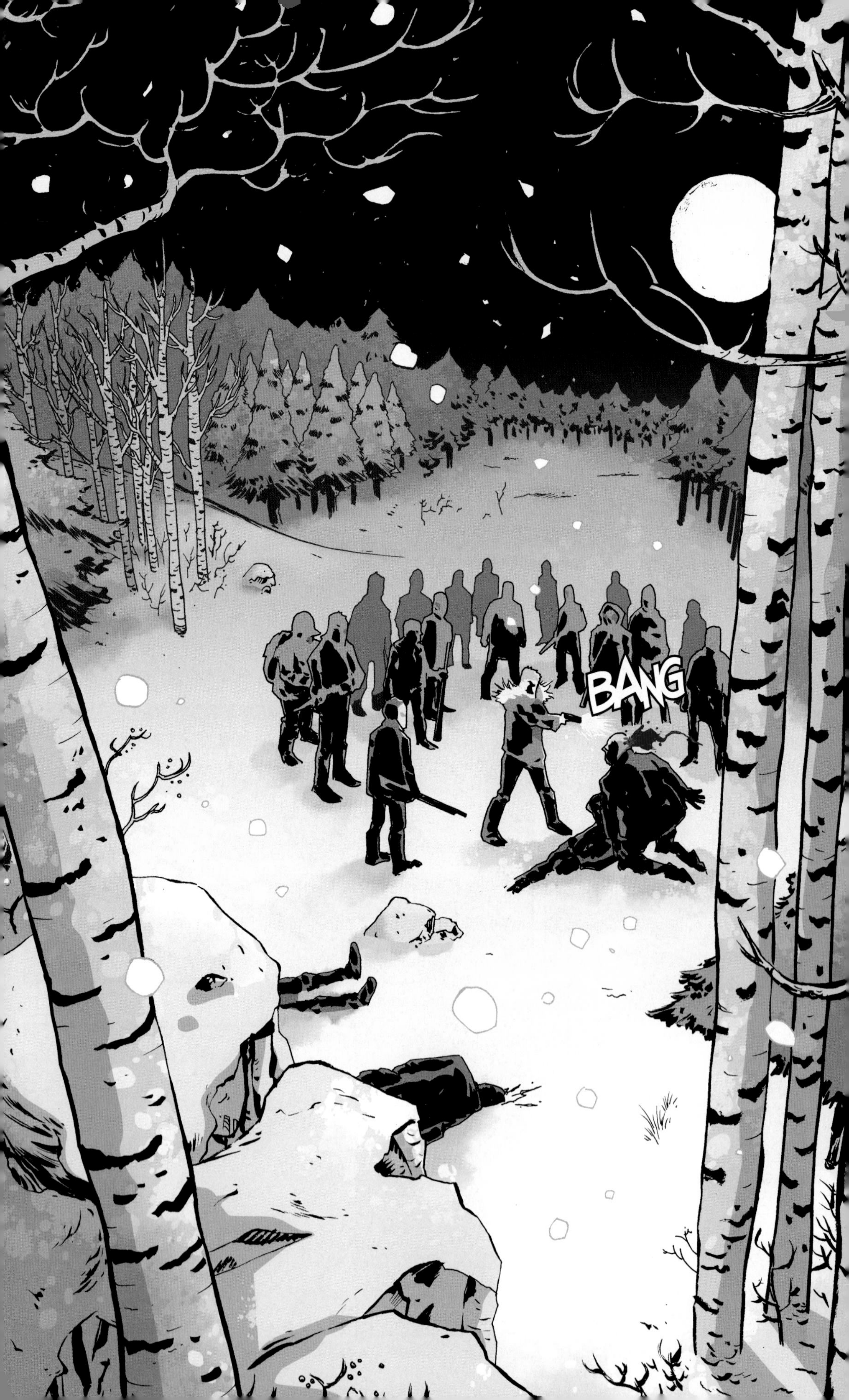
BANG

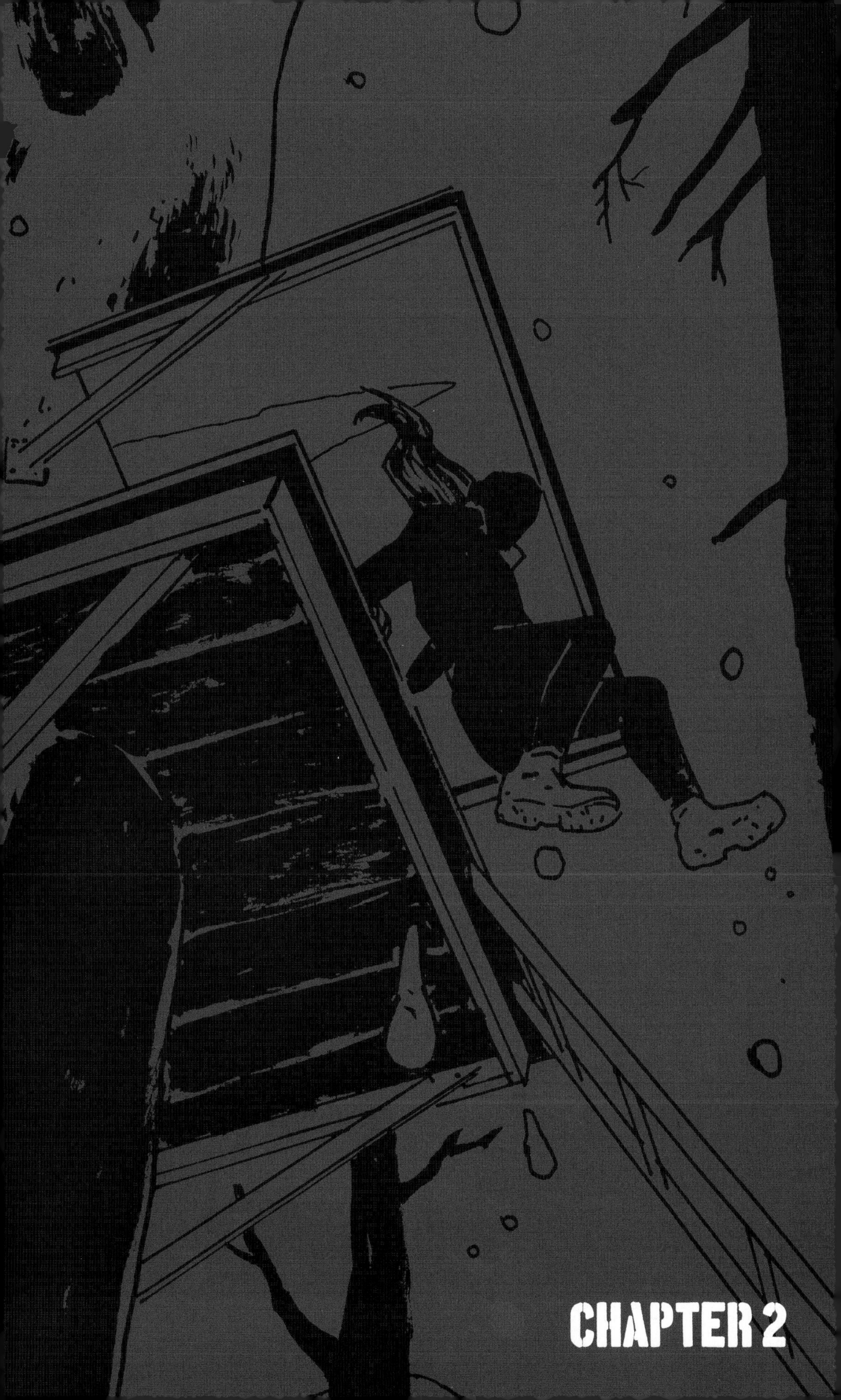

CHAPTER 2

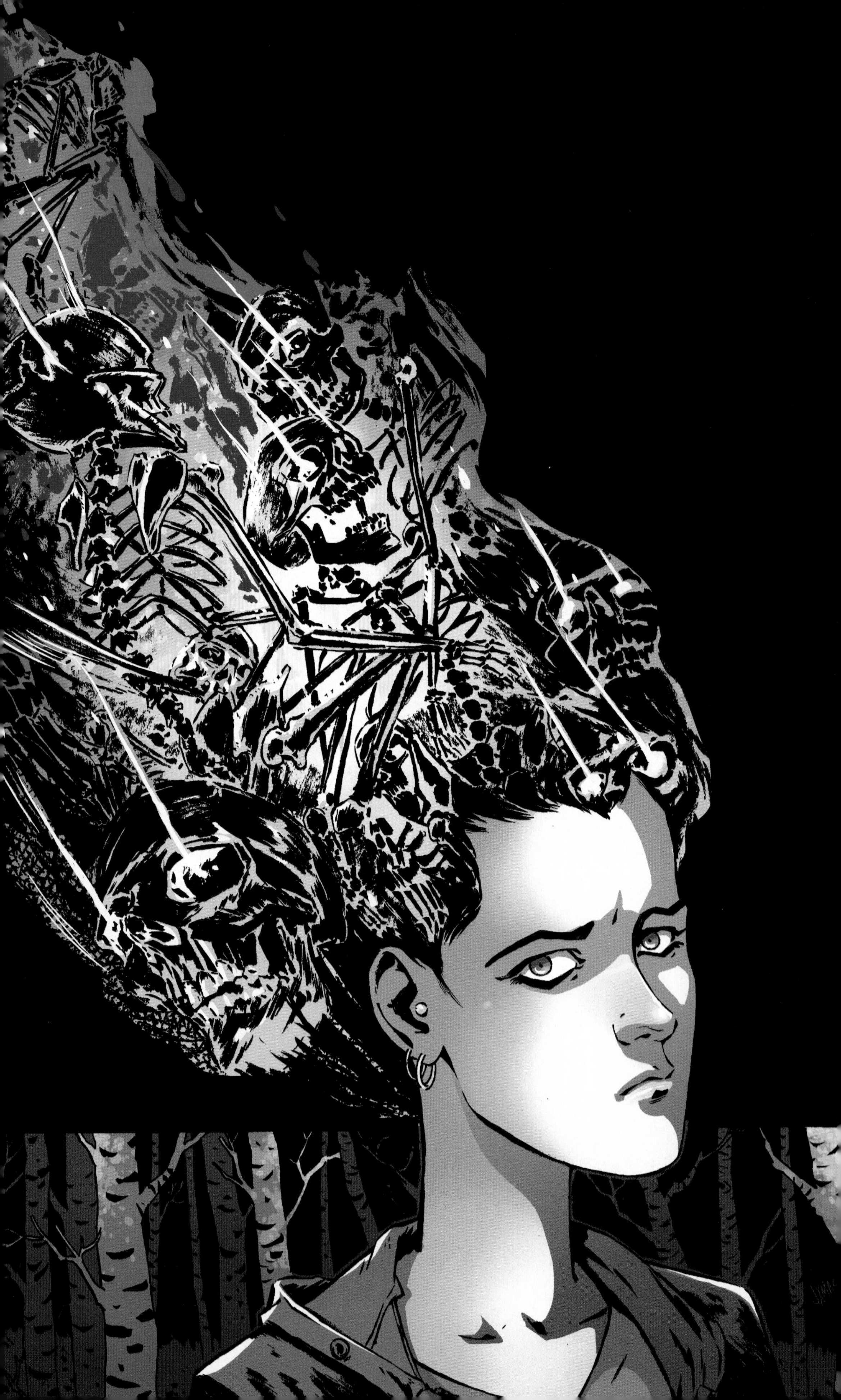

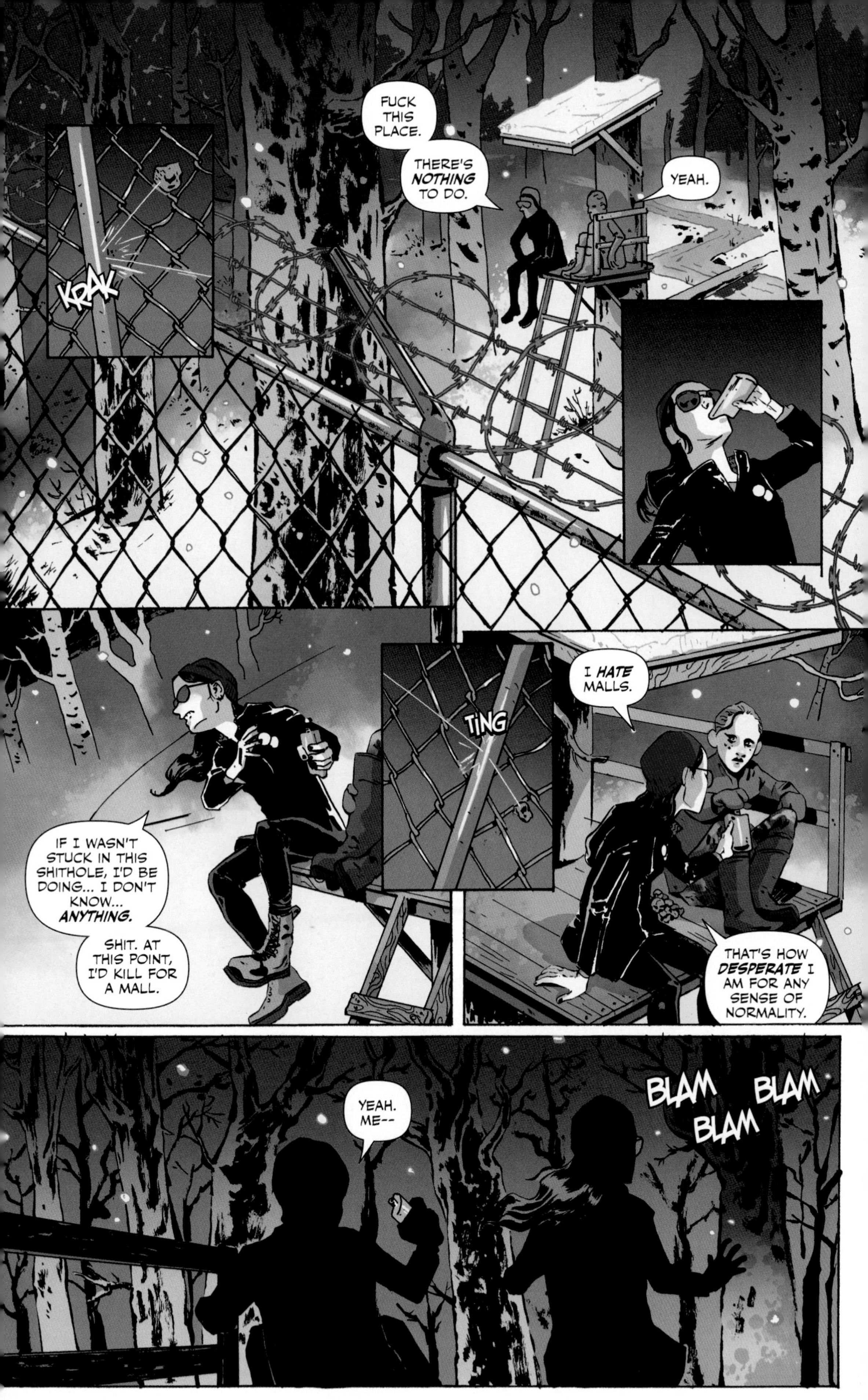

KRAK
FUCK THIS PLACE.
THERE'S NOTHING TO DO.
YEAH.
IF I WASN'T STUCK IN THIS SHITHOLE, I'D BE DOING... I DON'T KNOW... ANYTHING.
SHIT. AT THIS POINT, I'D KILL FOR A MALL.
TING
I HATE MALLS.
THAT'S HOW DESPERATE I AM FOR ANY SENSE OF NORMALITY.
YEAH. ME--
BLAM BLAM
BLAM

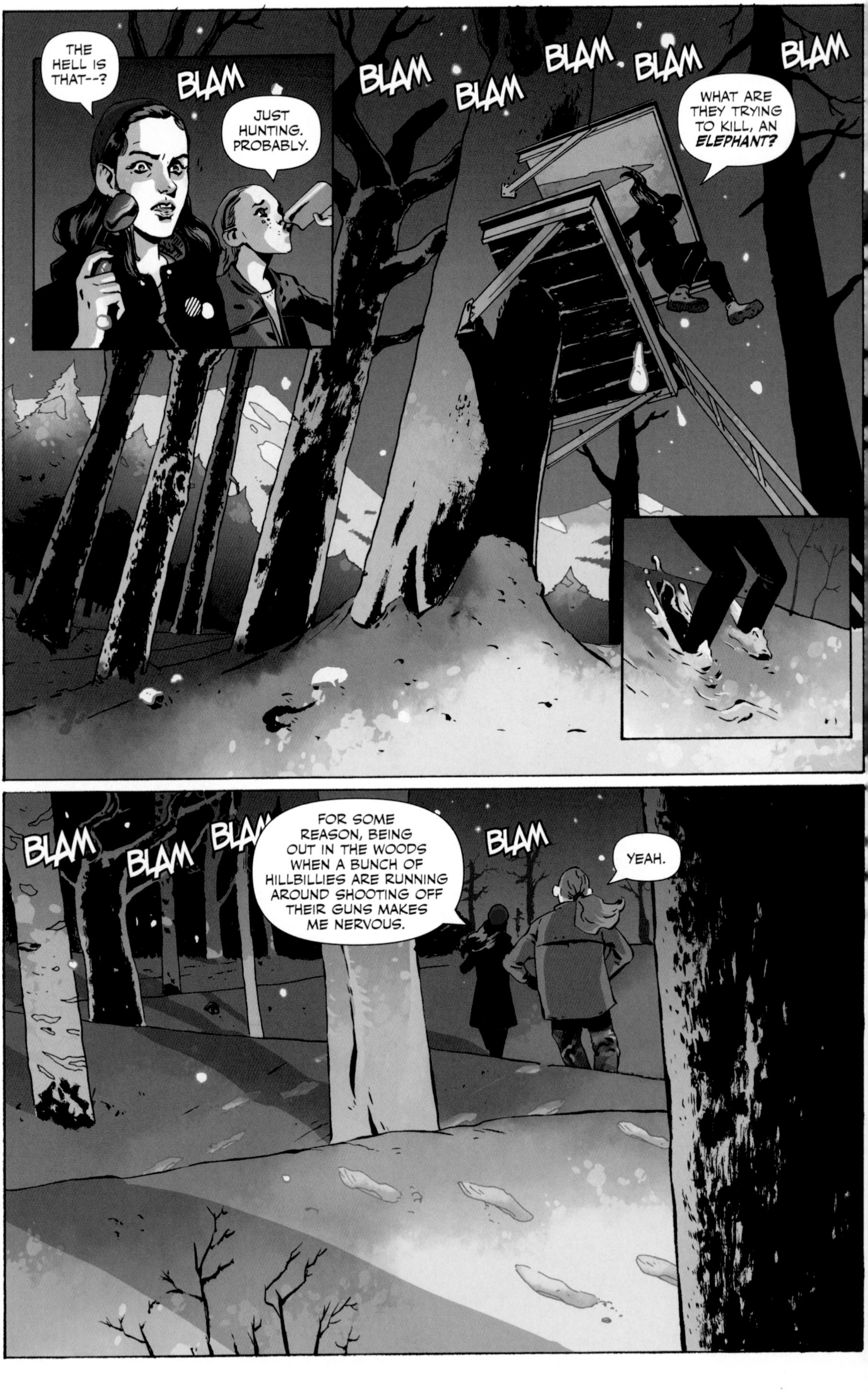
THE HELL IS THAT--?
BLAM
JUST HUNTING. PROBABLY.
BLAM
BLAM
BLAM
BLAM
BLAM
WHAT ARE THEY TRYING TO KILL, AN *ELEPHANT?*
BLAM
BLAM
BLAM
FOR SOME REASON, BEING OUT IN THE WOODS WHEN A BUNCH OF HILLBILLIES ARE RUNNING AROUND SHOOTING OFF THEIR GUNS MAKES ME NERVOUS.
BLAM
YEAH.

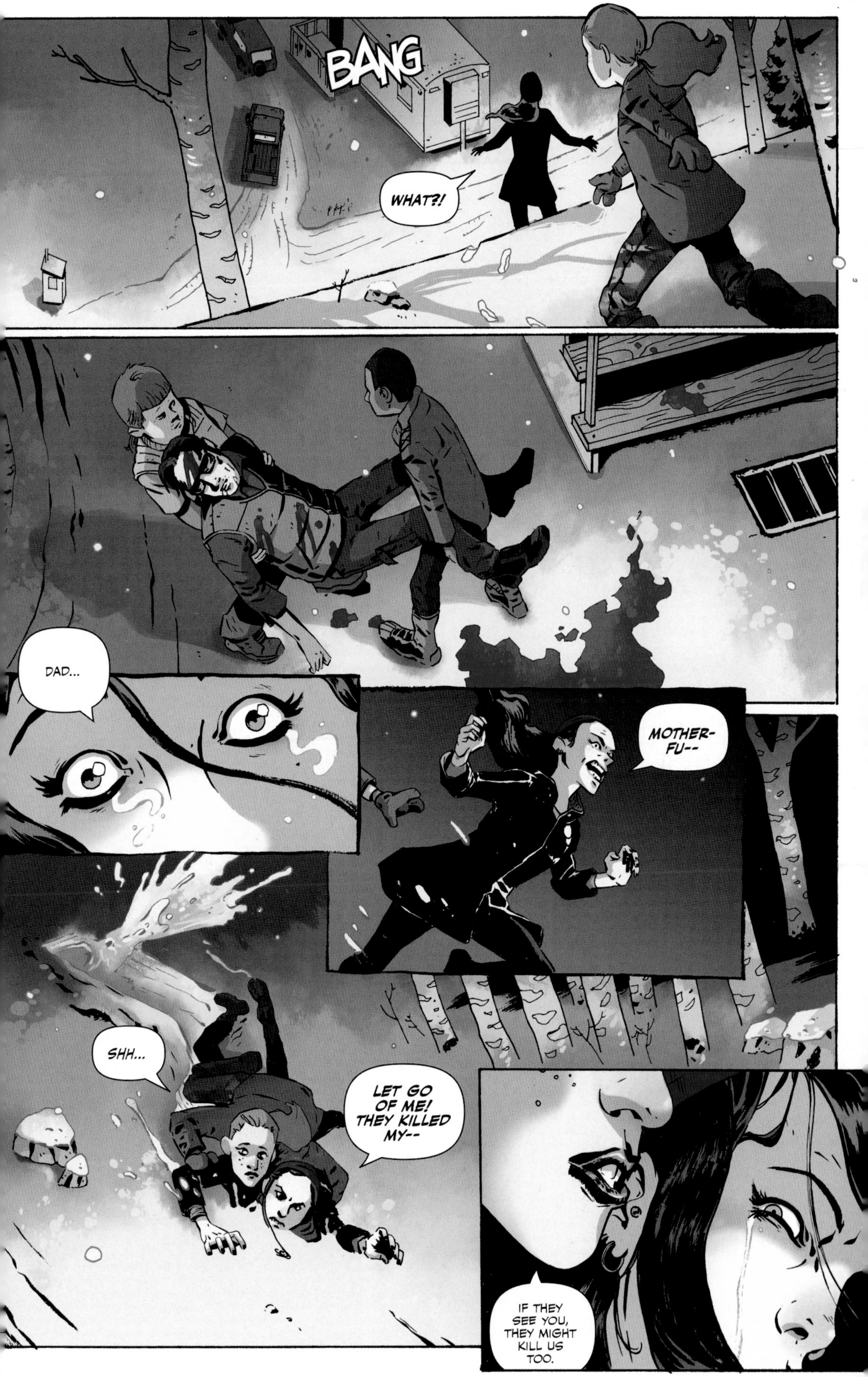
BANG
WHAT?!
DAD...
MOTHER-FU--
SHH...
LET GO OF ME! THEY KILLED MY--
IF THEY SEE YOU, THEY MIGHT KILL US TOO.

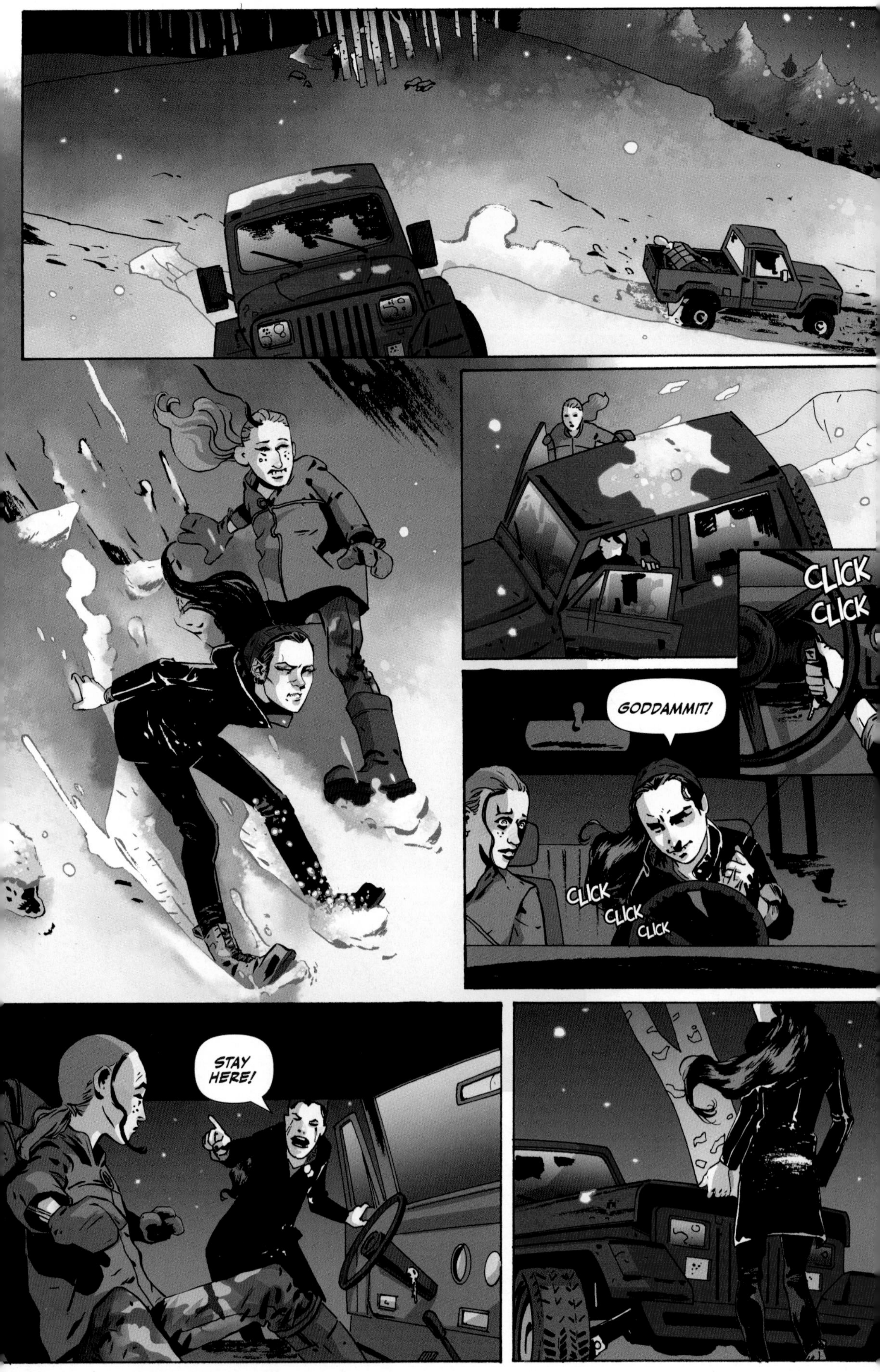
CLICK
CLICK
GODDAMMIT!
CLICK
CLICK
CLICK
STAY HERE!

SHIT.

THEY TOOK THE BATTERY! WE HAVE TO GET INSIDE.

NOW!

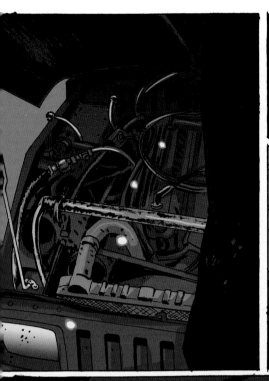

LOCK THE DOOR.

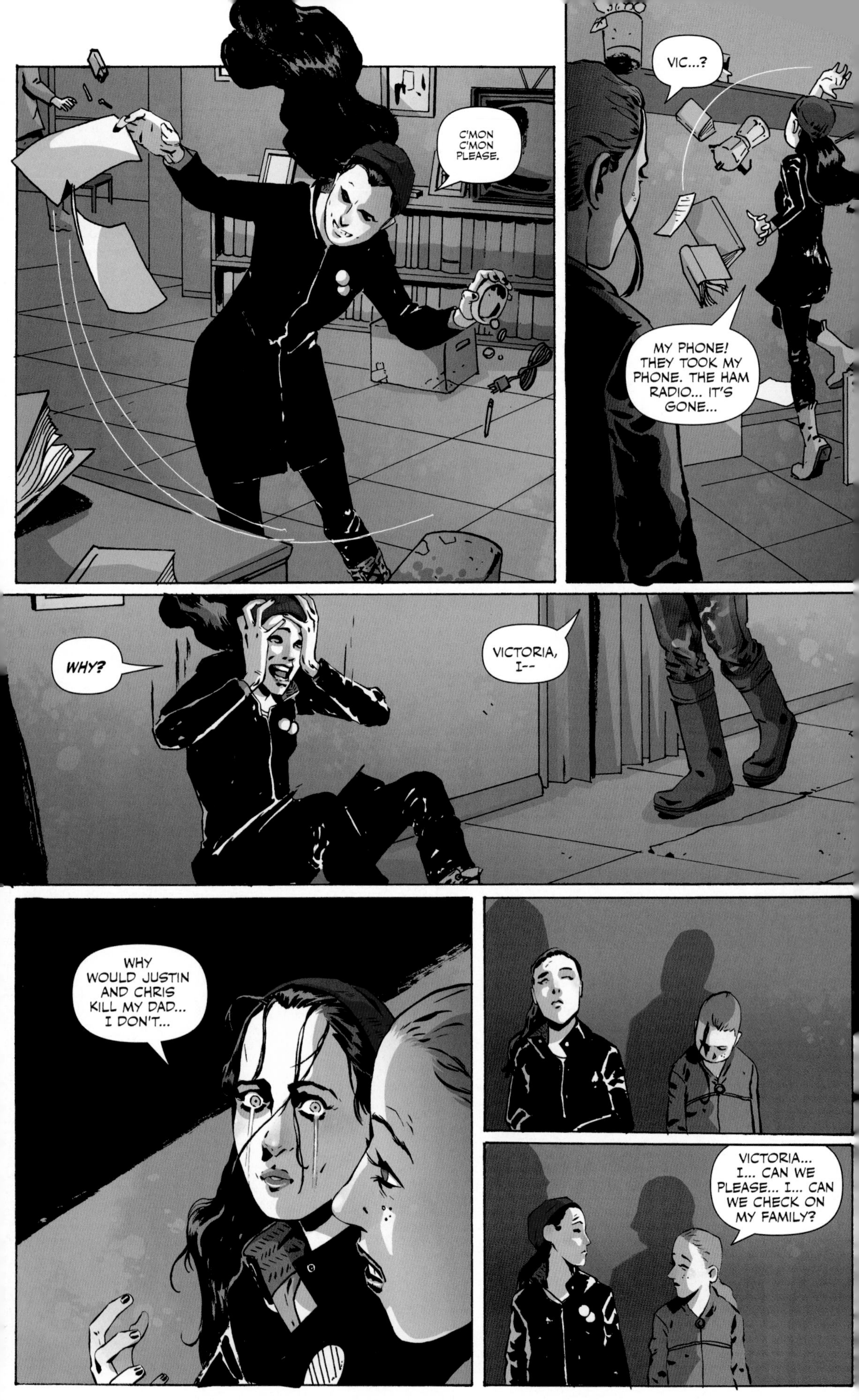
C'MON C'MON PLEASE.
VIC...?
MY PHONE! THEY TOOK MY PHONE. THE HAM RADIO... IT'S GONE...
WHY?
VICTORIA, I--
WHY WOULD JUSTIN AND CHRIS KILL MY DAD... I DON'T...
VICTORIA... I... CAN WE PLEASE... I... CAN WE CHECK ON MY FAMILY?

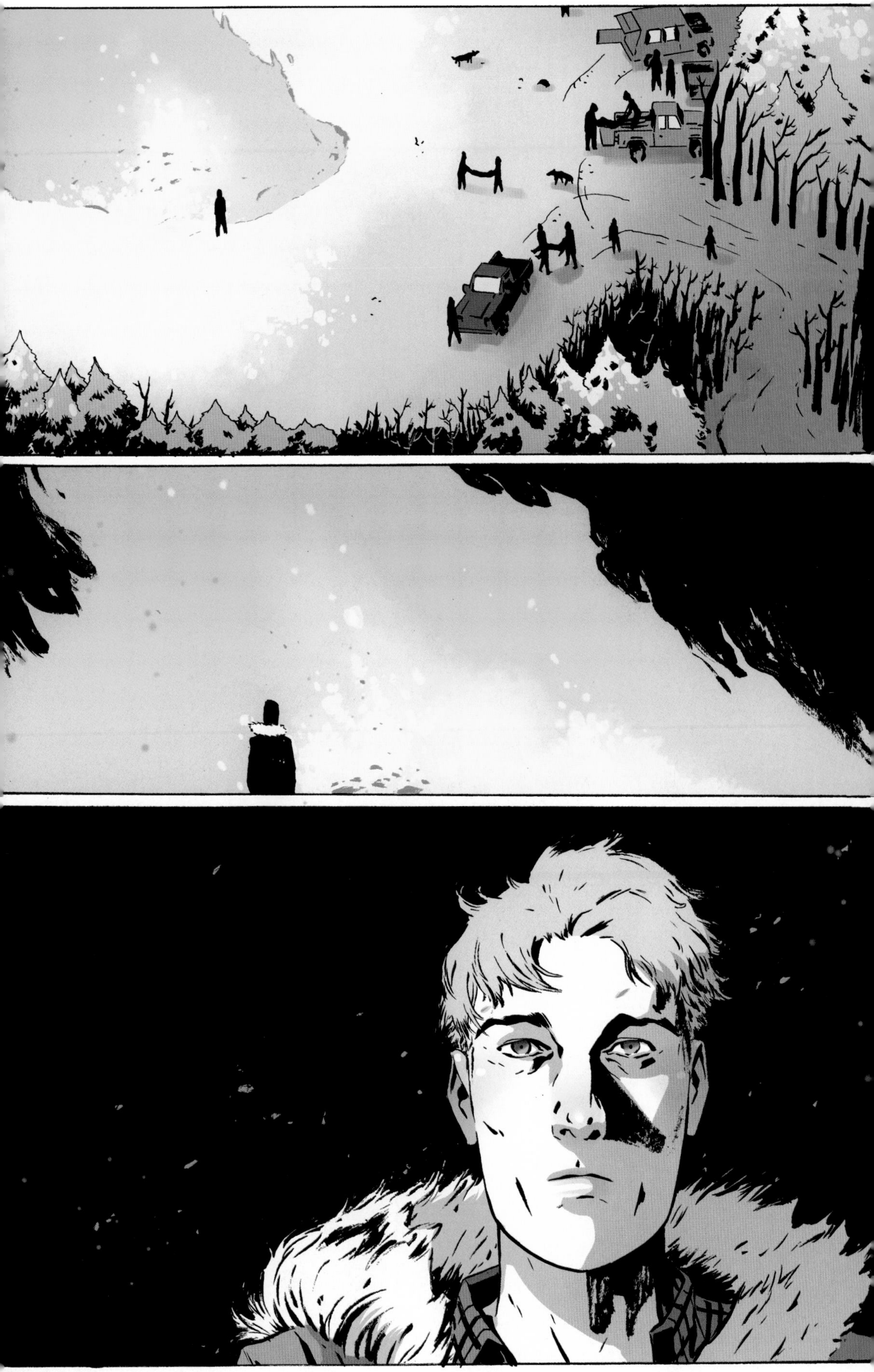

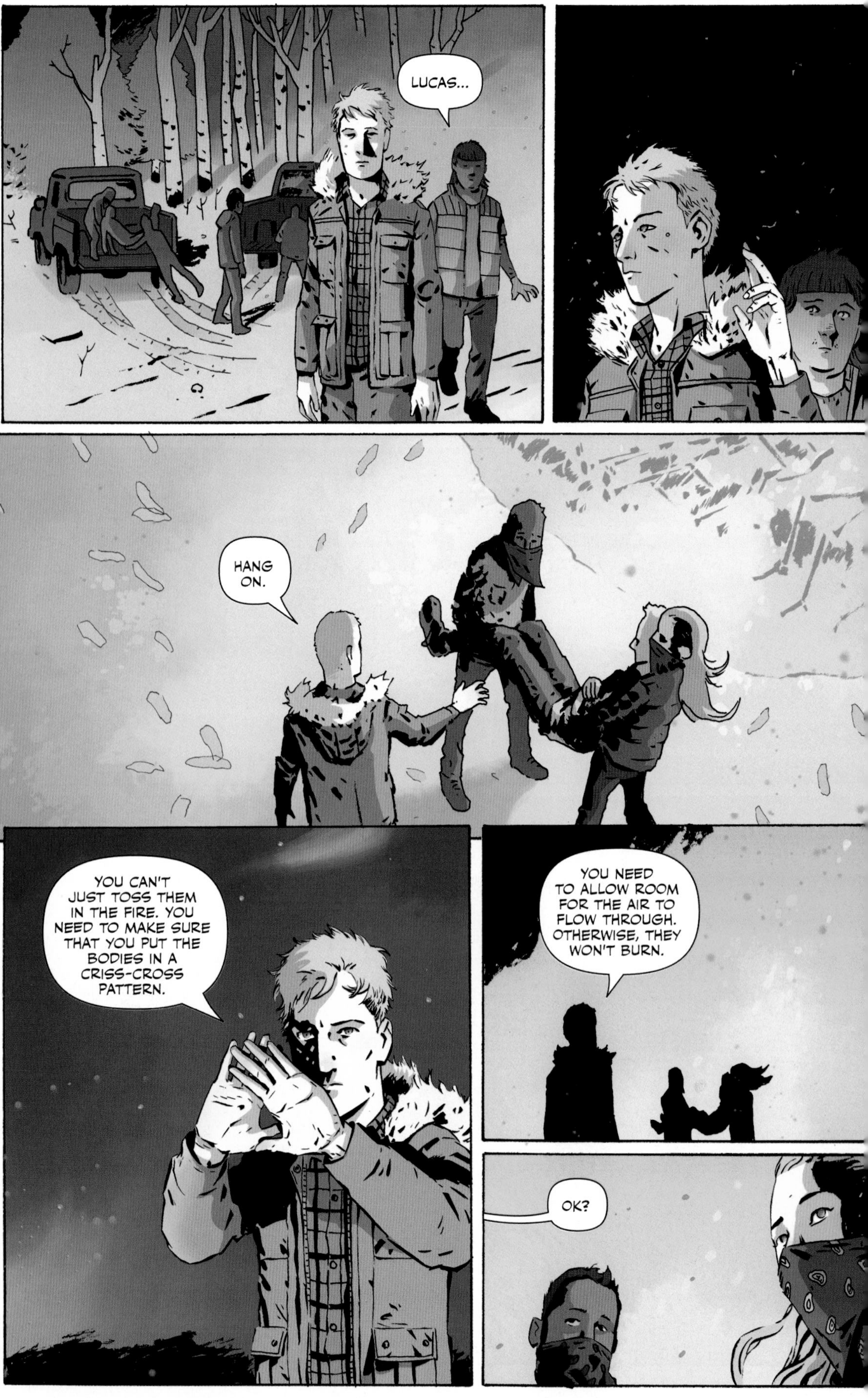
LUCAS...
HANG ON.
YOU CAN'T JUST TOSS THEM IN THE FIRE. YOU NEED TO MAKE SURE THAT YOU PUT THE BODIES IN A CRISS-CROSS PATTERN.
YOU NEED TO ALLOW ROOM FOR THE AIR TO FLOW THROUGH. OTHERWISE, THEY WON'T BURN.
OK?

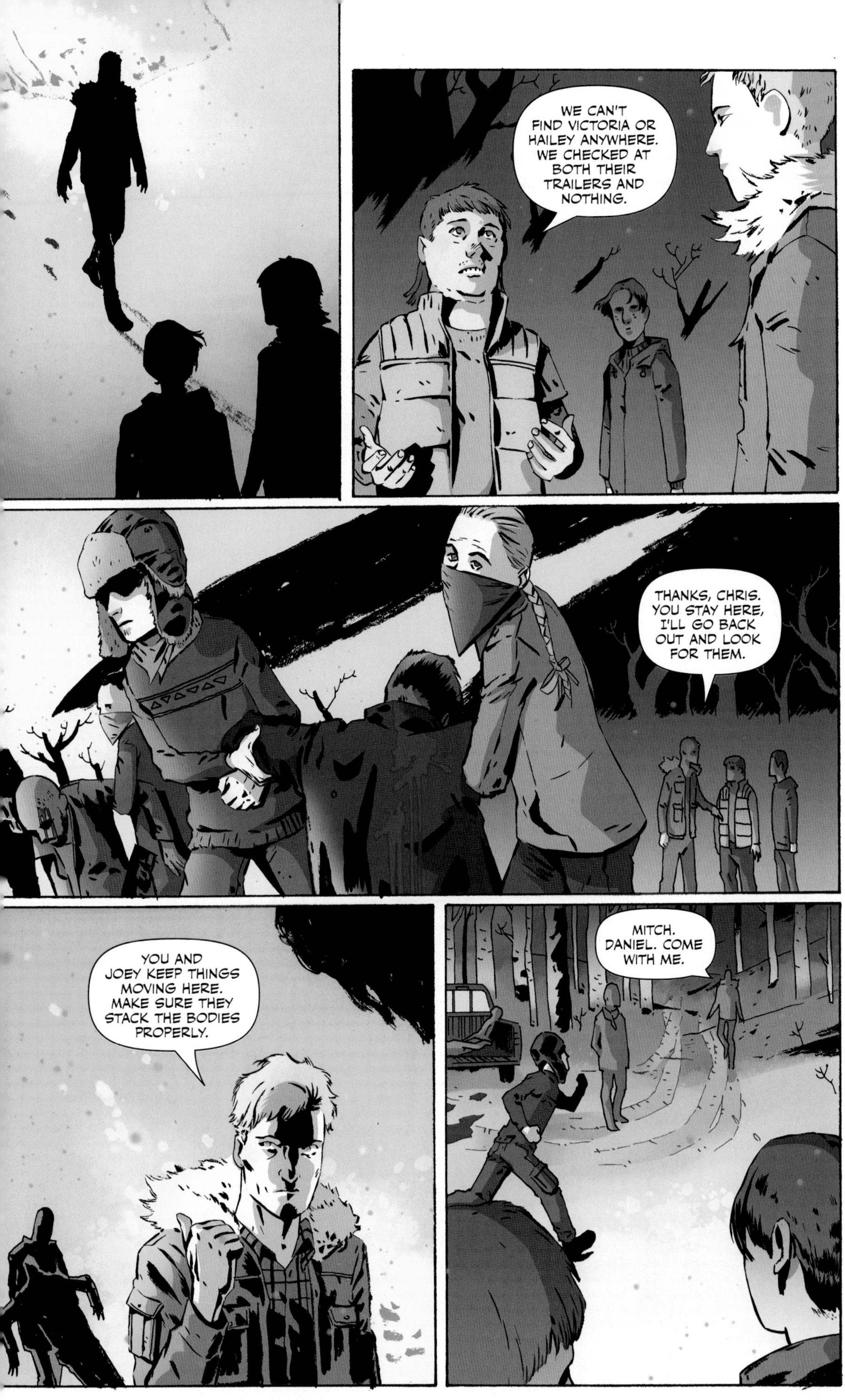
WE CAN'T FIND VICTORIA OR HAILEY ANYWHERE. WE CHECKED AT BOTH THEIR TRAILERS AND NOTHING.
THANKS, CHRIS. YOU STAY HERE, I'LL GO BACK OUT AND LOOK FOR THEM.
YOU AND JOEY KEEP THINGS MOVING HERE. MAKE SURE THEY STACK THE BODIES PROPERLY.
MITCH. DANIEL. COME WITH ME.

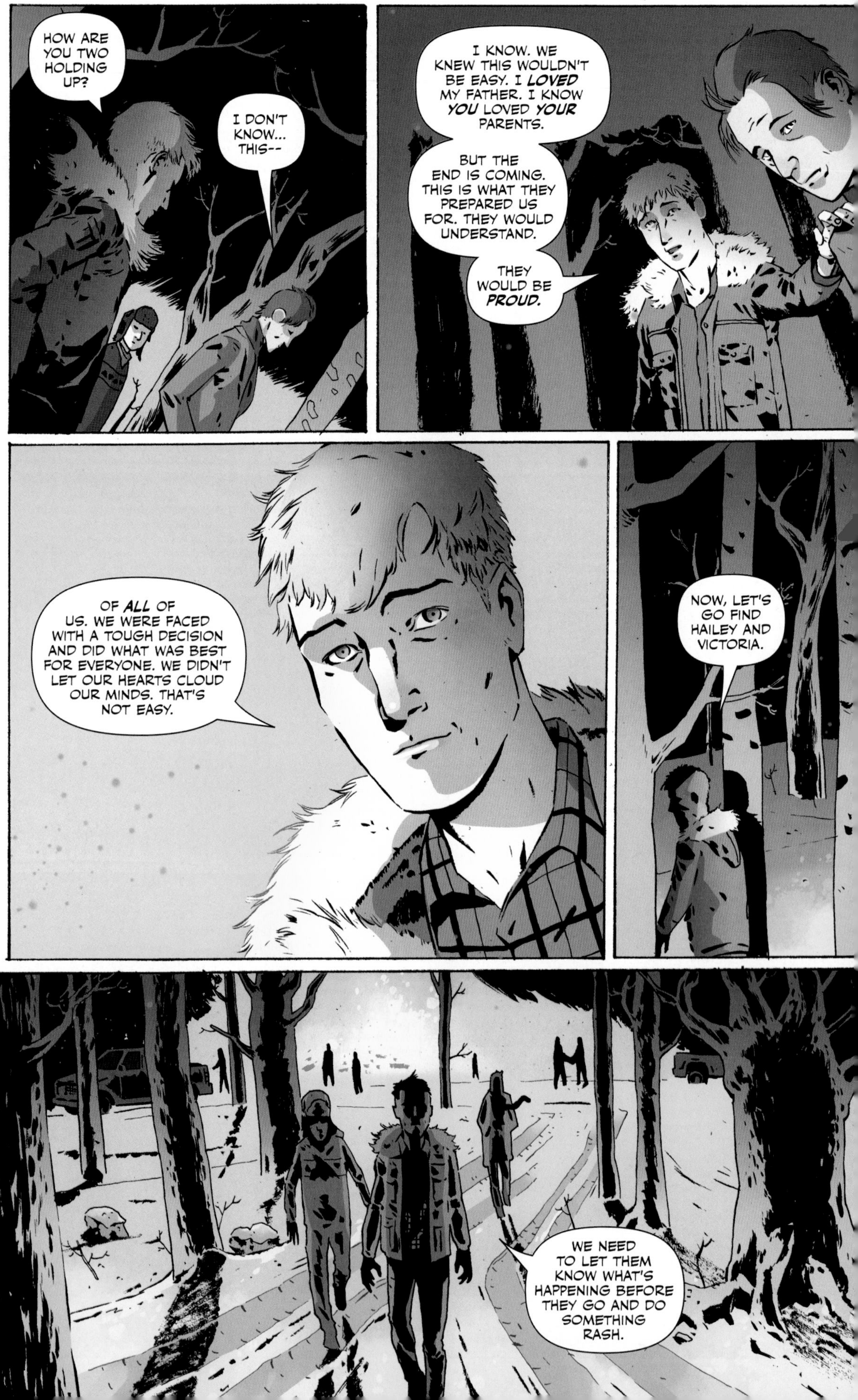
HOW ARE YOU TWO HOLDING UP?
I DON'T KNOW... THIS--
I KNOW. WE KNEW THIS WOULDN'T BE EASY. I LOVED MY FATHER. I KNOW YOU LOVED YOUR PARENTS.
BUT THE END IS COMING. THIS IS WHAT THEY PREPARED US FOR. THEY WOULD UNDERSTAND.
THEY WOULD BE PROUD.
OF ALL OF US. WE WERE FACED WITH A TOUGH DECISION AND DID WHAT WAS BEST FOR EVERYONE. WE DIDN'T LET OUR HEARTS CLOUD OUR MINDS. THAT'S NOT EASY.
NOW, LET'S GO FIND HAILEY AND VICTORIA.
WE NEED TO LET THEM KNOW WHAT'S HAPPENING BEFORE THEY GO AND DO SOMETHING RASH.

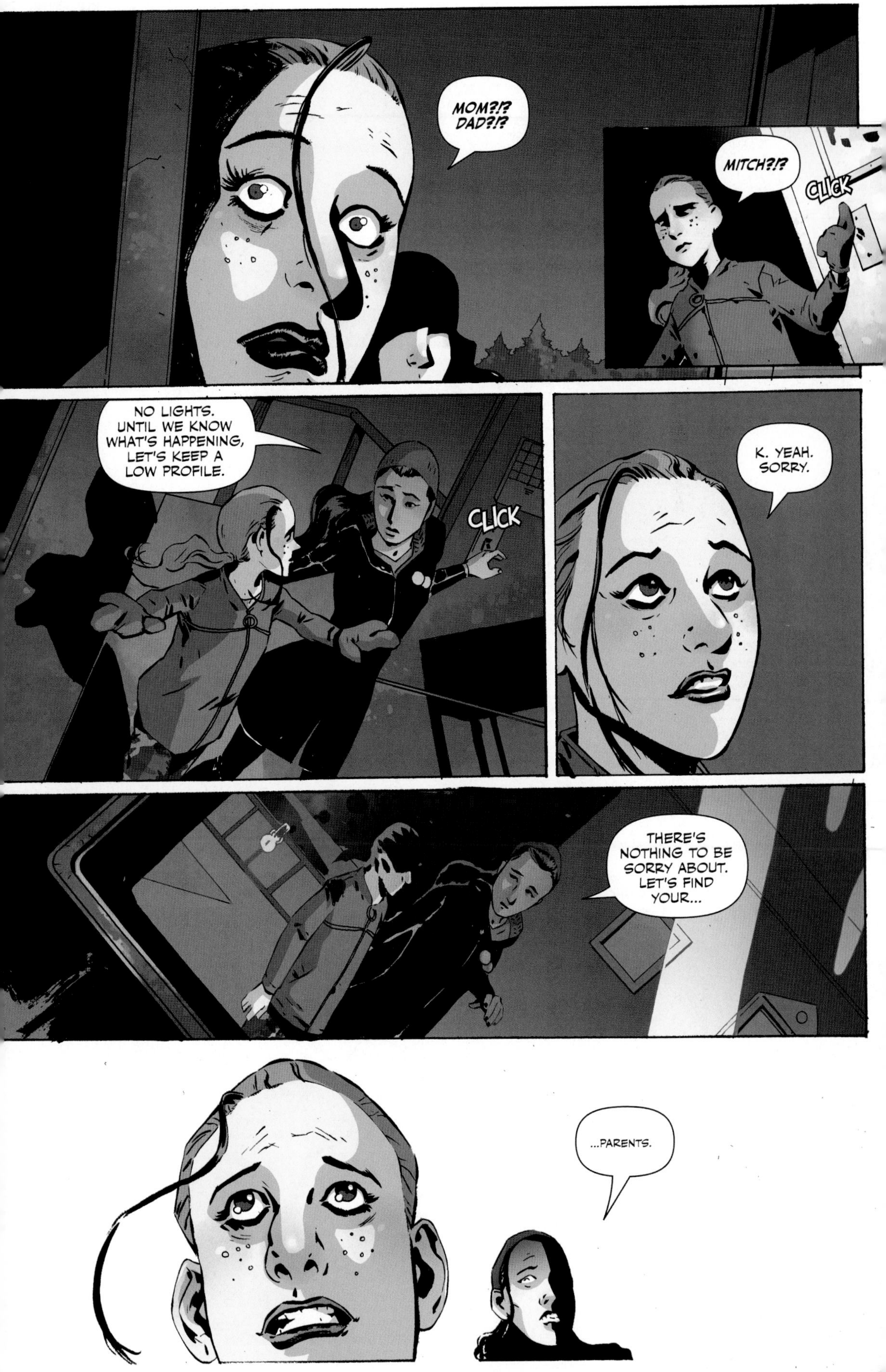
MOM?!?
DAD?!?
MITCH?!?
CLICK
NO LIGHTS. UNTIL WE KNOW WHAT'S HAPPENING, LET'S KEEP A LOW PROFILE.
CLICK
K. YEAH. SORRY.
THERE'S NOTHING TO BE SORRY ABOUT. LET'S FIND YOUR...
...PARENTS.

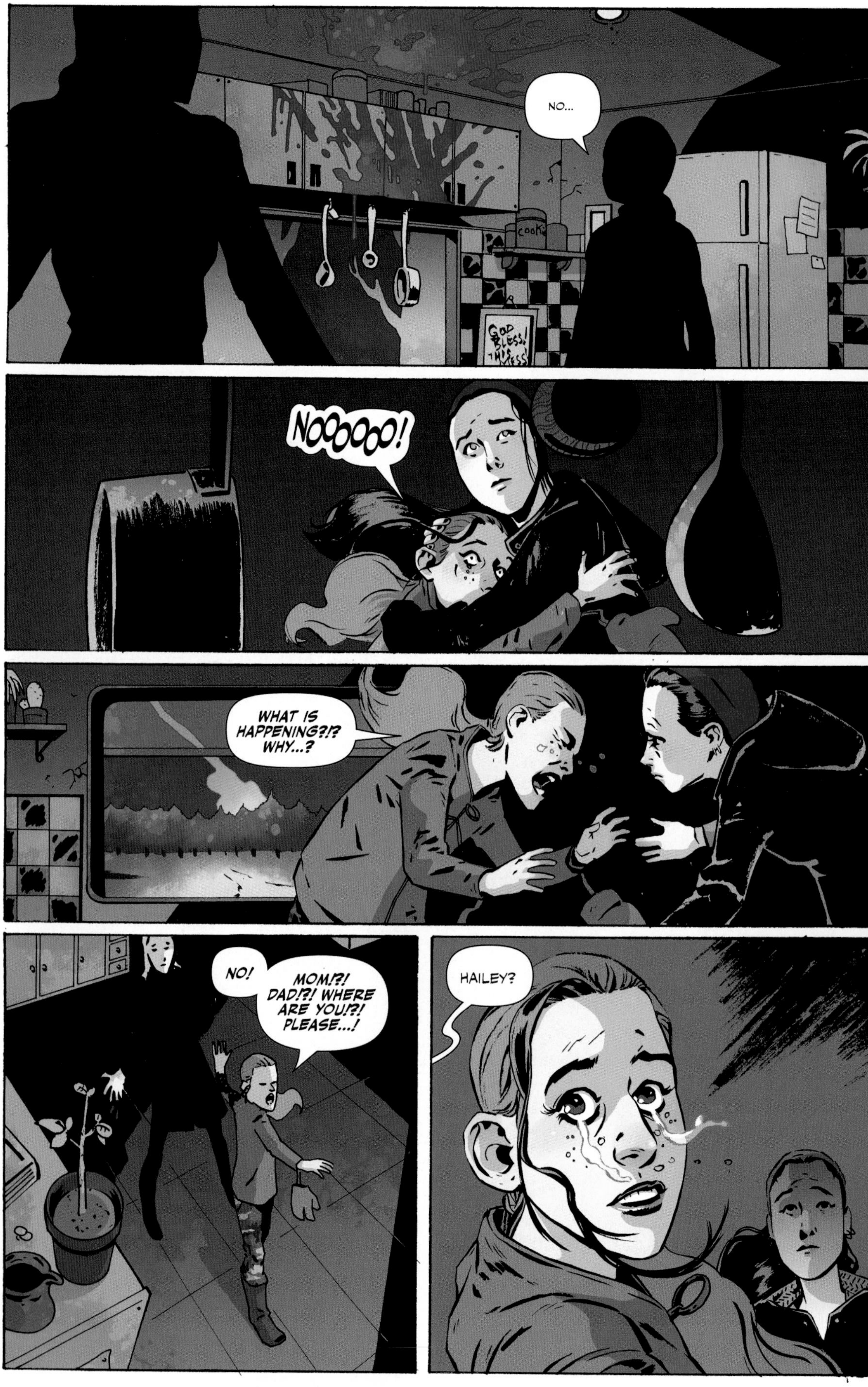
NO...
NOOOOOO!
WHAT IS HAPPENING?!? WHY...?
NO!
MOM!?! DAD!?! WHERE ARE YOU!?! PLEASE...!
HAILEY?

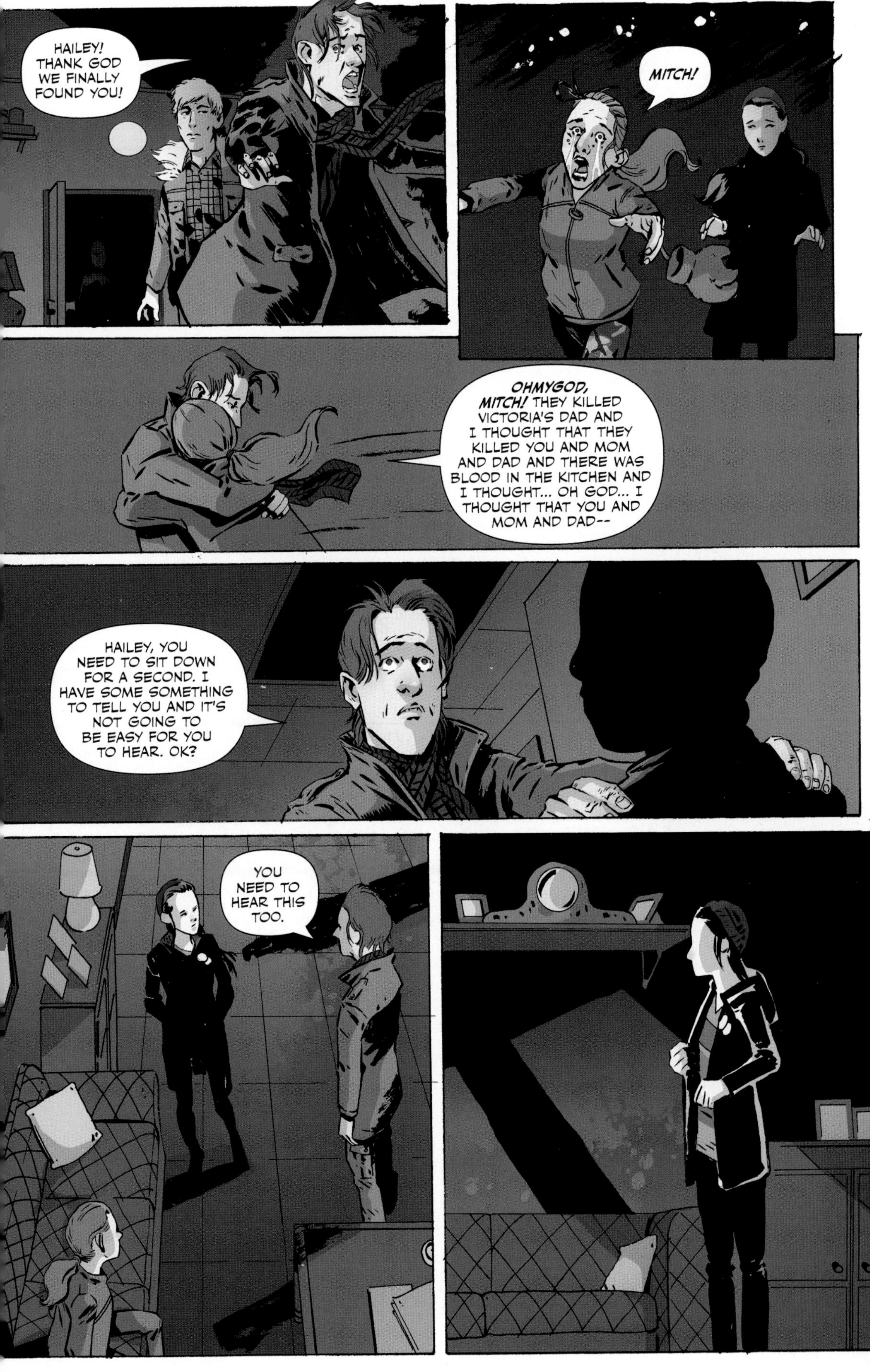
HAILEY! THANK GOD WE FINALLY FOUND YOU!
MITCH!
OHMYGOD, MITCH! THEY KILLED VICTORIA'S DAD AND I THOUGHT THAT THEY KILLED YOU AND MOM AND DAD AND THERE WAS BLOOD IN THE KITCHEN AND I THOUGHT... OH GOD... I THOUGHT THAT YOU AND MOM AND DAD--
HAILEY, YOU NEED TO SIT DOWN FOR A SECOND. I HAVE SOME SOMETHING TO TELL YOU AND IT'S NOT GOING TO BE EASY FOR YOU TO HEAR. OK?
YOU NEED TO HEAR THIS TOO.

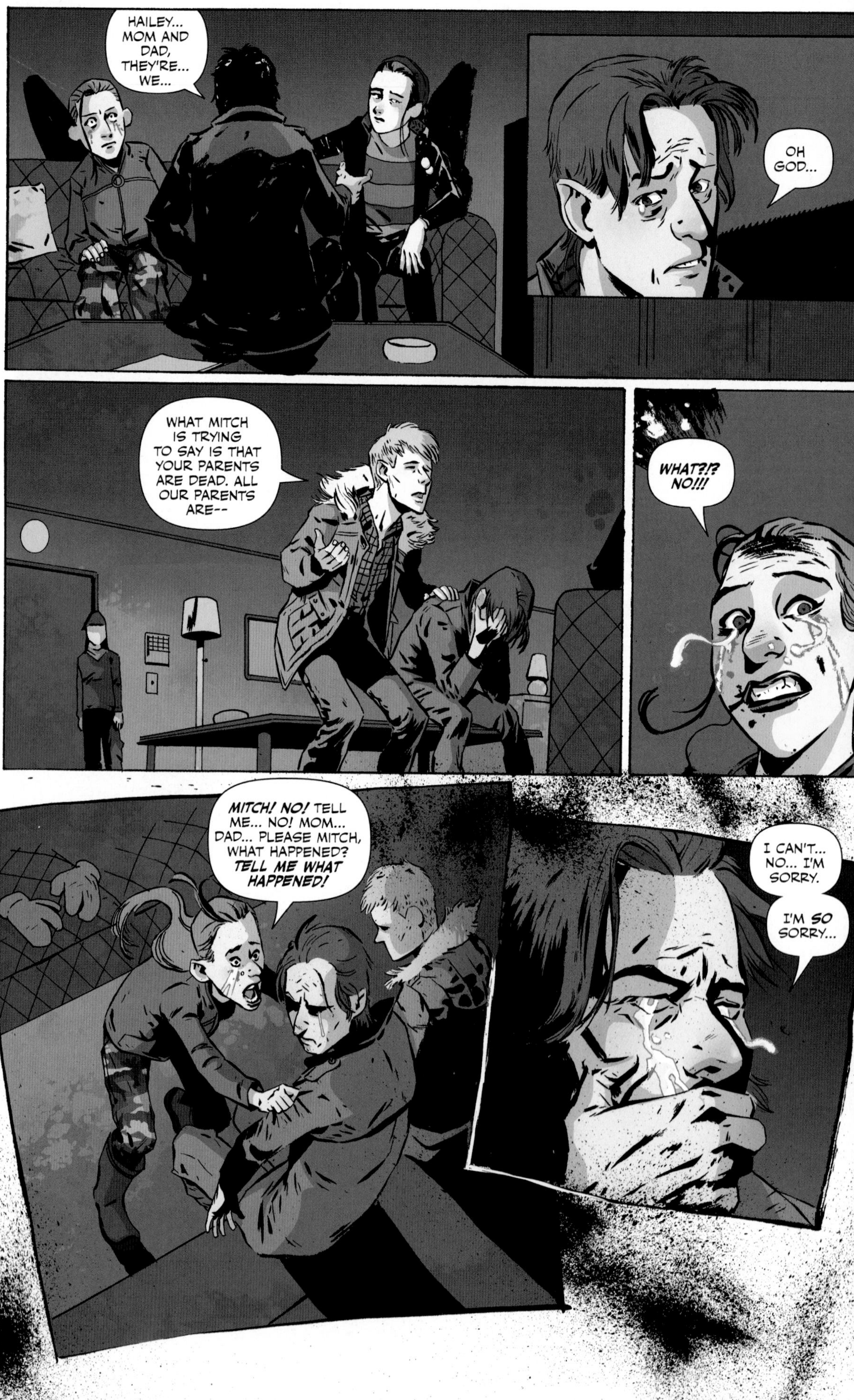
HAILEY... MOM AND DAD, THEY'RE... WE...
OH GOD...
WHAT MITCH IS TRYING TO SAY IS THAT YOUR PARENTS ARE DEAD. ALL OUR PARENTS ARE--
WHAT?!? NO!!!
MITCH! NO! TELL ME... NO! MOM... DAD... PLEASE MITCH, WHAT HAPPENED? TELL ME WHAT HAPPENED!
I CAN'T... NO... I'M SORRY.
I'M SO SORRY...

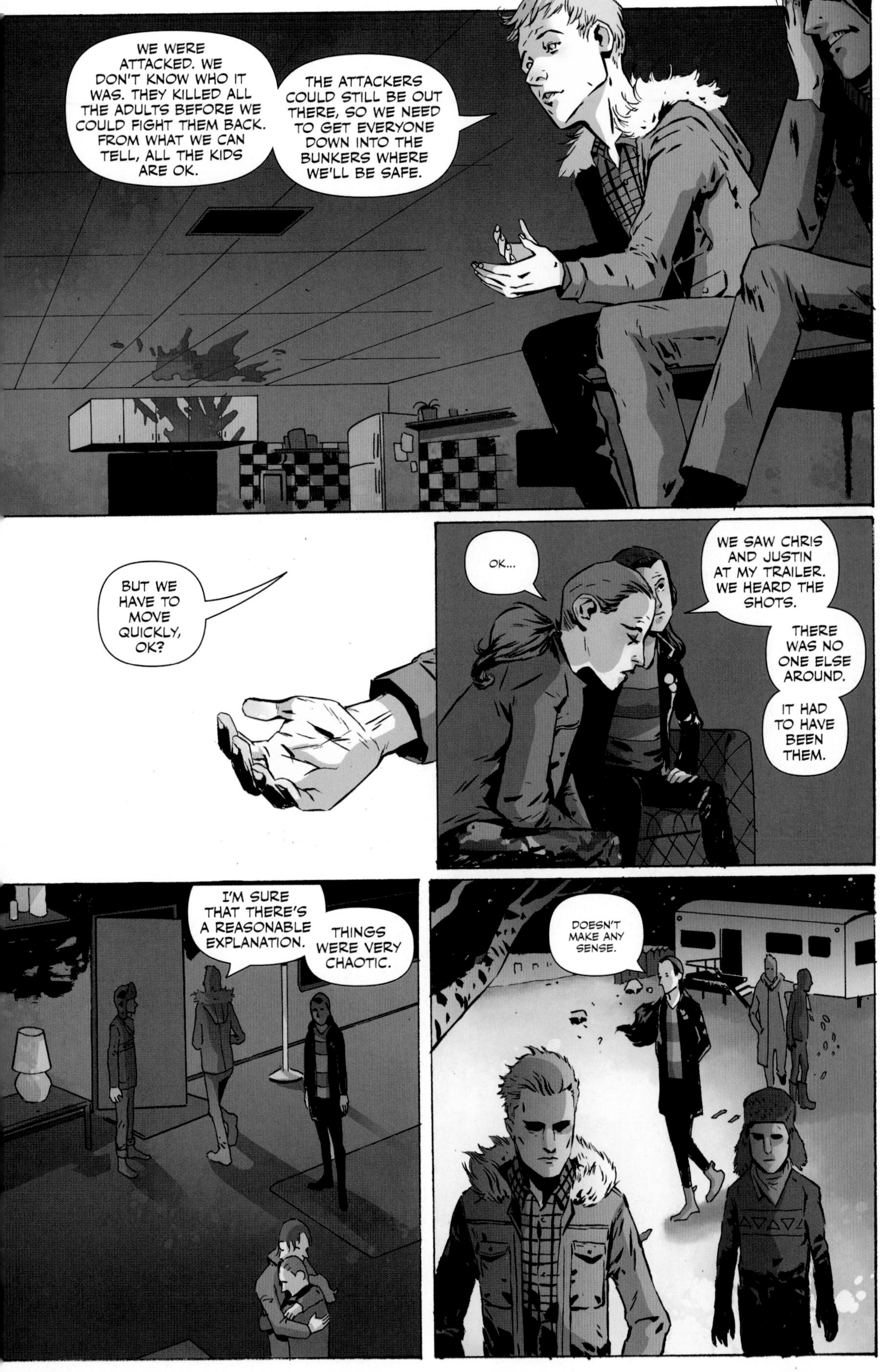
WE WERE ATTACKED. WE DON'T KNOW WHO IT WAS. THEY KILLED ALL THE ADULTS BEFORE WE COULD FIGHT THEM BACK. FROM WHAT WE CAN TELL, ALL THE KIDS ARE OK.
THE ATTACKERS COULD STILL BE OUT THERE, SO WE NEED TO GET EVERYONE DOWN INTO THE BUNKERS WHERE WE'LL BE SAFE.
BUT WE HAVE TO MOVE QUICKLY, OK?
OK...
WE SAW CHRIS AND JUSTIN AT MY TRAILER. WE HEARD THE SHOTS.
THERE WAS NO ONE ELSE AROUND.
IT HAD TO HAVE BEEN THEM.
I'M SURE THAT THERE'S A REASONABLE EXPLANATION.
THINGS WERE VERY CHAOTIC.
DOESN'T MAKE ANY SENSE.

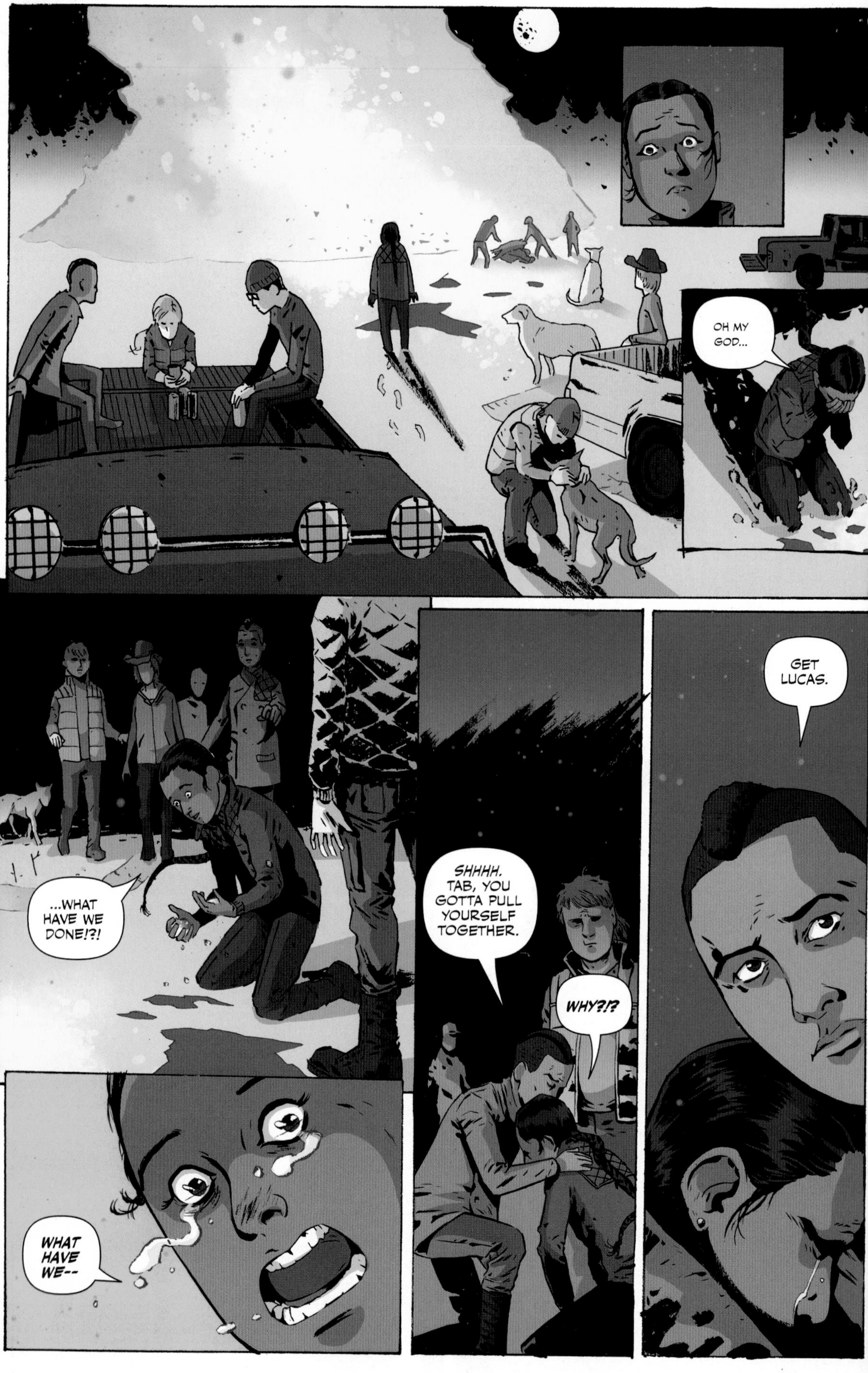
OH MY GOD...
...WHAT HAVE WE DONE!?!
WHAT HAVE WE--
SHHHH. TAB, YOU GOTTA PULL YOURSELF TOGETHER.
WHY?!?
GET LUCAS.

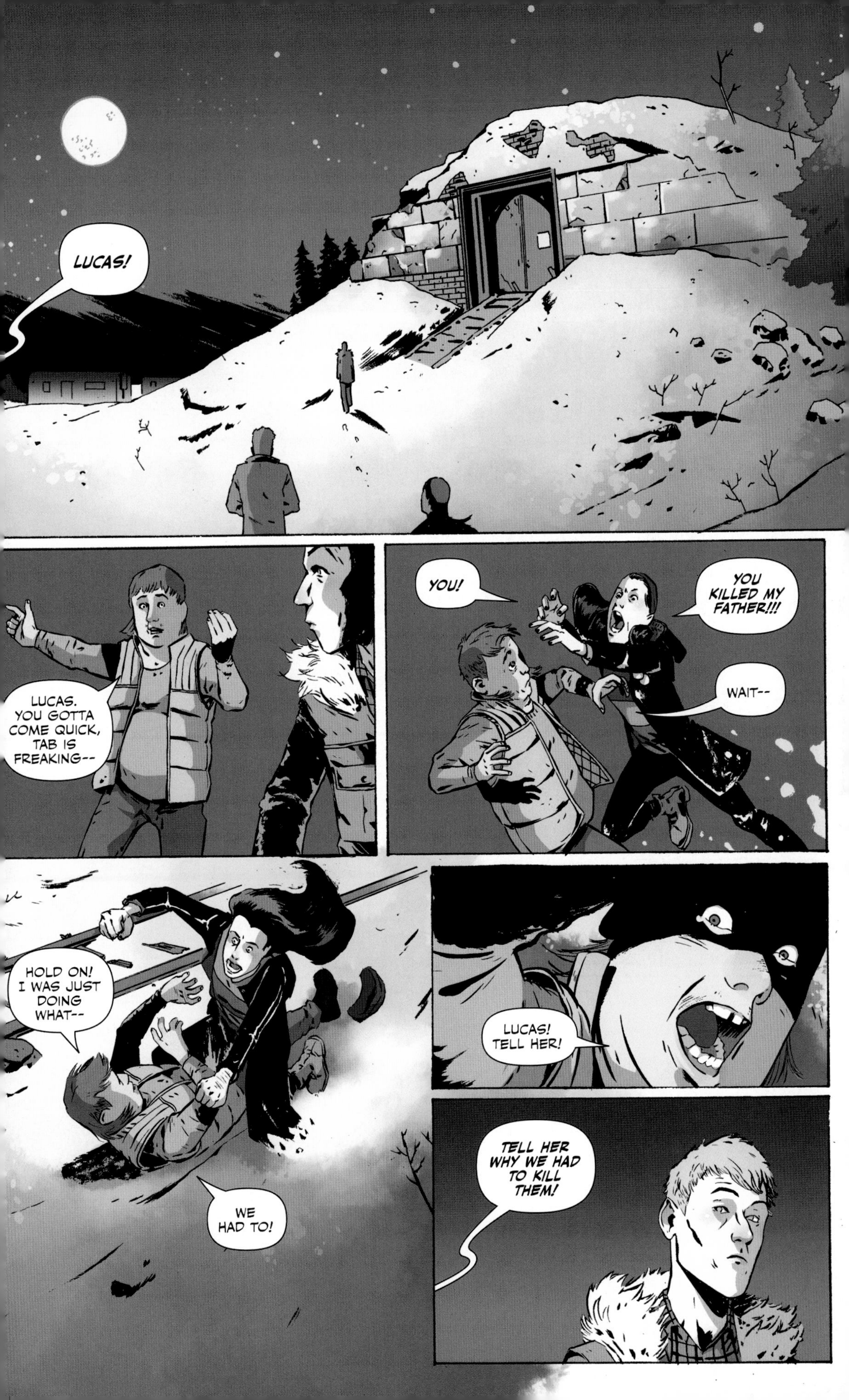
LUCAS!
LUCAS. YOU GOTTA COME QUICK, TAB IS FREAKING--
YOU!
YOU KILLED MY FATHER!!!
WAIT--
HOLD ON! I WAS JUST DOING WHAT--
WE HAD TO!
LUCAS! TELL HER!
TELL HER WHY WE HAD TO KILL THEM!

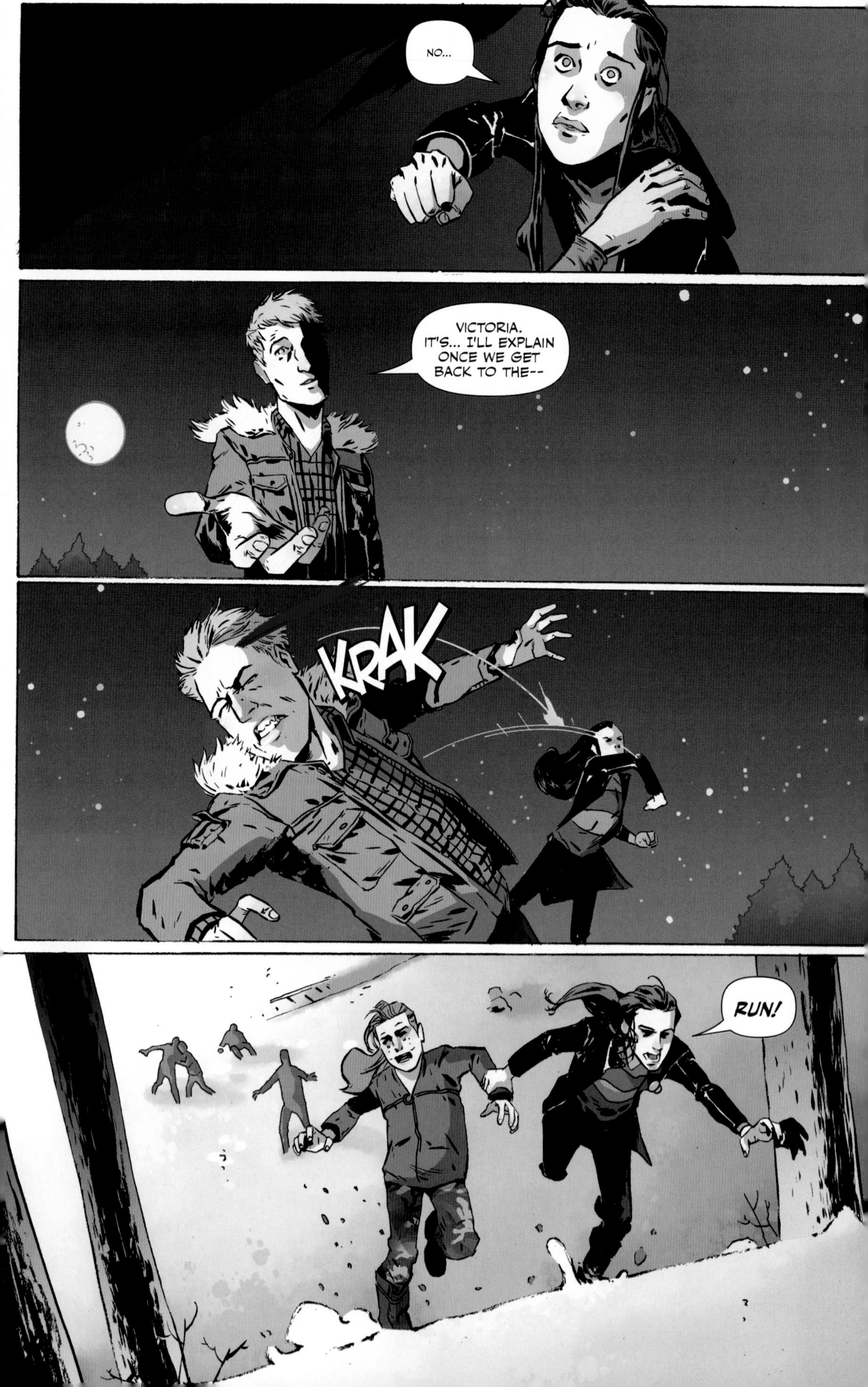
NO...
VICTORIA. IT'S... I'LL EXPLAIN ONCE WE GET BACK TO THE--
KRAK
RUN!

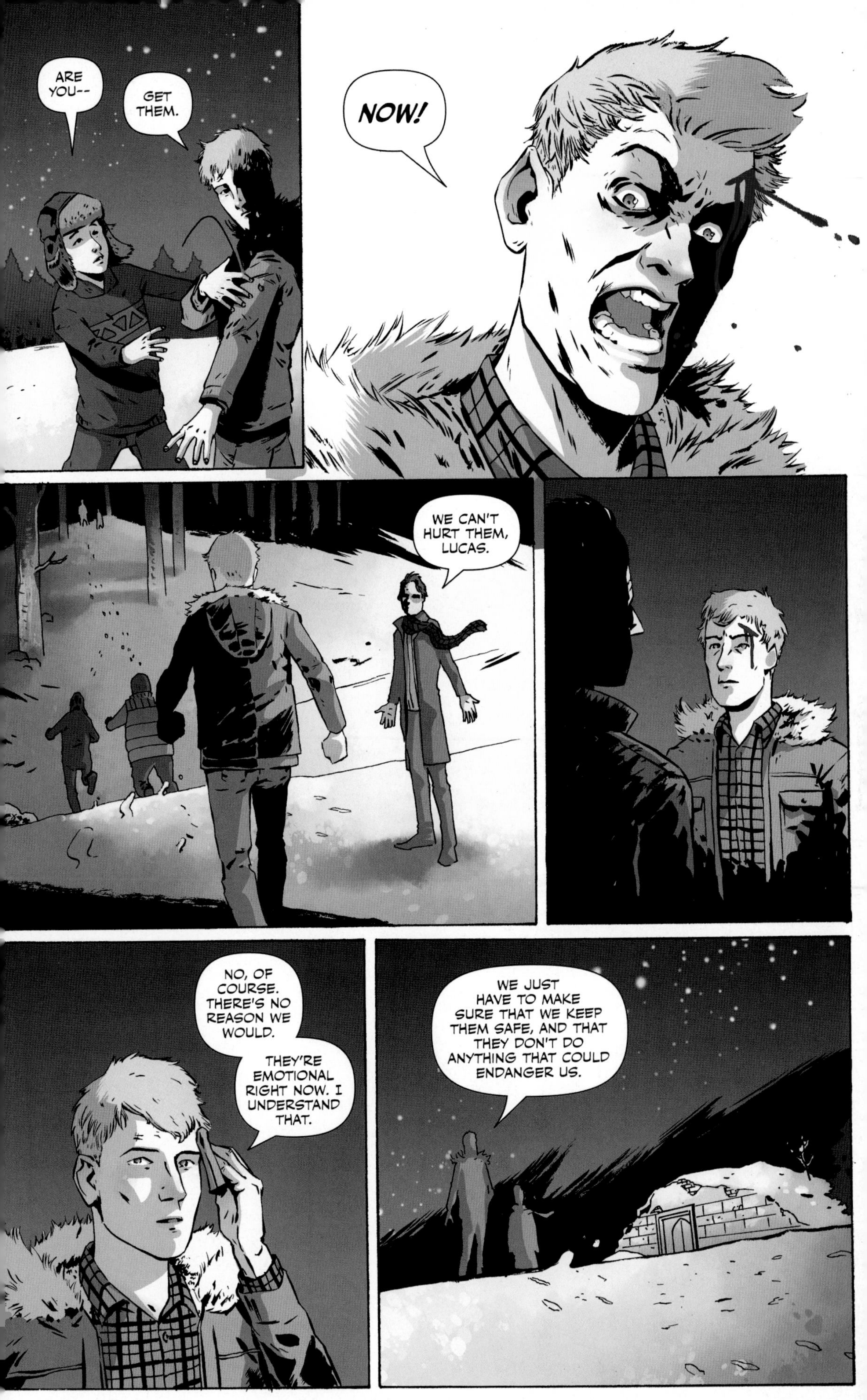
ARE YOU--
GET THEM.
NOW!
WE CAN'T HURT THEM, LUCAS.
NO, OF COURSE. THERE'S NO REASON WE WOULD.
THEY'RE EMOTIONAL RIGHT NOW. I UNDERSTAND THAT.
WE JUST HAVE TO MAKE SURE THAT WE KEEP THEM SAFE, AND THAT THEY DON'T DO ANYTHING THAT COULD ENDANGER US.

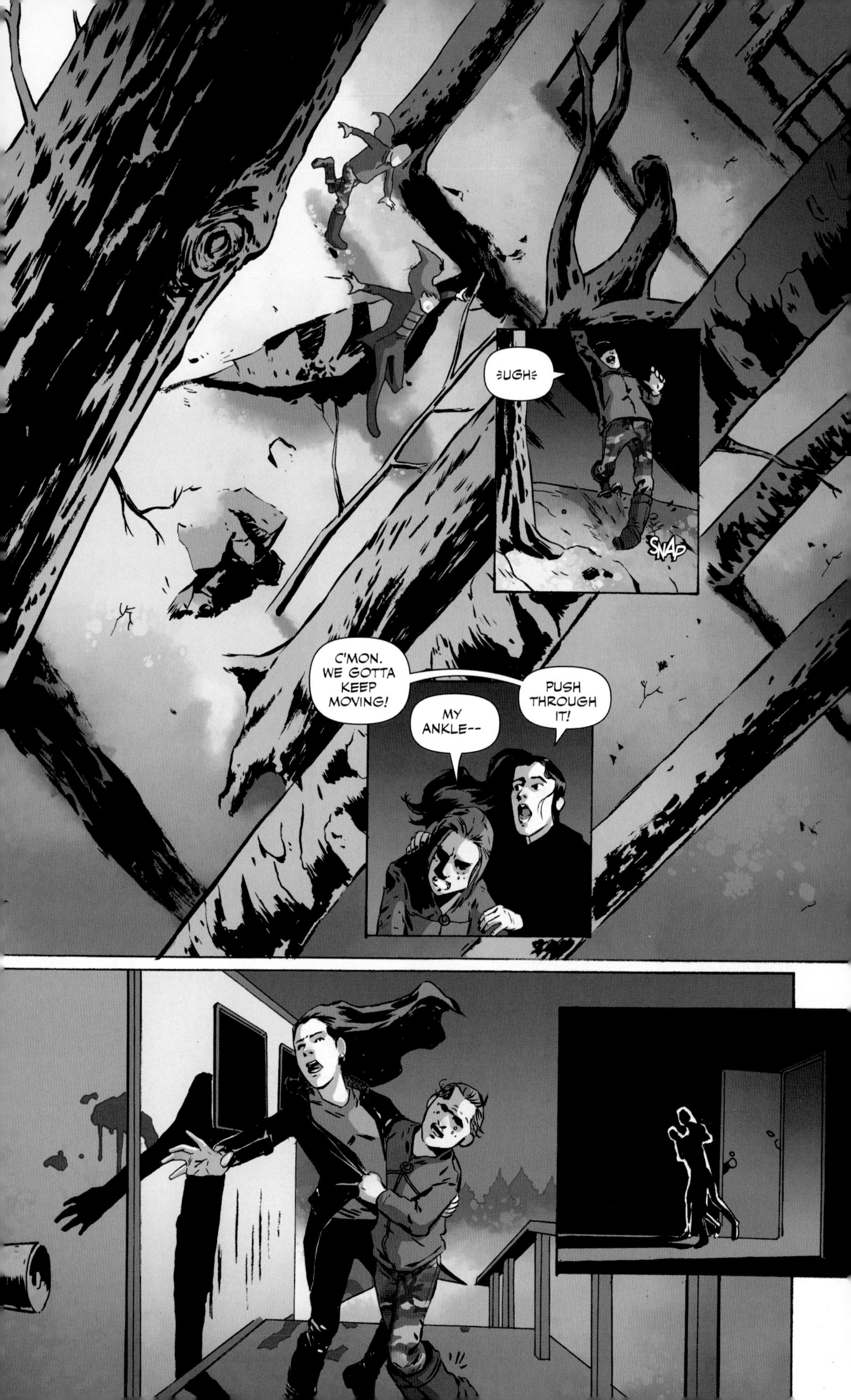

UGH
SNAP
C'MON. WE GOTTA KEEP MOVING!
MY ANKLE--
PUSH THROUGH IT!

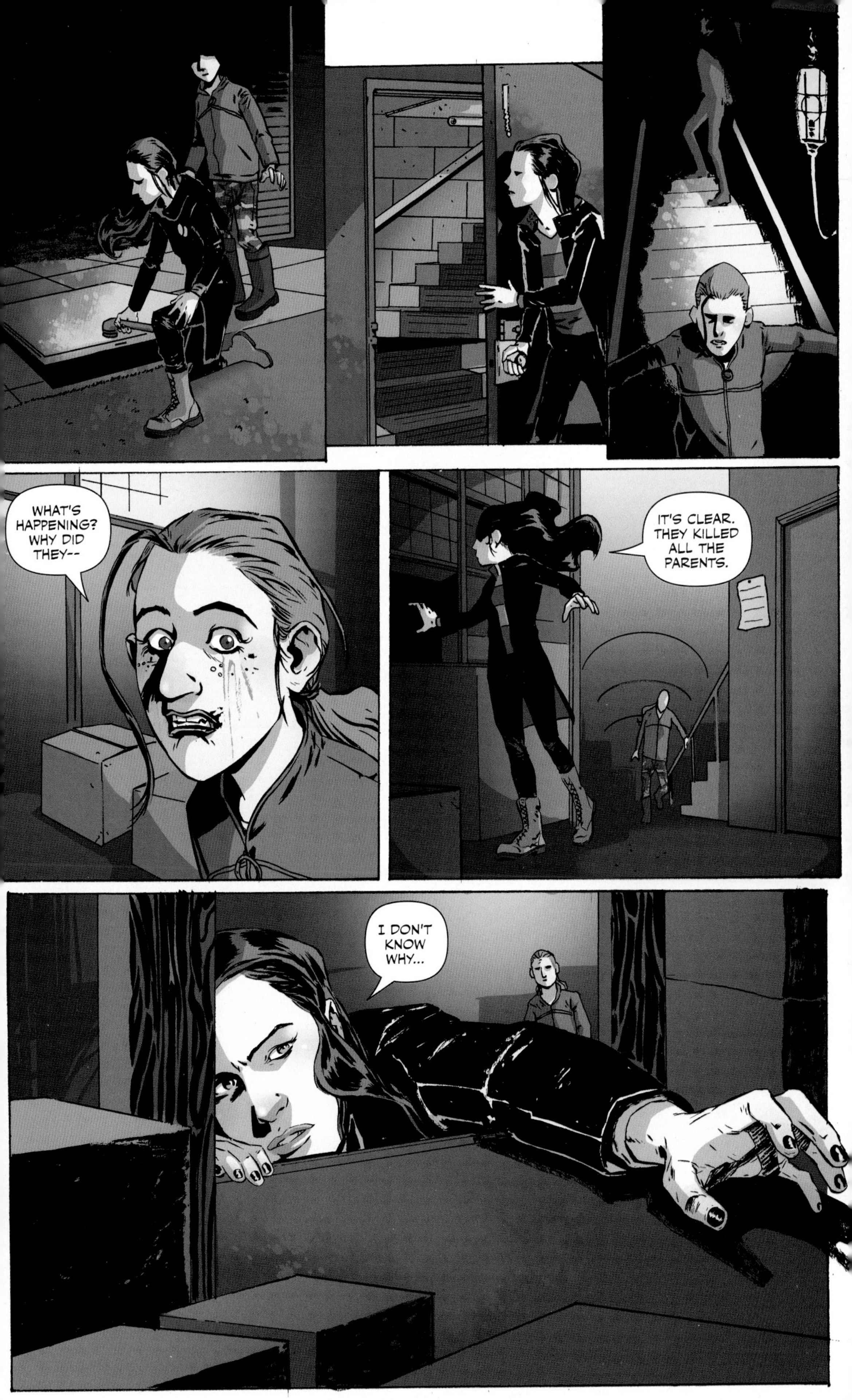
WHAT'S HAPPENING? WHY DID THEY--
IT'S CLEAR. THEY KILLED ALL THE PARENTS.
I DON'T KNOW WHY...

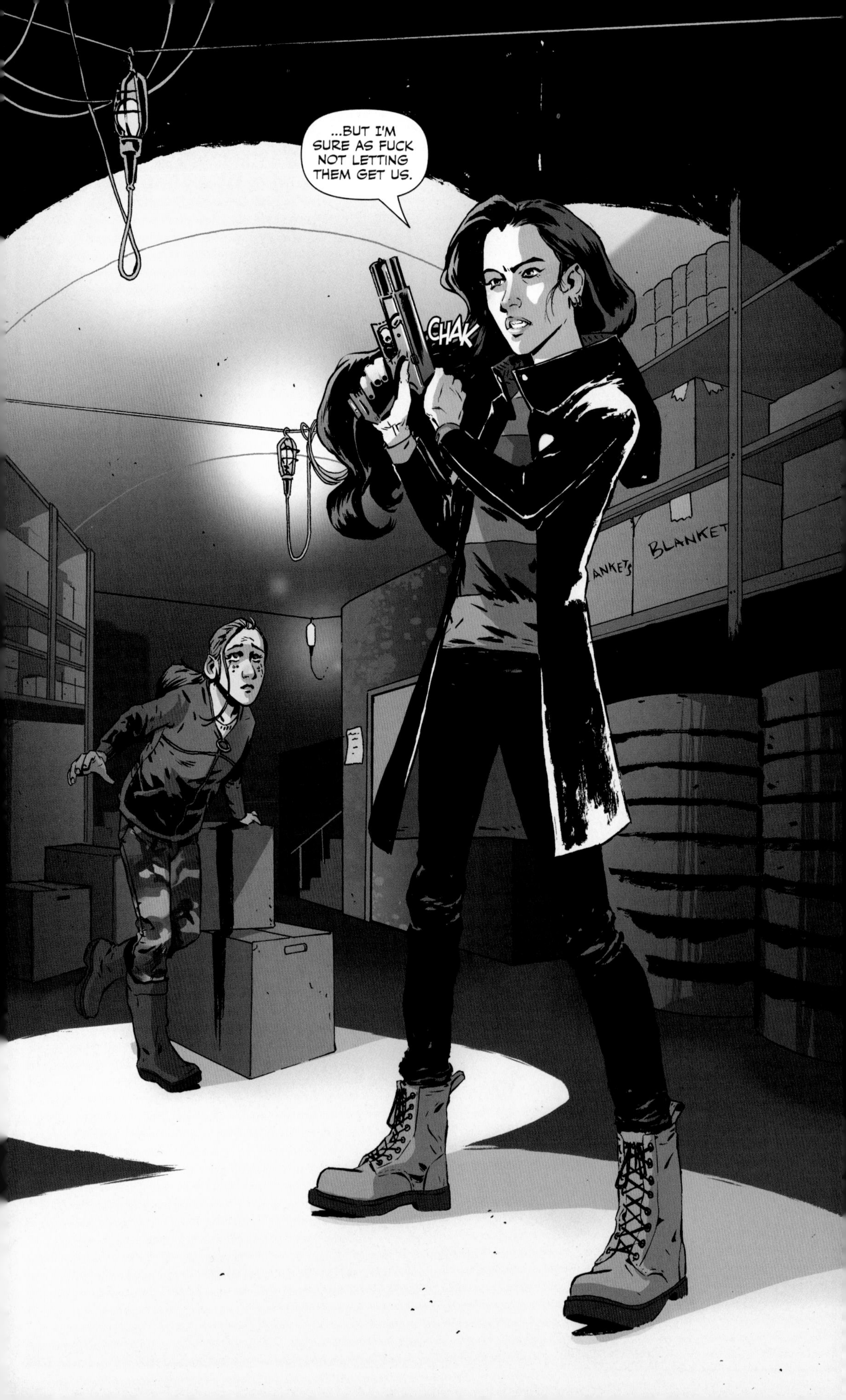

...BUT I'M SURE AS FUCK NOT LETTING THEM GET US.
CHAK
BLANKET
ANKETS

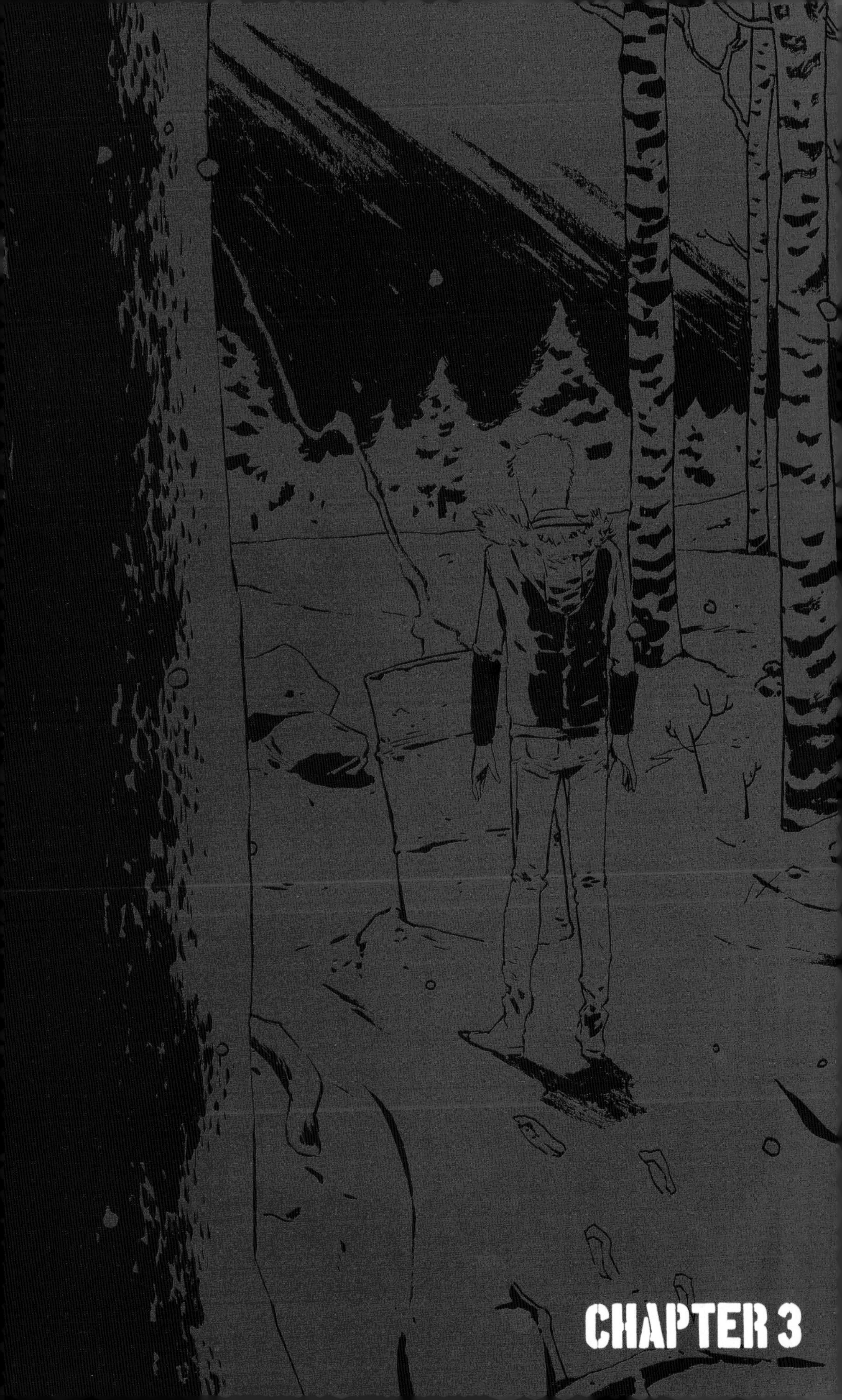

CHAPTER 3

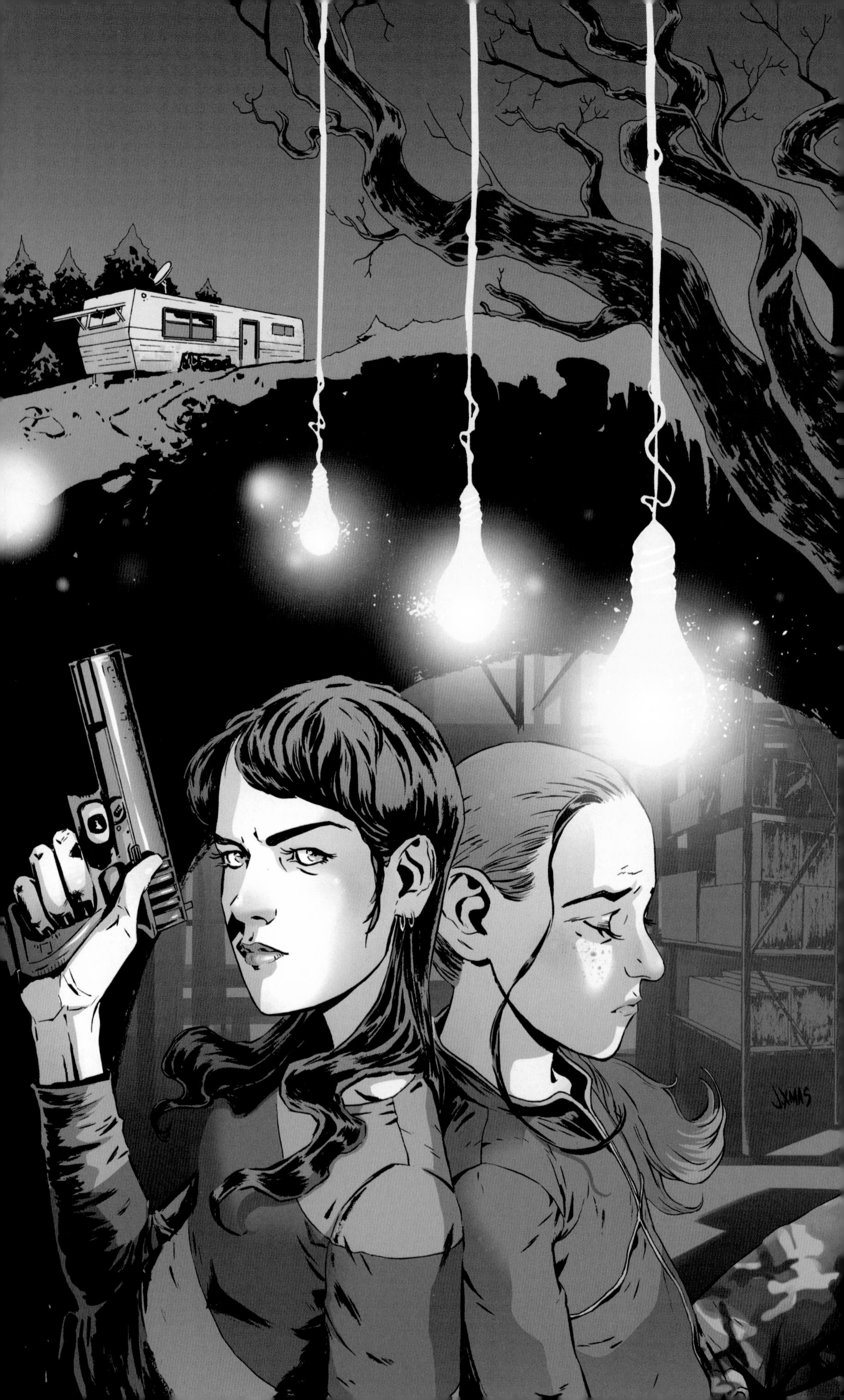

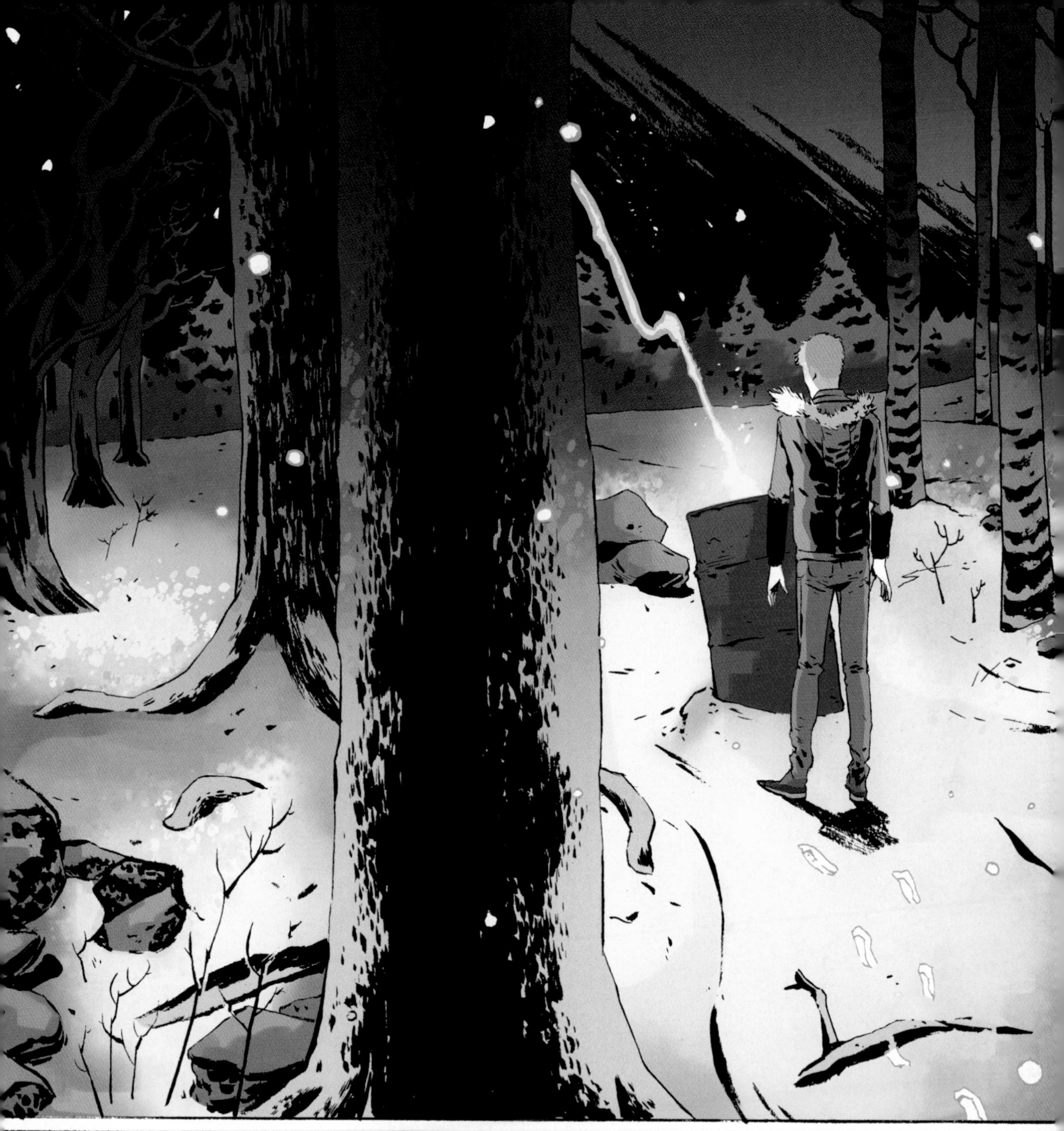

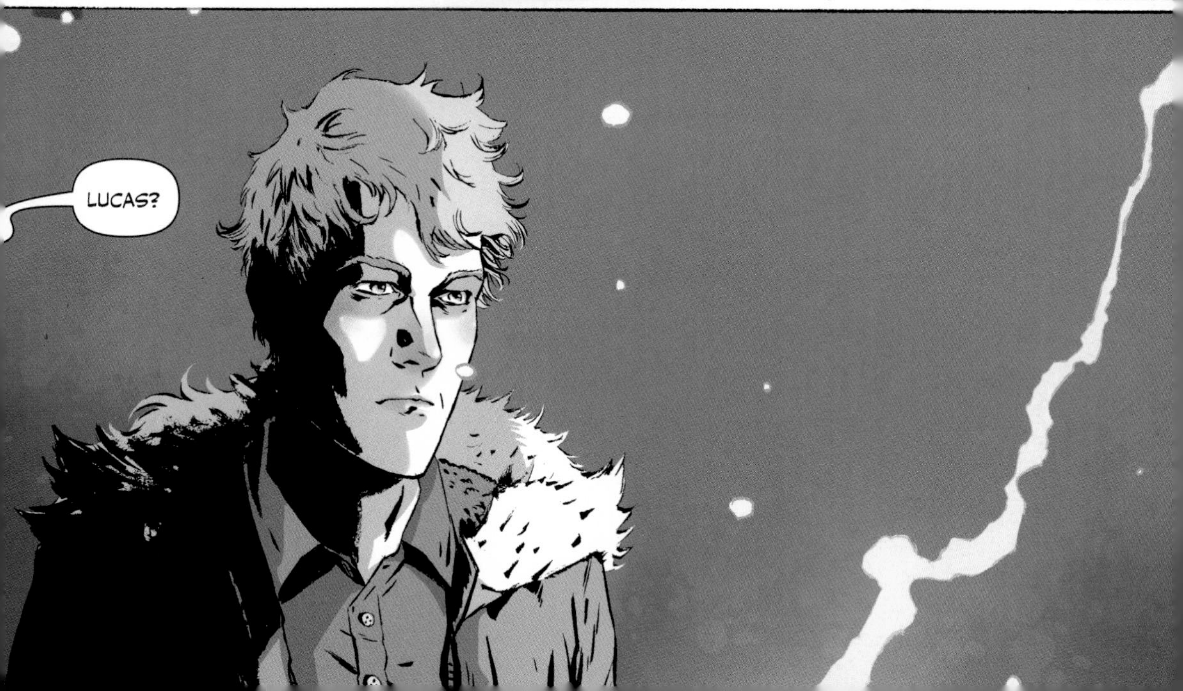
LUCAS?

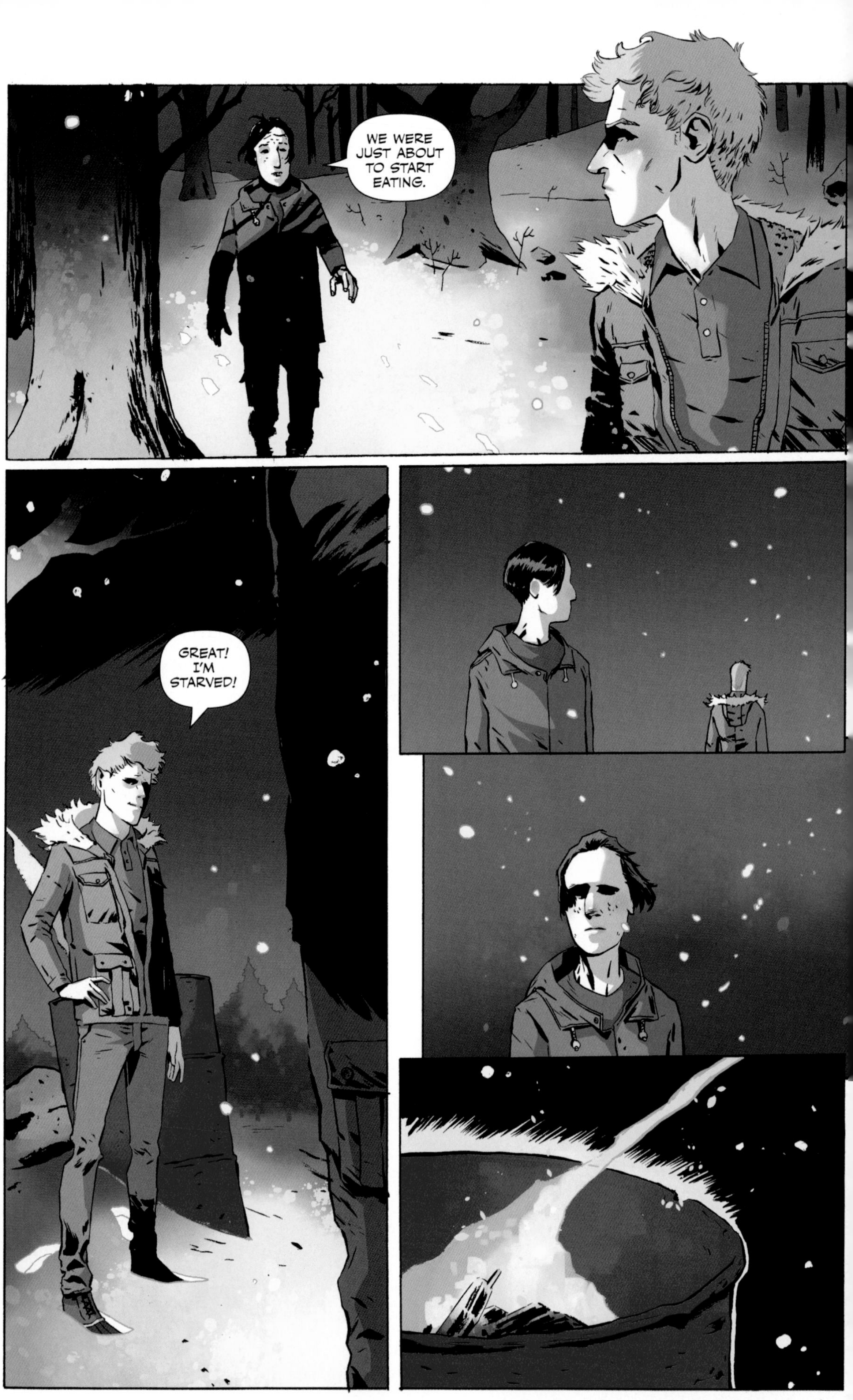
WE WERE JUST ABOUT TO START EATING.
GREAT! I'M STARVED!

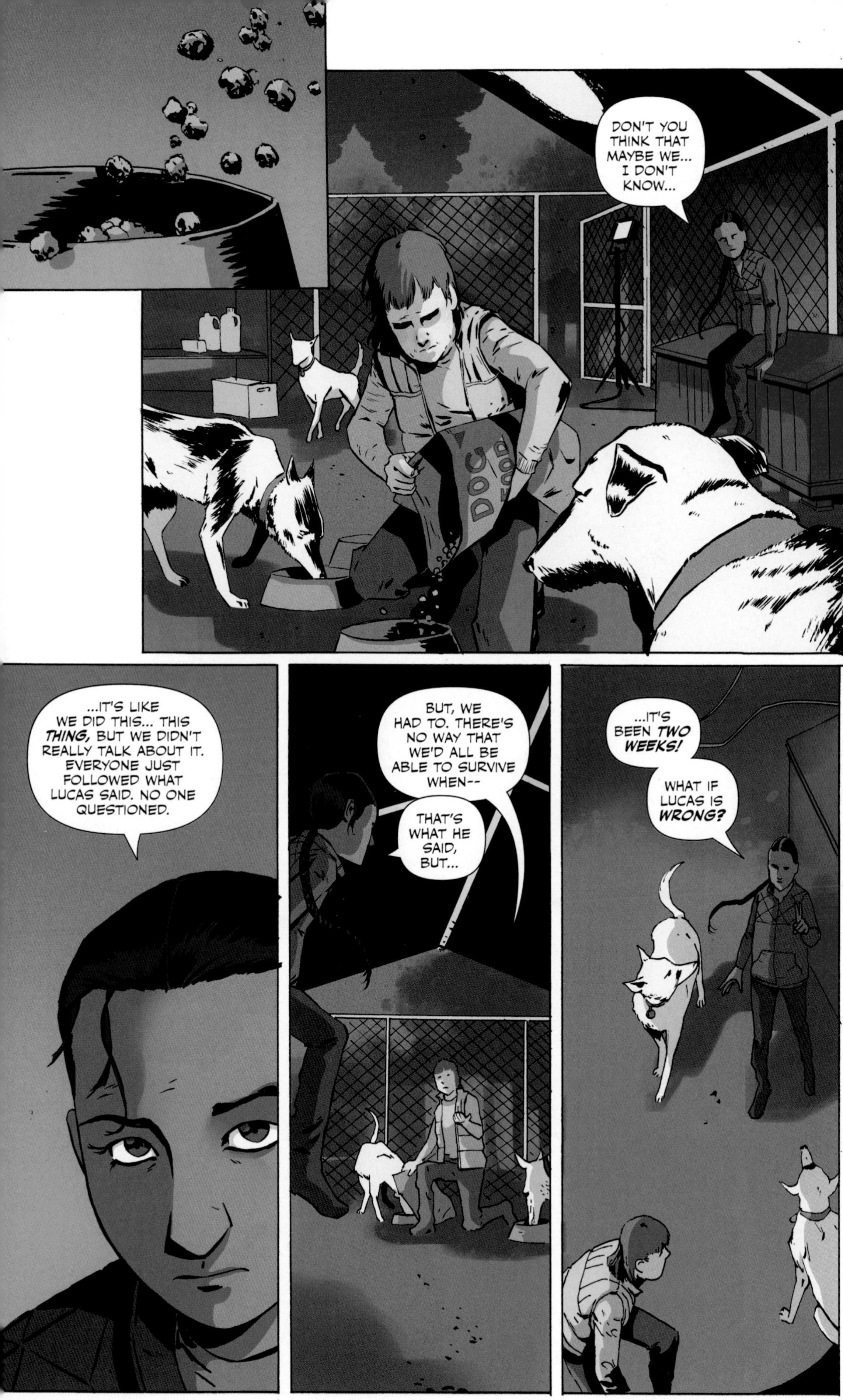
DON'T YOU THINK THAT MAYBE WE... I DON'T KNOW...
DOG FOOD
...IT'S LIKE WE DID THIS... THIS *THING,* BUT WE DIDN'T REALLY TALK ABOUT IT. EVERYONE JUST FOLLOWED WHAT LUCAS SAID. NO ONE QUESTIONED.
BUT, WE HAD TO. THERE'S NO WAY THAT WE'D ALL BE ABLE TO SURVIVE WHEN--
THAT'S WHAT HE SAID, BUT...
...IT'S BEEN *TWO WEEKS!*
WHAT IF LUCAS IS *WRONG?*

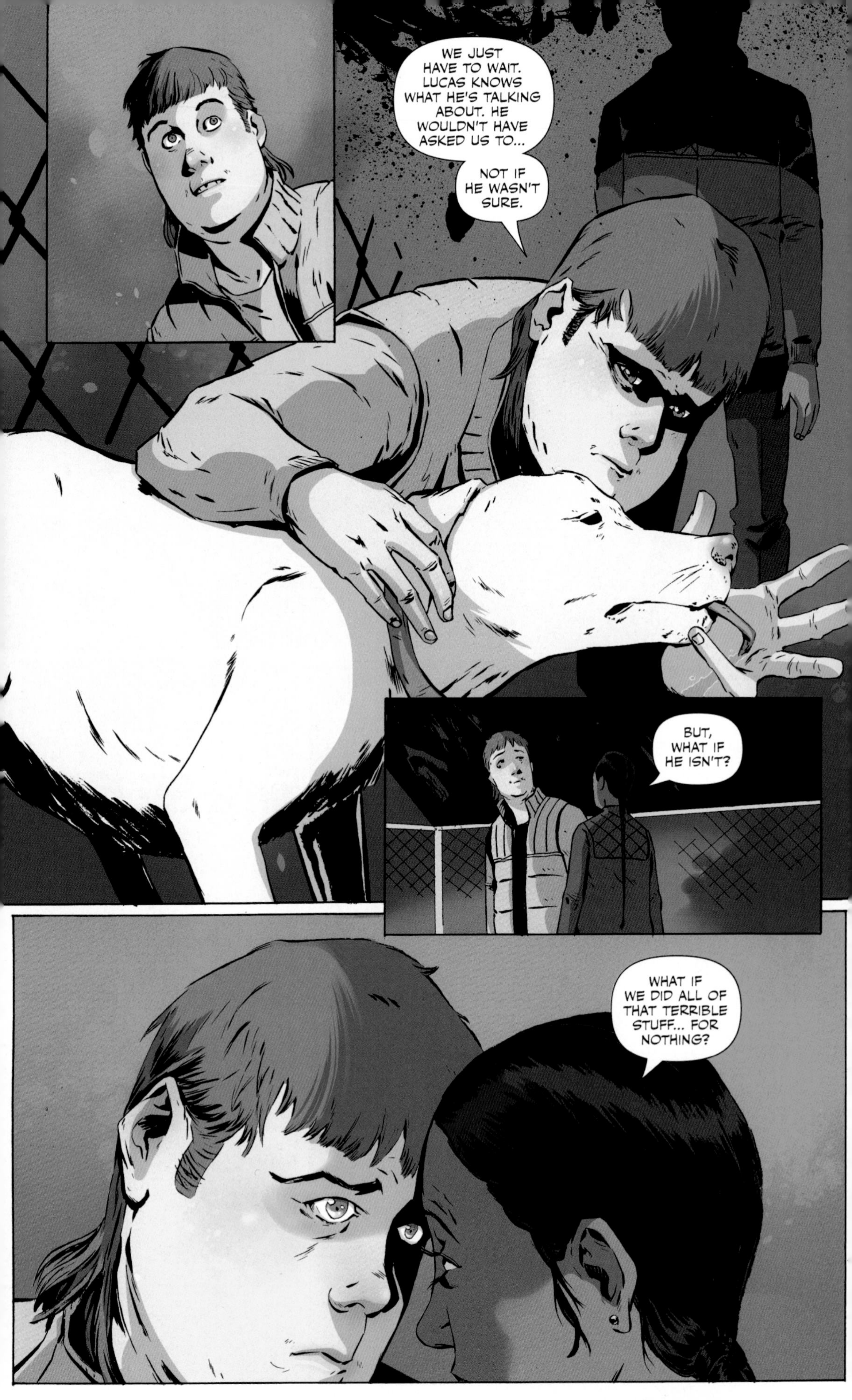

WE JUST HAVE TO WAIT. LUCAS KNOWS WHAT HE'S TALKING ABOUT. HE WOULDN'T HAVE ASKED US TO...
NOT IF HE WASN'T SURE.
BUT, WHAT IF HE ISN'T?
WHAT IF WE DID ALL OF THAT TERRIBLE STUFF... FOR NOTHING?

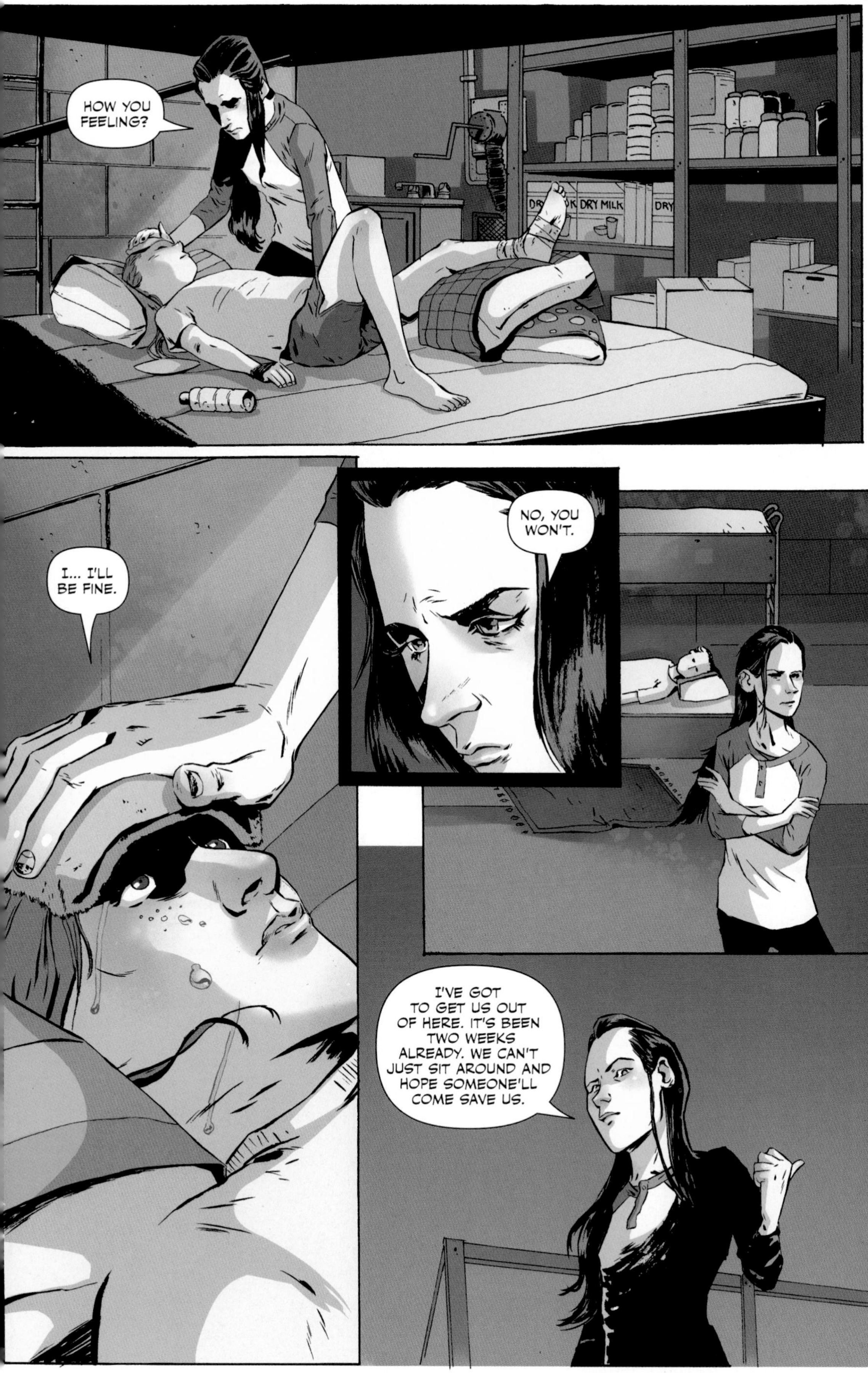
HOW YOU FEELING?
I... I'LL BE FINE.
NO, YOU WON'T.
I'VE GOT TO GET US OUT OF HERE. IT'S BEEN TWO WEEKS ALREADY. WE CAN'T JUST SIT AROUND AND HOPE SOMEONE'LL COME SAVE US.
DRY MILK

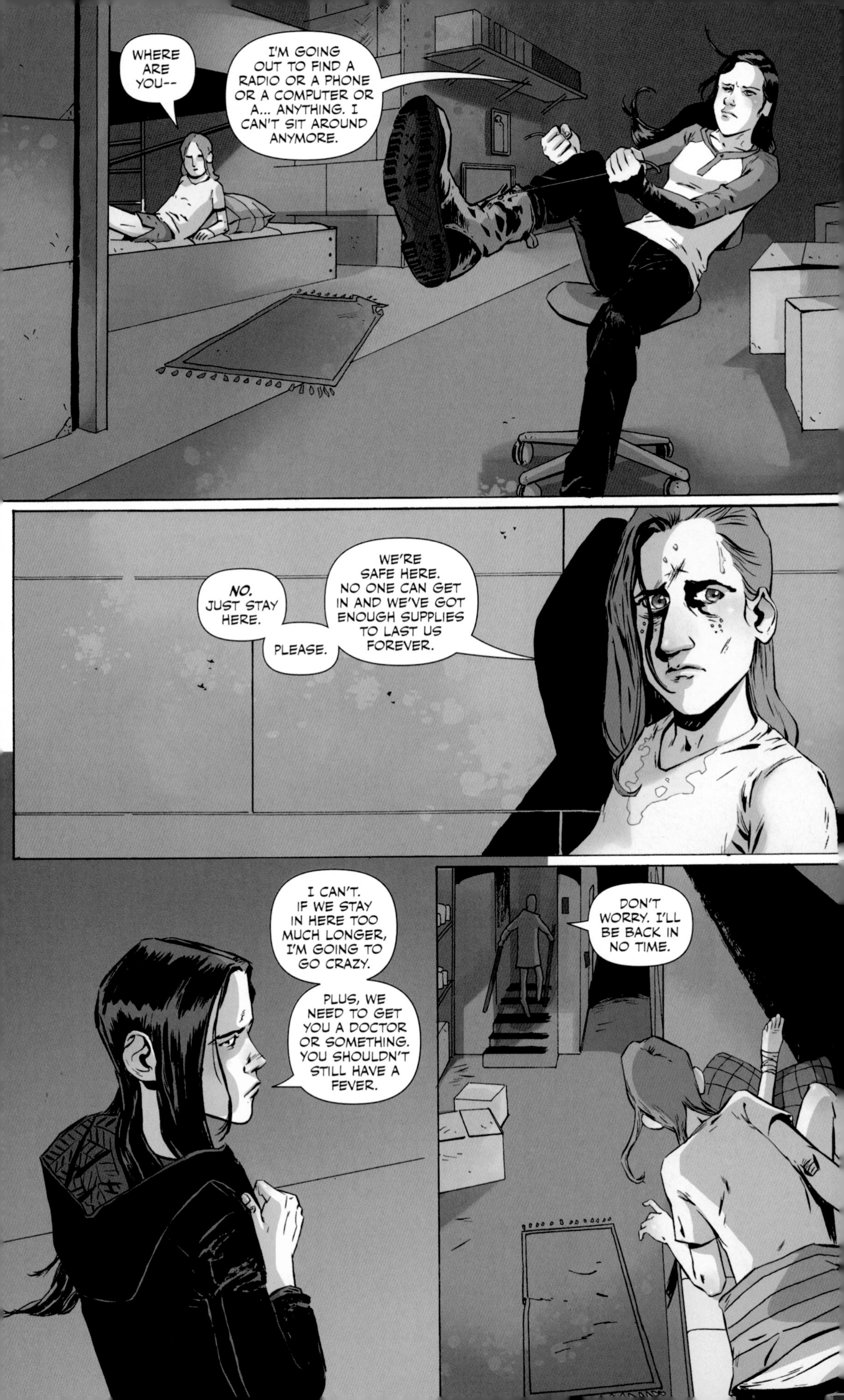
WHERE ARE YOU--
I'M GOING OUT TO FIND A RADIO OR A PHONE OR A COMPUTER OR A... ANYTHING. I CAN'T SIT AROUND ANYMORE.
NO. JUST STAY HERE.
PLEASE.
WE'RE SAFE HERE. NO ONE CAN GET IN AND WE'VE GOT ENOUGH SUPPLIES TO LAST US FOREVER.
I CAN'T. IF WE STAY IN HERE TOO MUCH LONGER, I'M GOING TO GO CRAZY.
PLUS, WE NEED TO GET YOU A DOCTOR OR SOMETHING. YOU SHOULDN'T STILL HAVE A FEVER.
DON'T WORRY. I'LL BE BACK IN NO TIME.

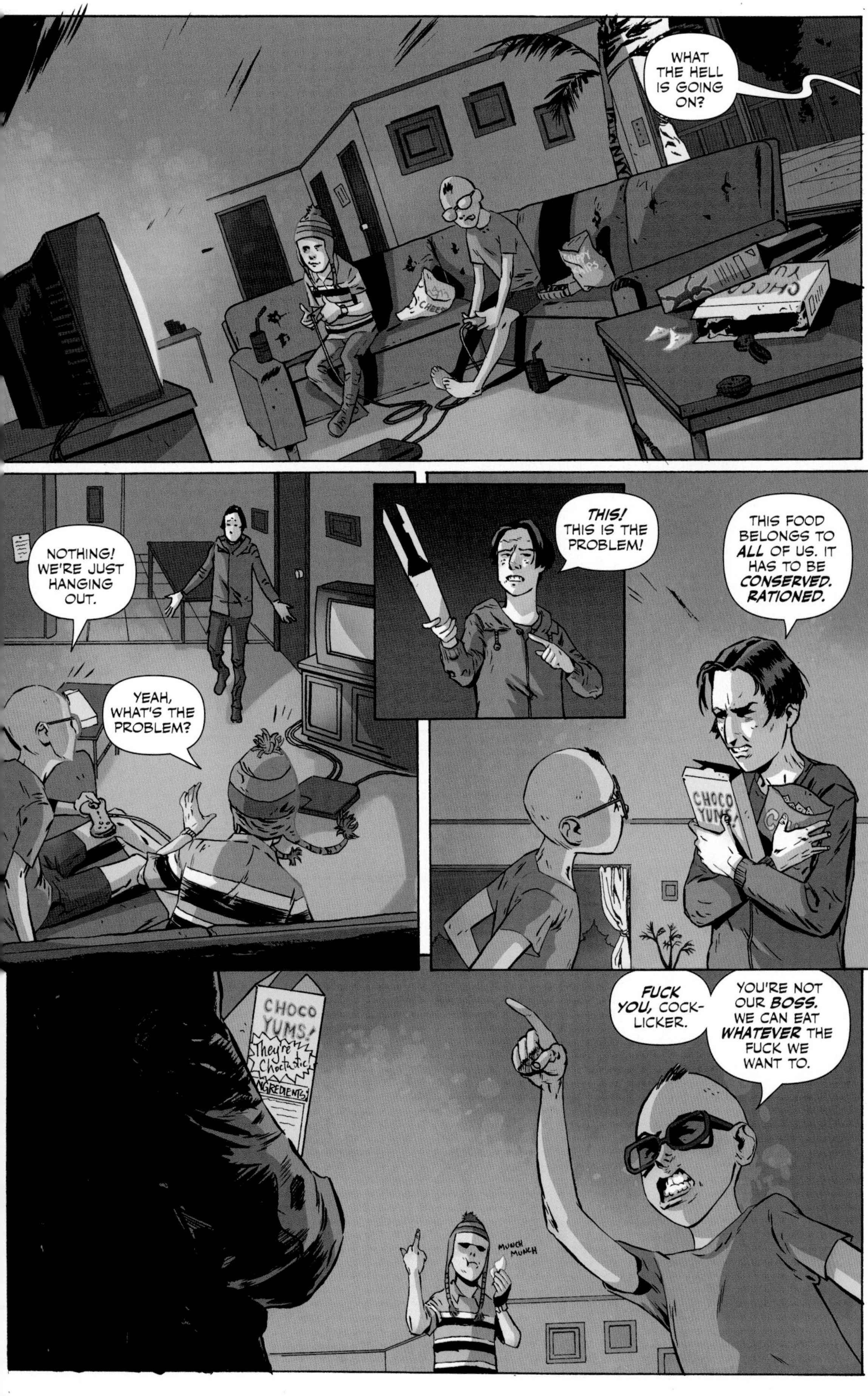
WHAT THE HELL IS GOING ON?
NOTHING! WE'RE JUST HANGING OUT.
YEAH, WHAT'S THE PROBLEM?
THIS! THIS IS THE PROBLEM!
THIS FOOD BELONGS TO ALL OF US. IT HAS TO BE CONSERVED. RATIONED.
CHOCO YUMS!
CHOCO YUMS!
They're Choctastic!
FUCK YOU, COCK-LICKER.
YOU'RE NOT OUR BOSS. WE CAN EAT WHATEVER THE FUCK WE WANT TO.
MUNCH MUNCH

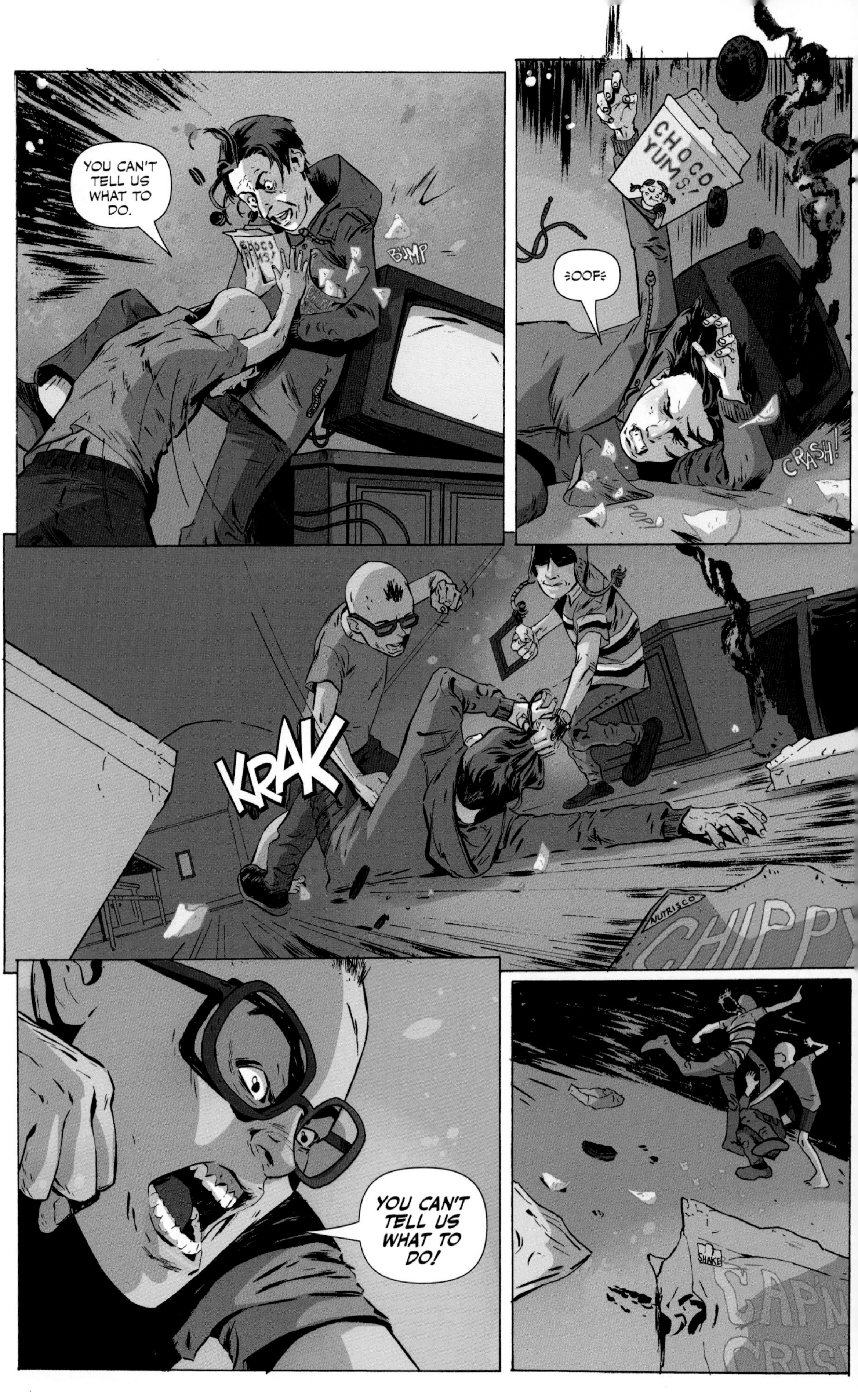
YOU CAN'T TELL US WHAT TO DO.
BUMP
CHOCO YUMS!
OOF
CRASH!
POP!
KRAK
NUTRISCO
CHIPPY
YOU CAN'T TELL US WHAT TO DO!
SHAKE
CAP'N

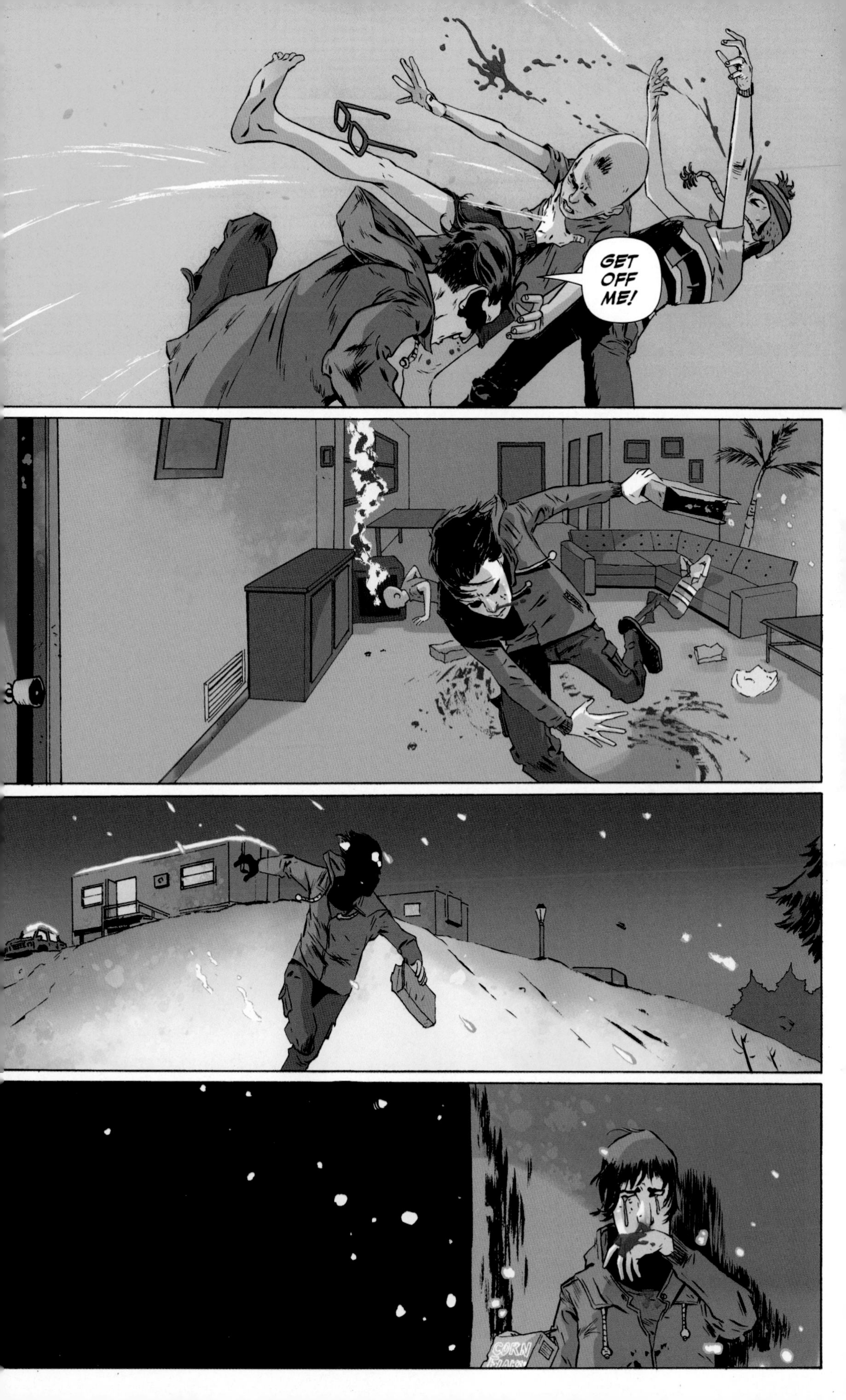
GET OFF ME!
CORN

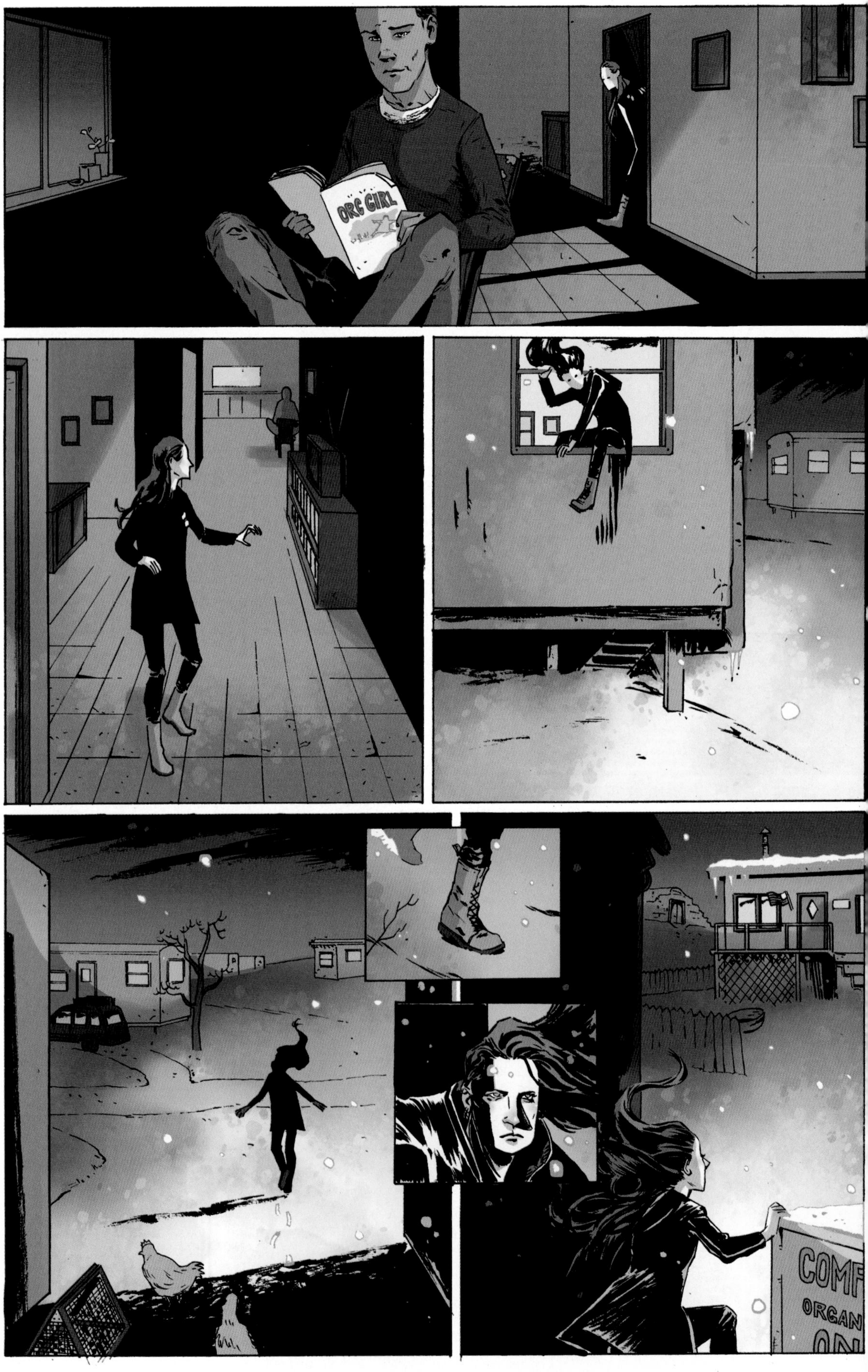
ORC GIRL
COMF
ORGAN

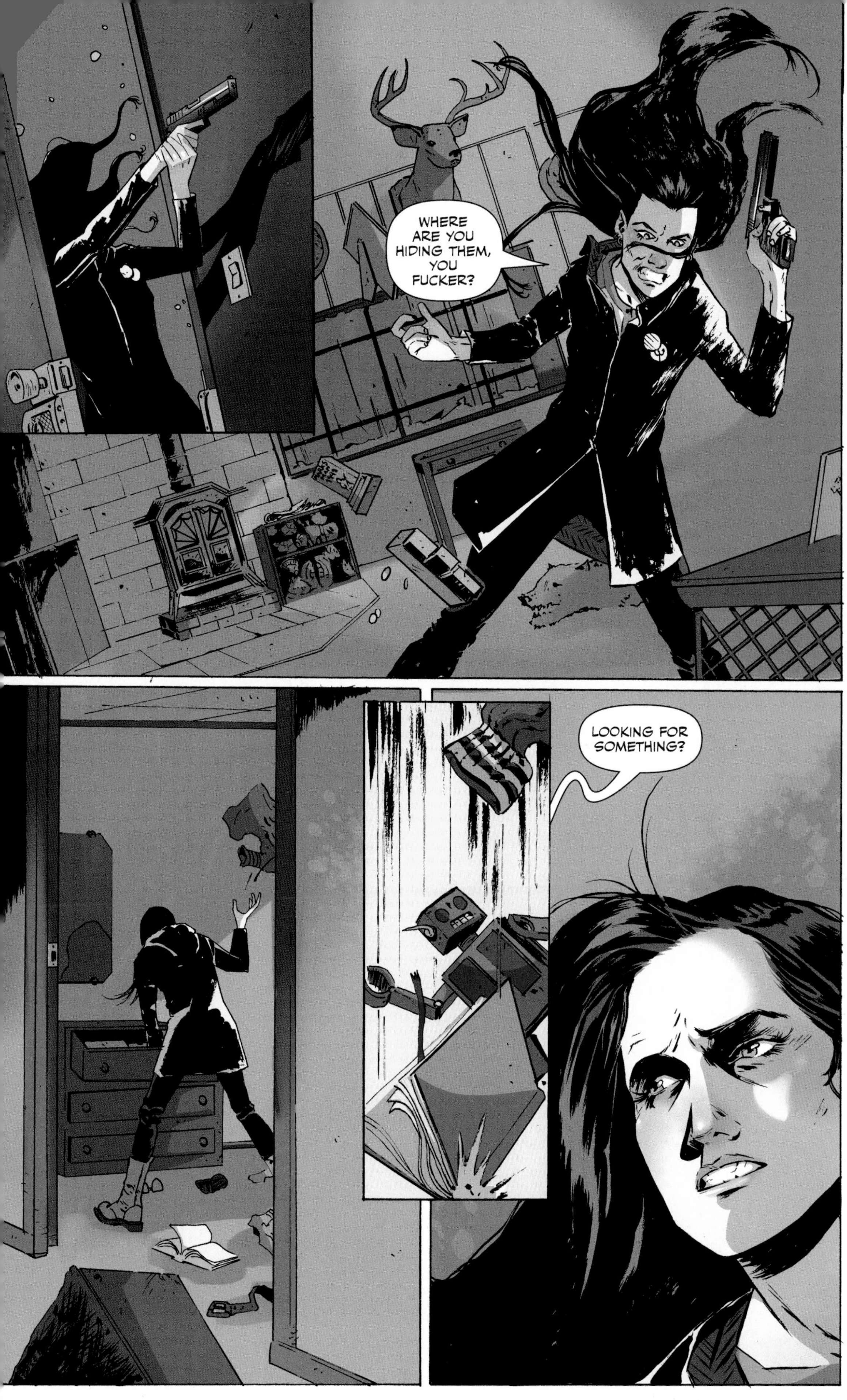
WHERE ARE YOU HIDING THEM, YOU FUCKER?
LOOKING FOR SOMETHING?

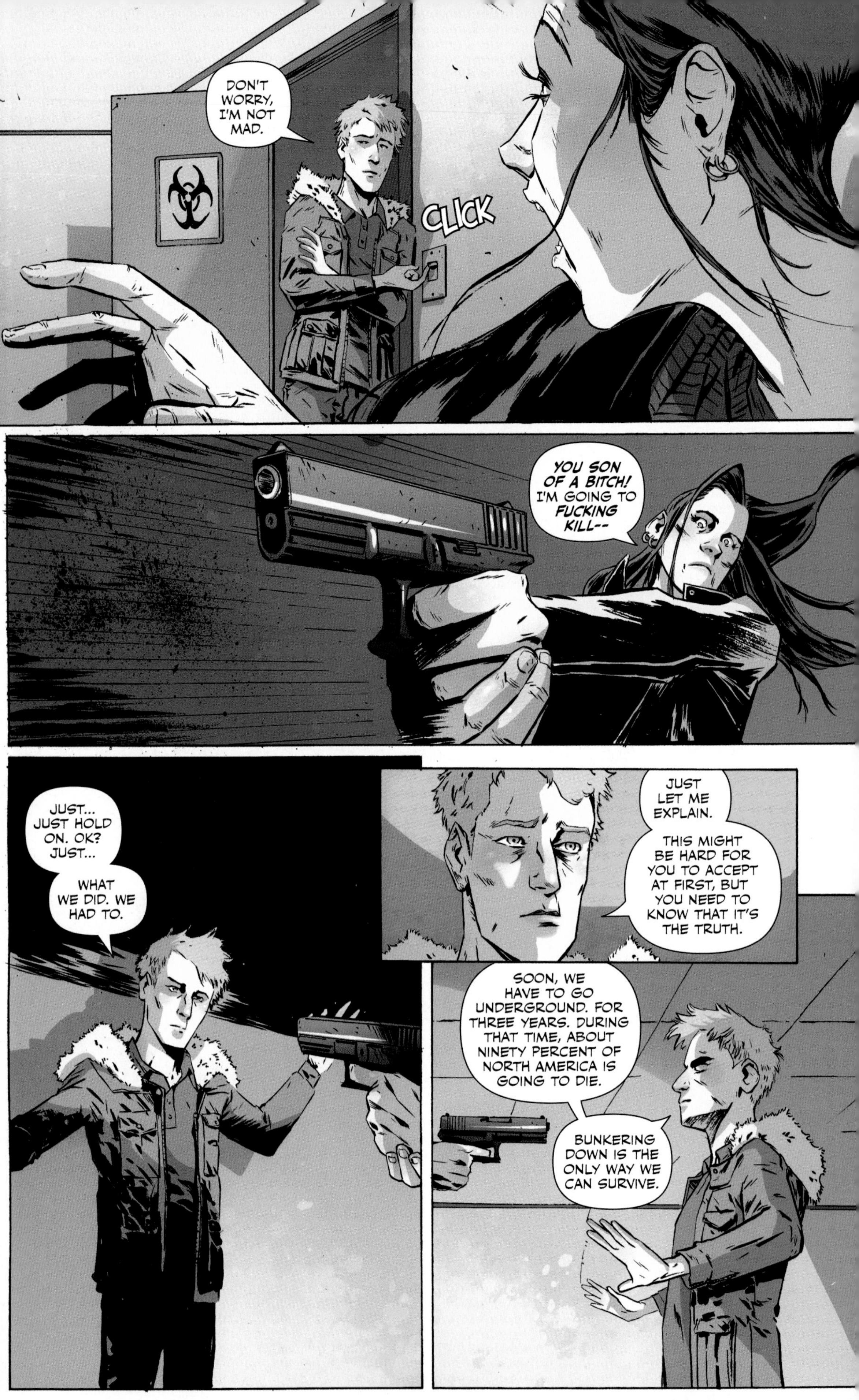
DON'T WORRY, I'M NOT MAD.
CLICK
YOU SON OF A BITCH! I'M GOING TO FUCKING KILL--
JUST... JUST HOLD ON. OK? JUST...
WHAT WE DID. WE HAD TO.
JUST LET ME EXPLAIN.
THIS MIGHT BE HARD FOR YOU TO ACCEPT AT FIRST, BUT YOU NEED TO KNOW THAT IT'S THE TRUTH.
SOON, WE HAVE TO GO UNDERGROUND. FOR THREE YEARS. DURING THAT TIME, ABOUT NINETY PERCENT OF NORTH AMERICA IS GOING TO DIE.
BUNKERING DOWN IS THE ONLY WAY WE CAN SURVIVE.

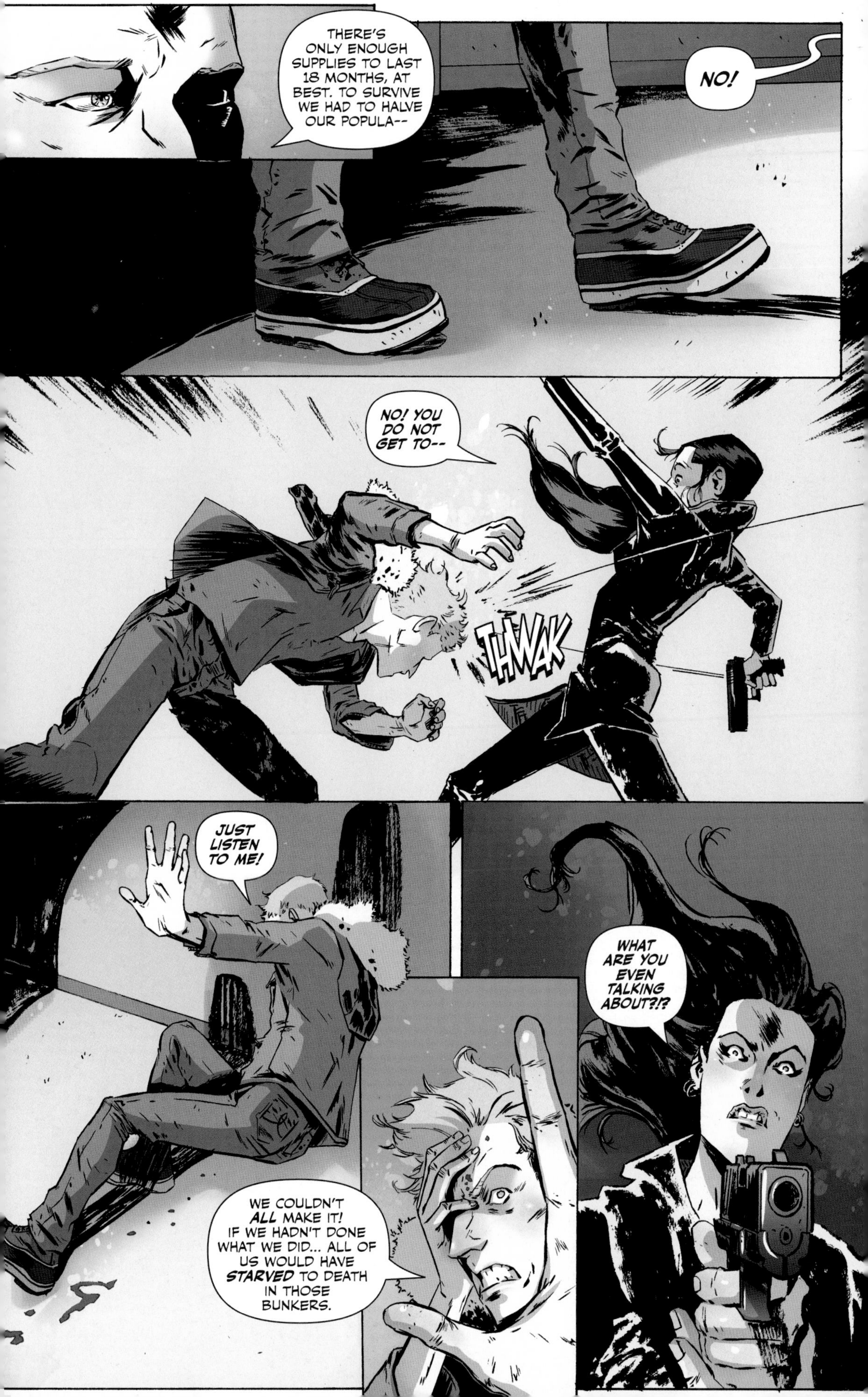
THERE'S ONLY ENOUGH SUPPLIES TO LAST 18 MONTHS, AT BEST. TO SURVIVE WE HAD TO HALVE OUR POPULA--
NO!
NO! YOU DO NOT GET TO--
THWAK
JUST LISTEN TO ME!
WHAT ARE YOU EVEN TALKING ABOUT?!?
WE COULDN'T ALL MAKE IT! IF WE HADN'T DONE WHAT WE DID... ALL OF US WOULD HAVE STARVED TO DEATH IN THOSE BUNKERS.

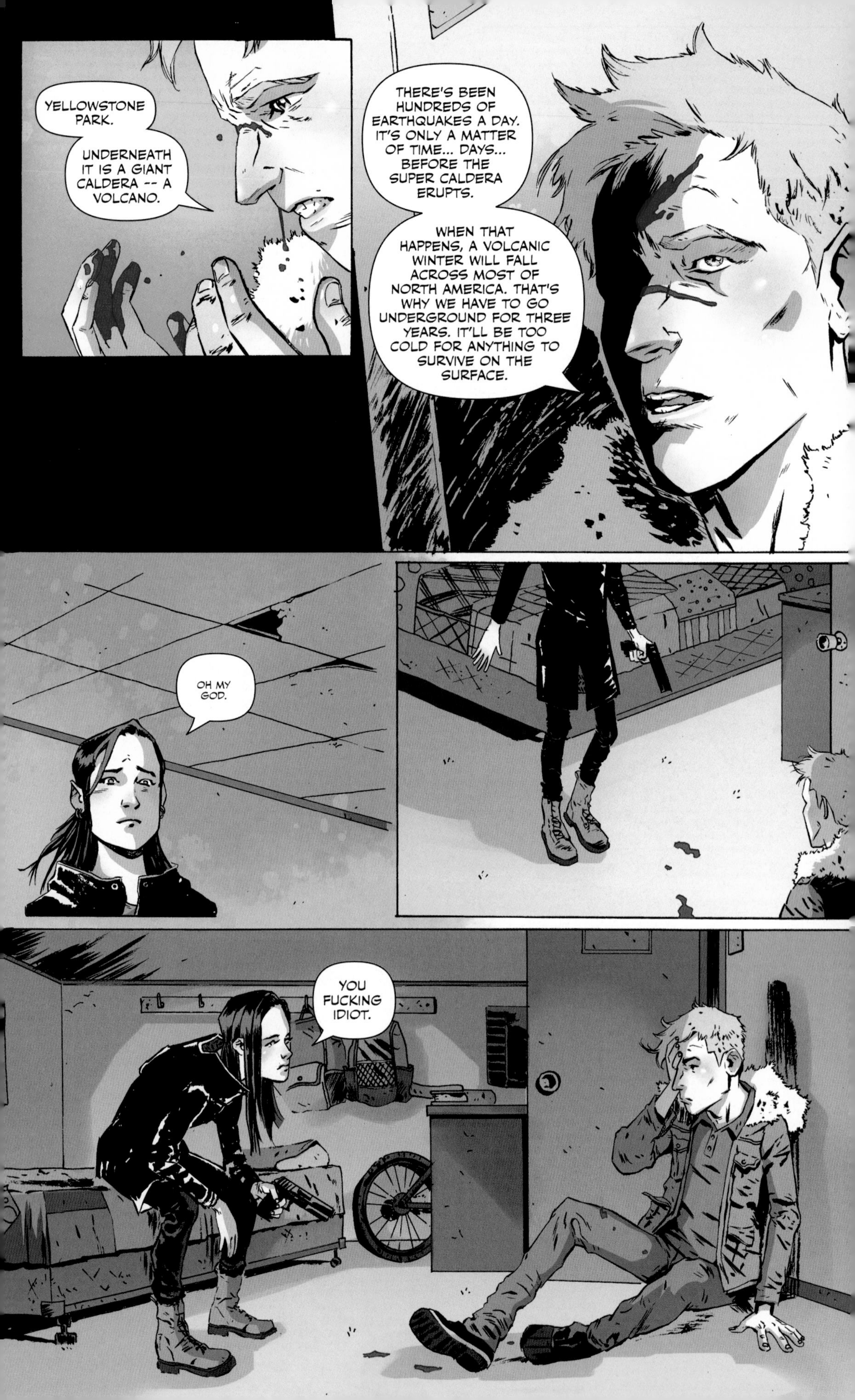
YELLOWSTONE PARK.
UNDERNEATH IT IS A GIANT CALDERA -- A VOLCANO.
THERE'S BEEN HUNDREDS OF EARTHQUAKES A DAY. IT'S ONLY A MATTER OF TIME... DAYS... BEFORE THE SUPER CALDERA ERUPTS.
WHEN THAT HAPPENS, A VOLCANIC WINTER WILL FALL ACROSS MOST OF NORTH AMERICA. THAT'S WHY WE HAVE TO GO UNDERGROUND FOR THREE YEARS. IT'LL BE TOO COLD FOR ANYTHING TO SURVIVE ON THE SURFACE.
OH MY GOD.
YOU FUCKING IDIOT.

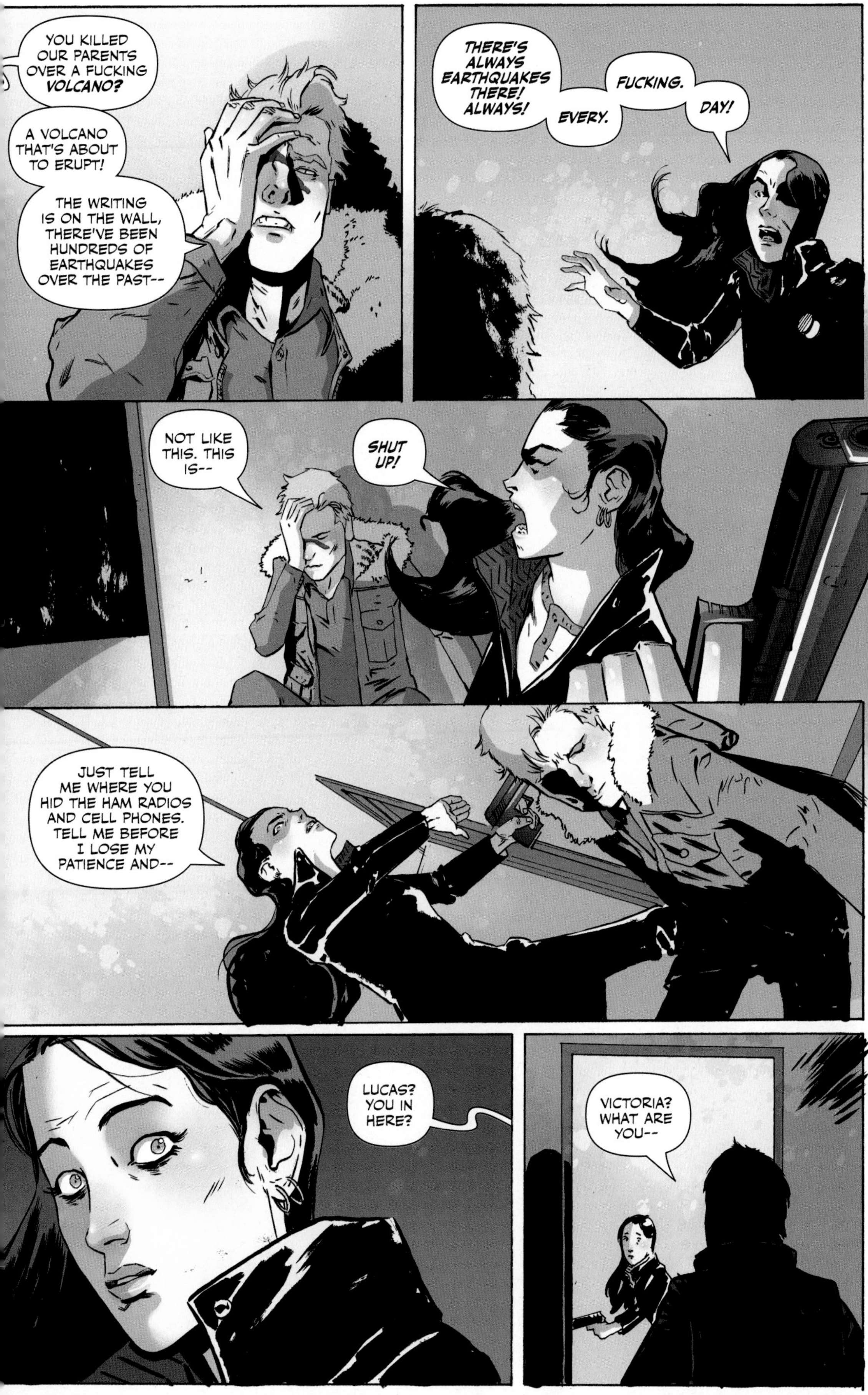
YOU KILLED OUR PARENTS OVER A FUCKING *VOLCANO?*
A VOLCANO THAT'S ABOUT TO ERUPT!
THE WRITING IS ON THE WALL, THERE'VE BEEN HUNDREDS OF EARTHQUAKES OVER THE PAST--
THERE'S ALWAYS EARTHQUAKES THERE! ALWAYS!
EVERY.
FUCKING.
DAY!
NOT LIKE THIS. THIS IS--
SHUT UP!
JUST TELL ME WHERE YOU HID THE HAM RADIOS AND CELL PHONES. TELL ME BEFORE I LOSE MY PATIENCE AND--
LUCAS? YOU IN HERE?
VICTORIA? WHAT ARE YOU--

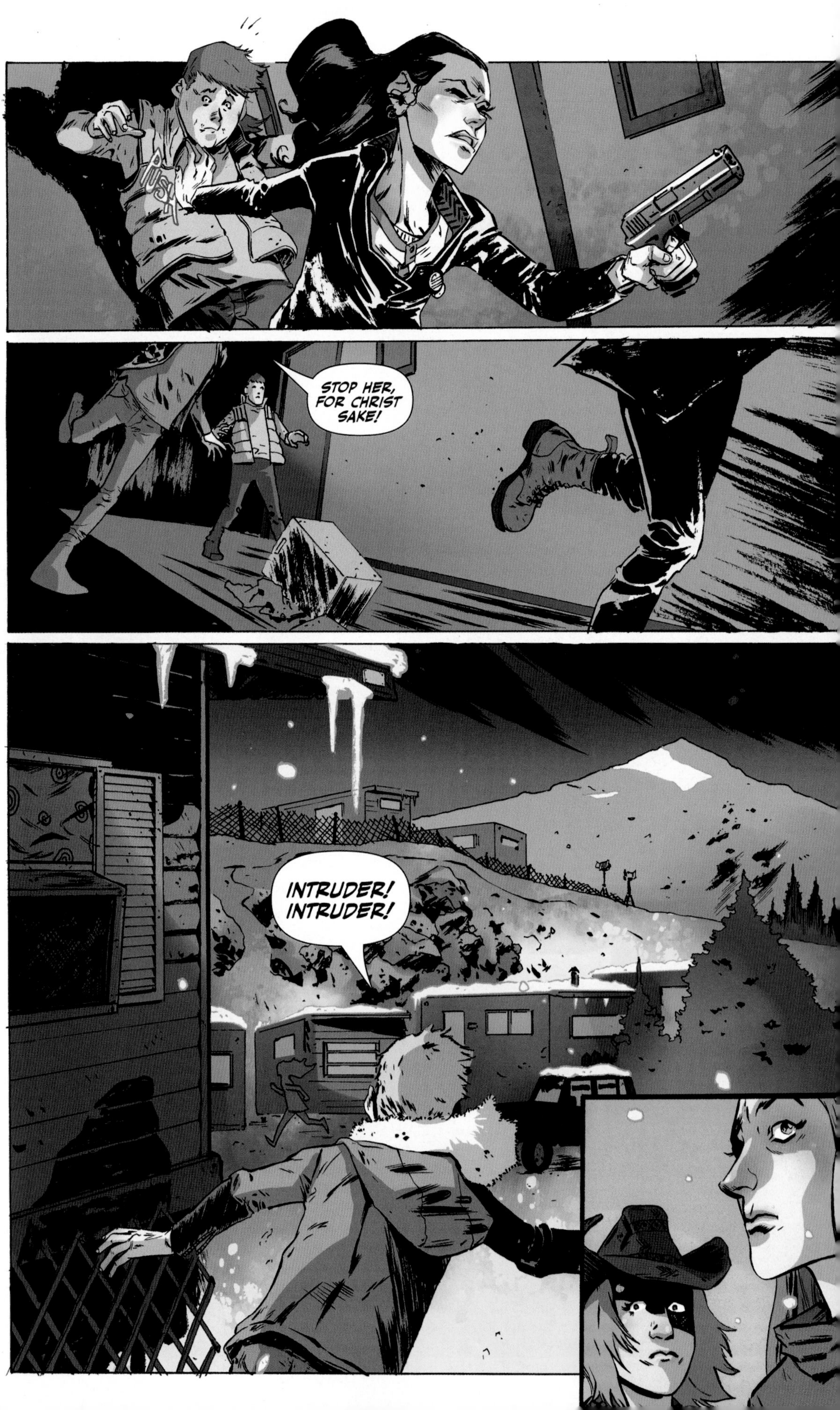
STOP HER, FOR CHRIST SAKE!
INTRUDER! INTRUDER!

BDUMP

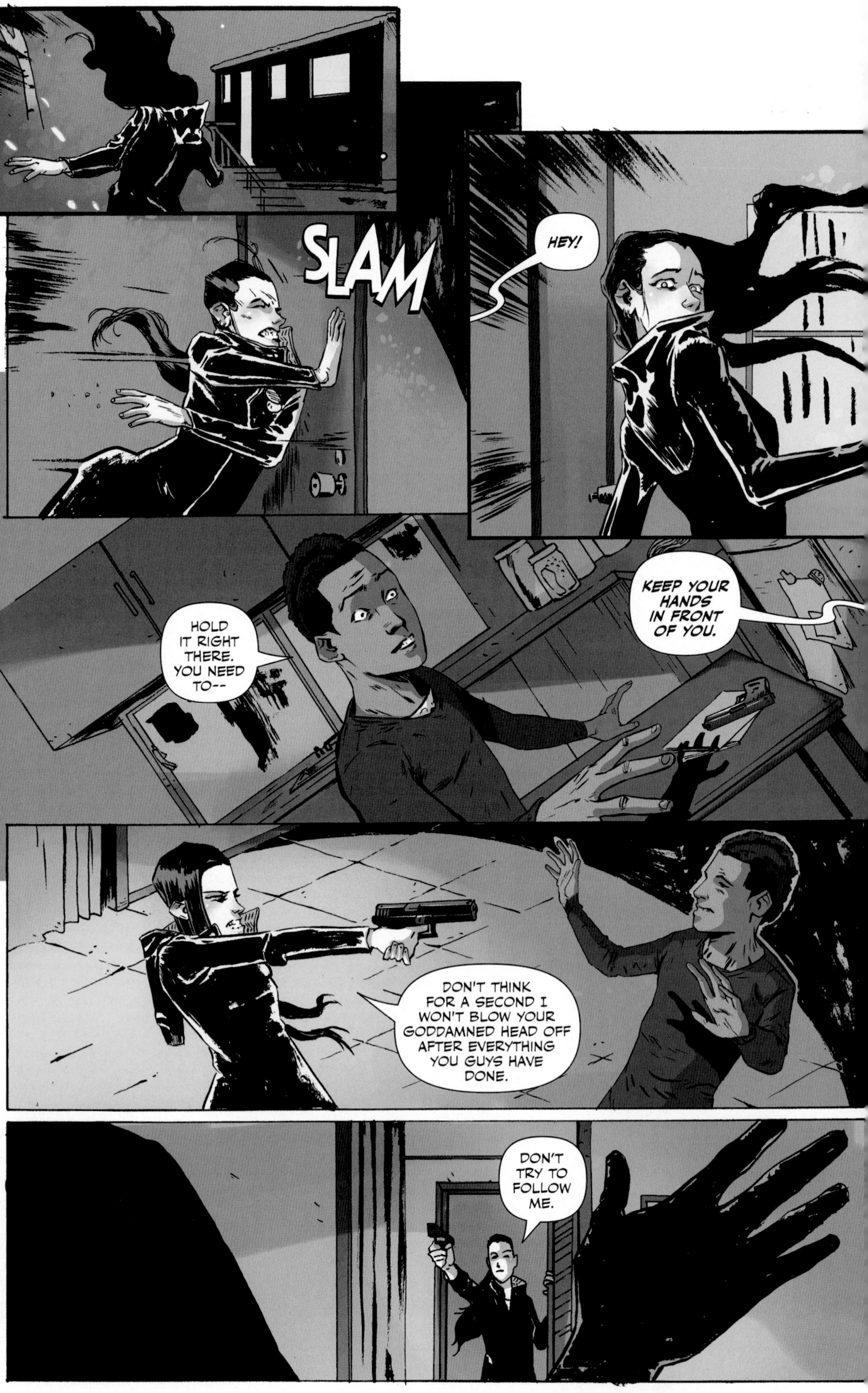
SLAM
HEY!
HOLD IT RIGHT THERE. YOU NEED TO--
KEEP YOUR HANDS IN FRONT OF YOU.
DON'T THINK FOR A SECOND I WON'T BLOW YOUR GODDAMNED HEAD OFF AFTER EVERYTHING YOU GUYS HAVE DONE.
DON'T TRY TO FOLLOW ME.

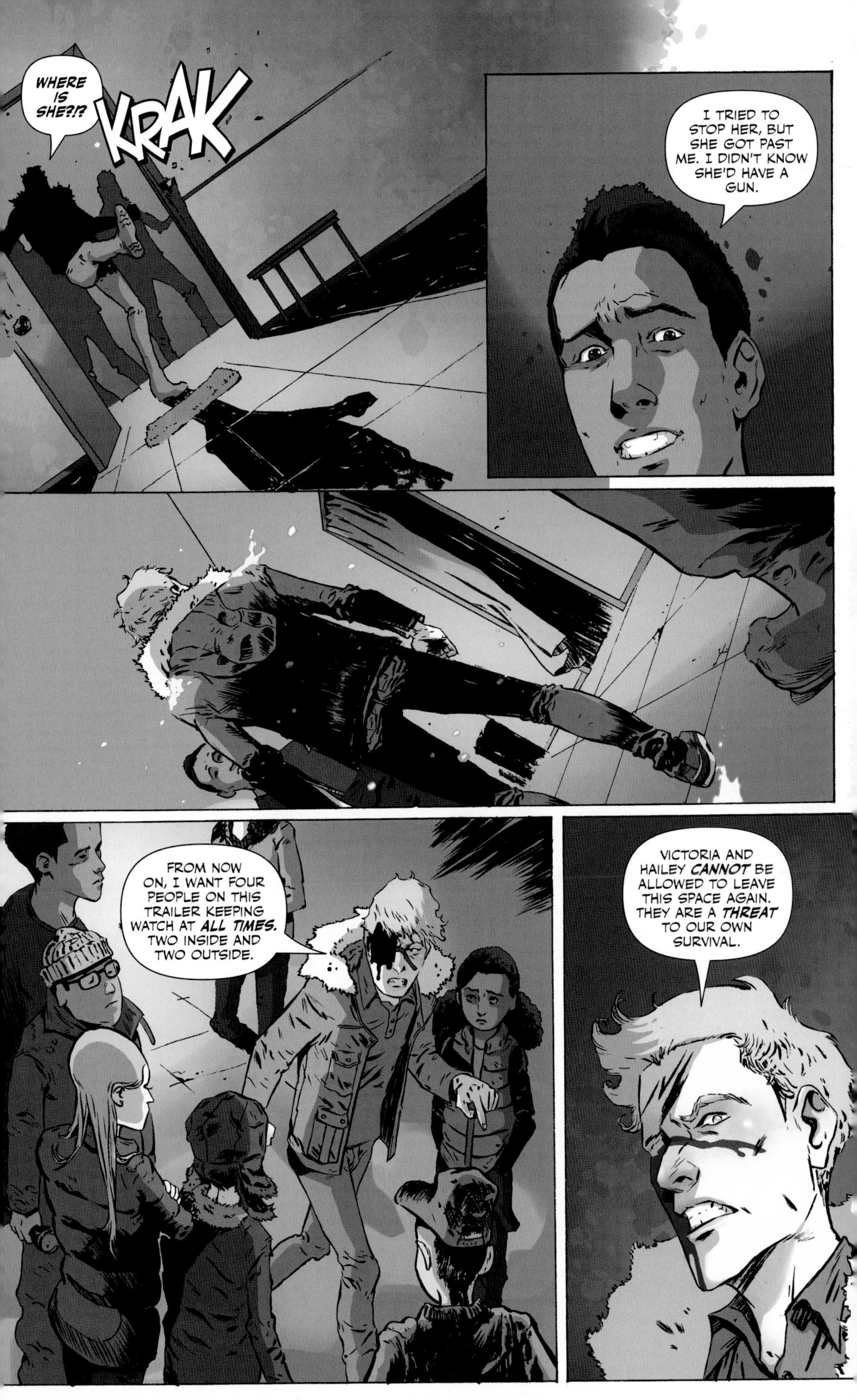
WHERE IS SHE?!?
KRAK
I TRIED TO STOP HER, BUT SHE GOT PAST ME. I DIDN'T KNOW SHE'D HAVE A GUN.
FROM NOW ON, I WANT FOUR PEOPLE ON THIS TRAILER KEEPING WATCH AT ALL TIMES. TWO INSIDE AND TWO OUTSIDE.
VICTORIA AND HAILEY CANNOT BE ALLOWED TO LEAVE THIS SPACE AGAIN. THEY ARE A THREAT TO OUR OWN SURVIVAL.

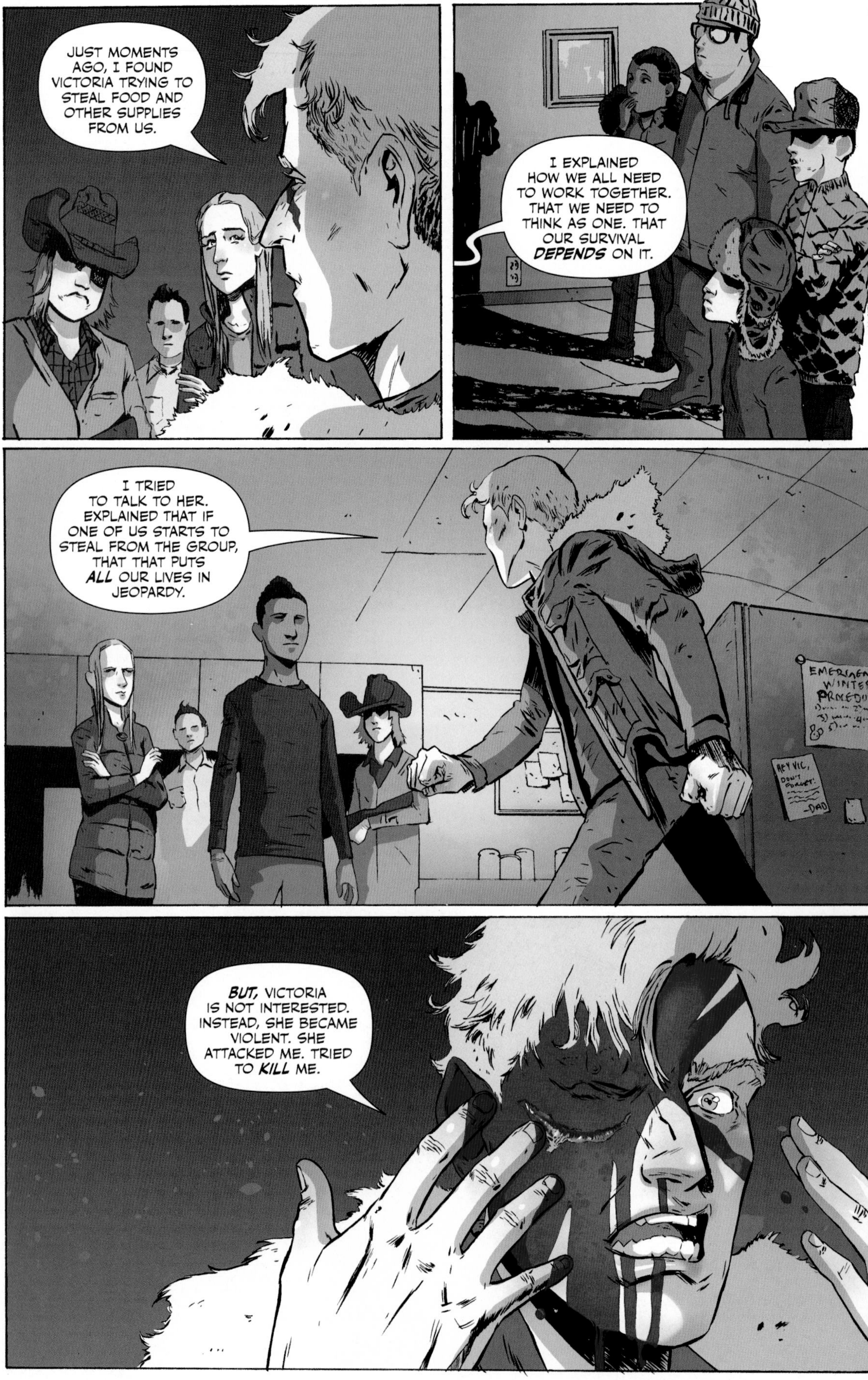
JUST MOMENTS AGO, I FOUND VICTORIA TRYING TO STEAL FOOD AND OTHER SUPPLIES FROM US.
I EXPLAINED HOW WE ALL NEED TO WORK TOGETHER. THAT WE NEED TO THINK AS ONE. THAT OUR SURVIVAL DEPENDS ON IT.
I TRIED TO TALK TO HER. EXPLAINED THAT IF ONE OF US STARTS TO STEAL FROM THE GROUP, THAT THAT PUTS ALL OUR LIVES IN JEOPARDY.
HEY VIC,
-DAD
BUT, VICTORIA IS NOT INTERESTED. INSTEAD, SHE BECAME VIOLENT. SHE ATTACKED ME. TRIED TO KILL ME.

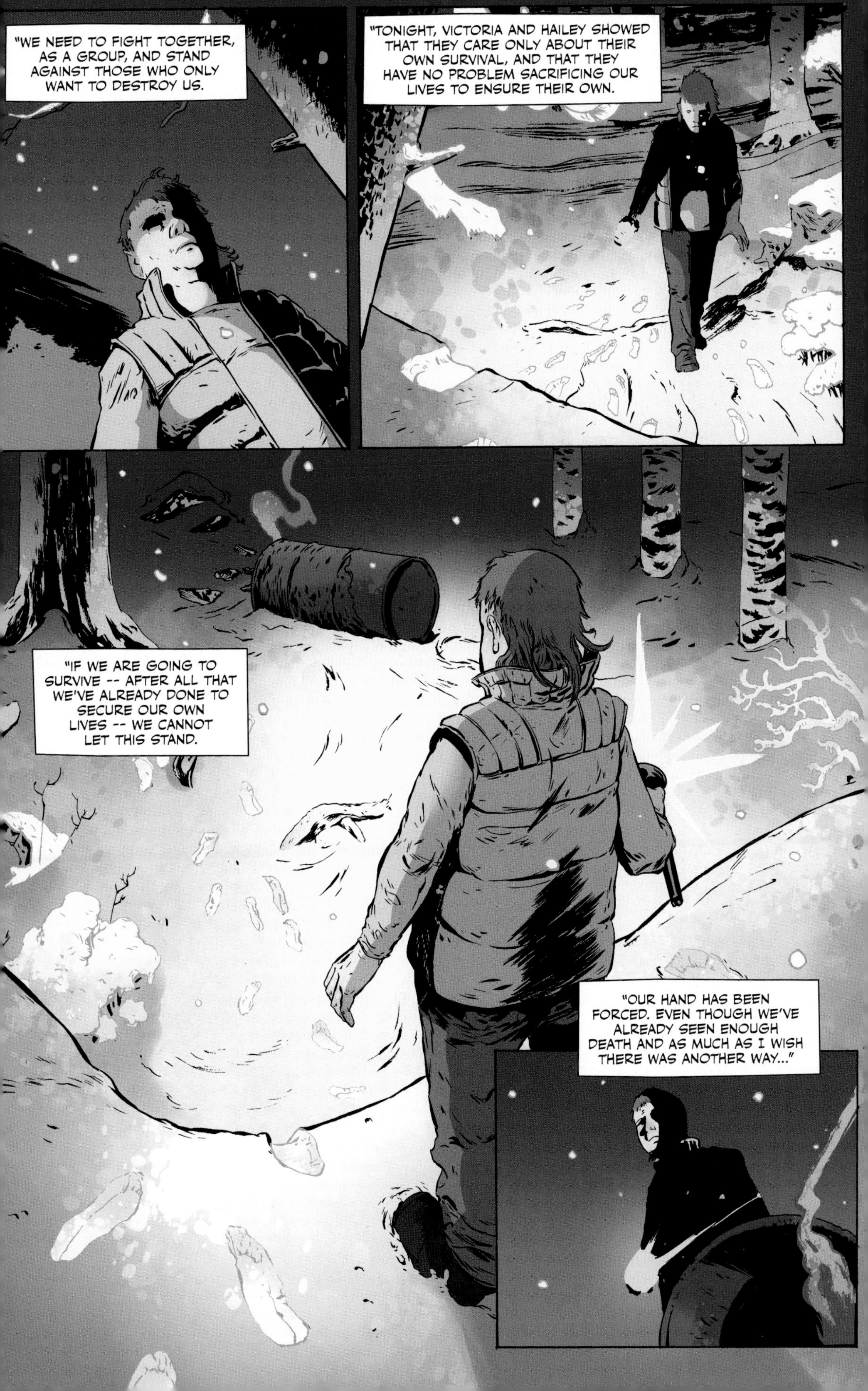
"WE NEED TO FIGHT TOGETHER, AS A GROUP, AND STAND AGAINST THOSE WHO ONLY WANT TO DESTROY US.
"TONIGHT, VICTORIA AND HAILEY SHOWED THAT THEY CARE ONLY ABOUT THEIR OWN SURVIVAL, AND THAT THEY HAVE NO PROBLEM SACRIFICING OUR LIVES TO ENSURE THEIR OWN.
"IF WE ARE GOING TO SURVIVE -- AFTER ALL THAT WE'VE ALREADY DONE TO SECURE OUR OWN LIVES -- WE CANNOT LET THIS STAND.
"OUR HAND HAS BEEN FORCED. EVEN THOUGH WE'VE ALREADY SEEN ENOUGH DEATH AND AS MUCH AS I WISH THERE WAS ANOTHER WAY..."

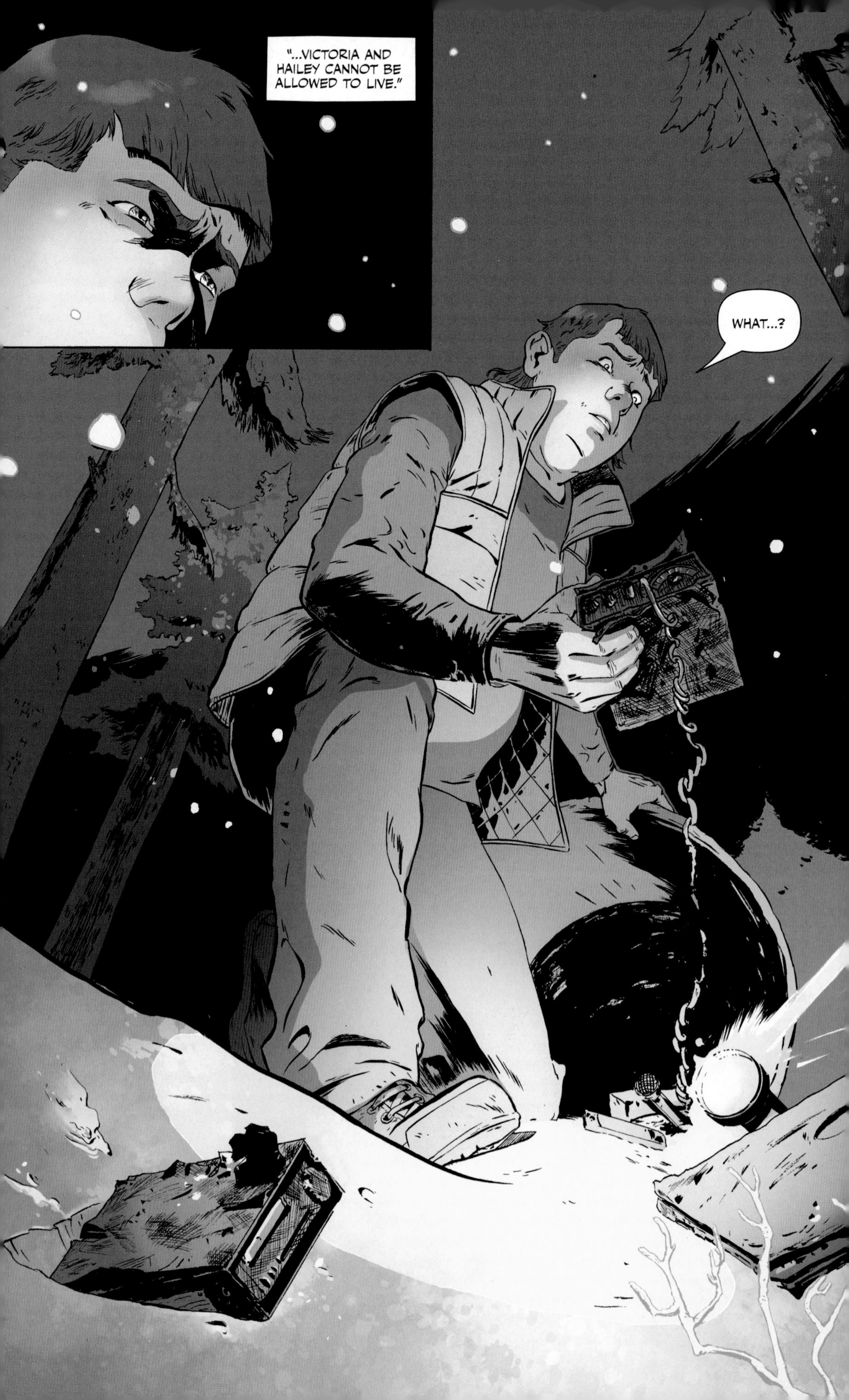
"...VICTORIA AND HAILEY CANNOT BE ALLOWED TO LIVE."
WHAT...?

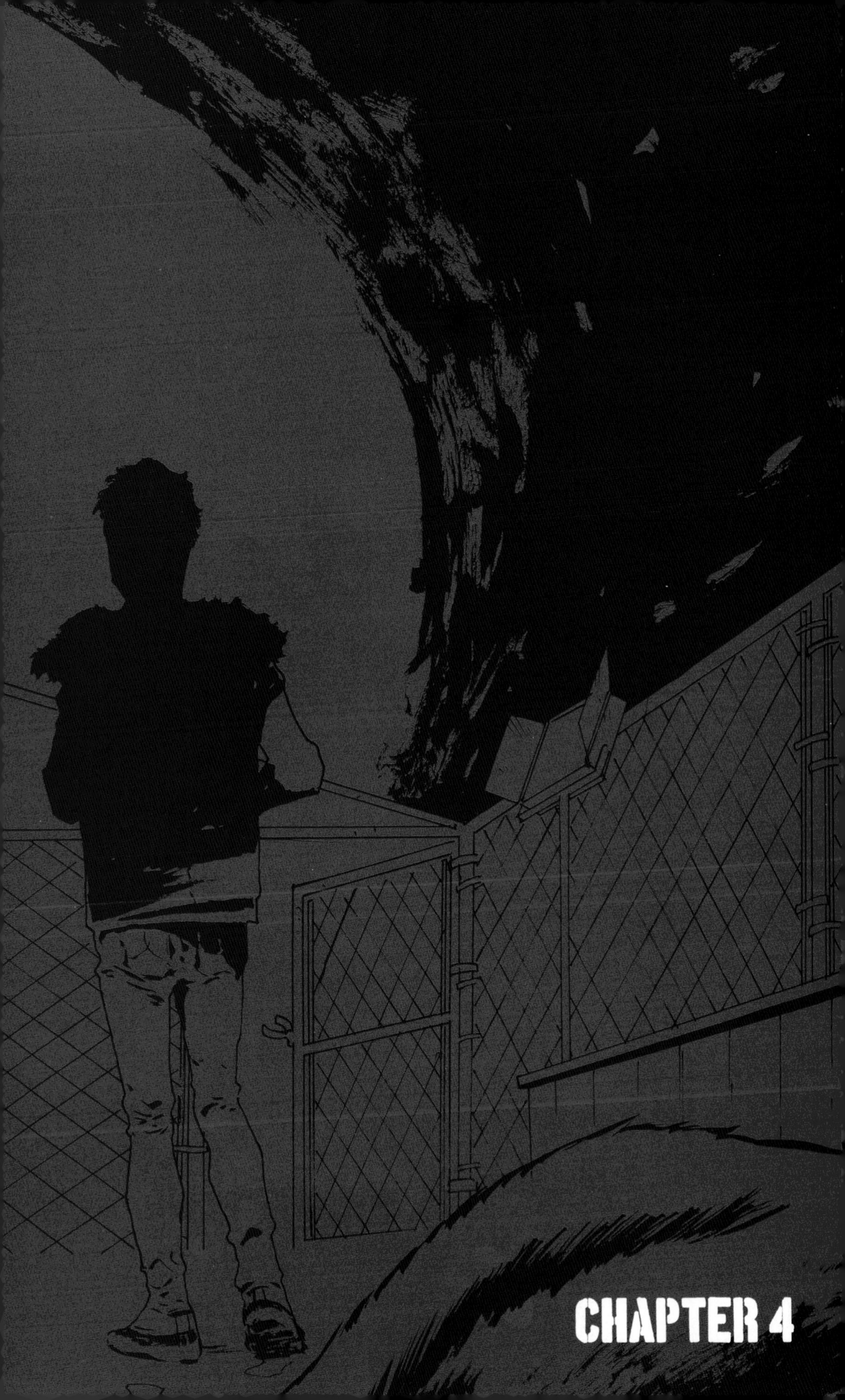
CHAPTER 4

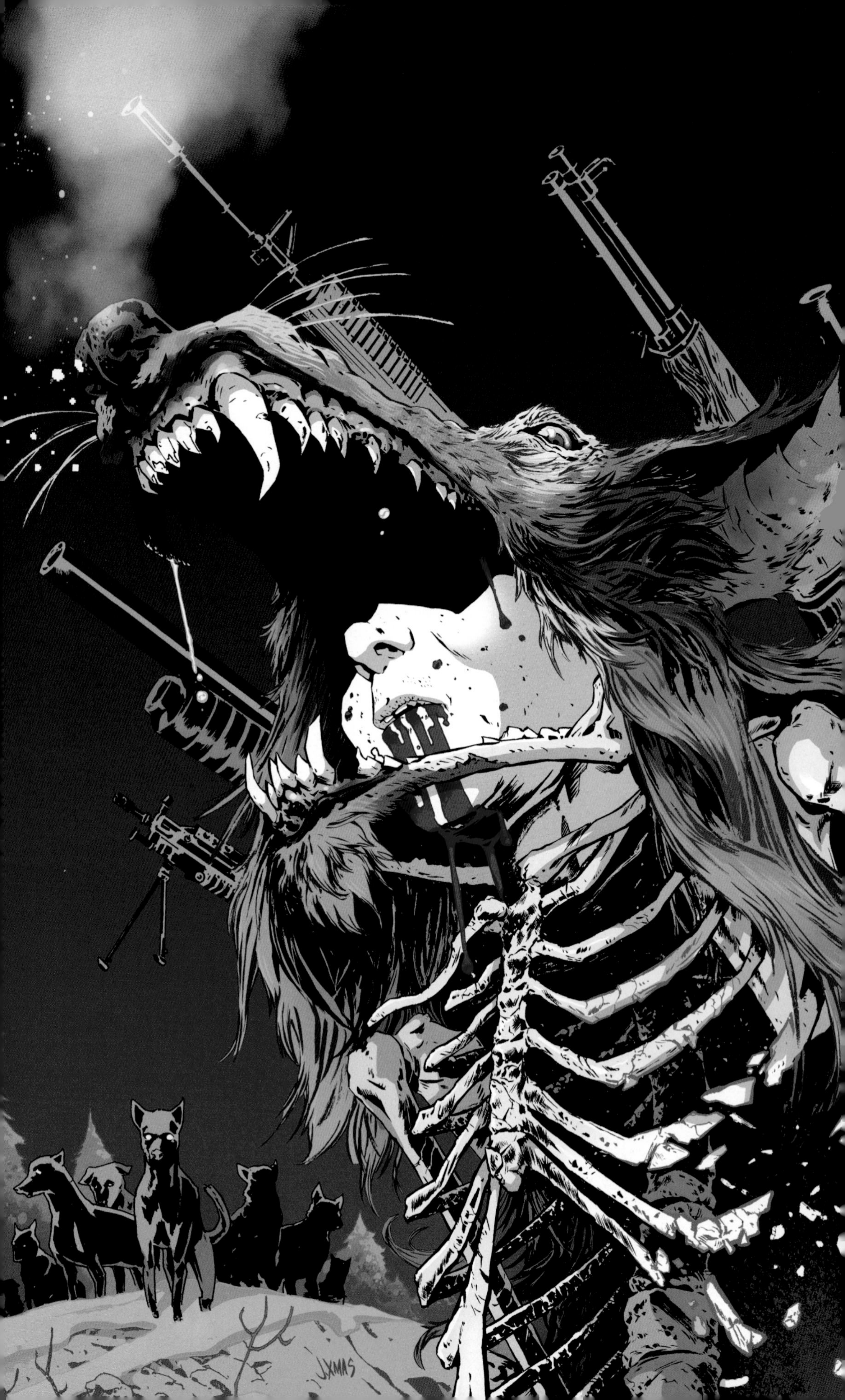
J.XMAS

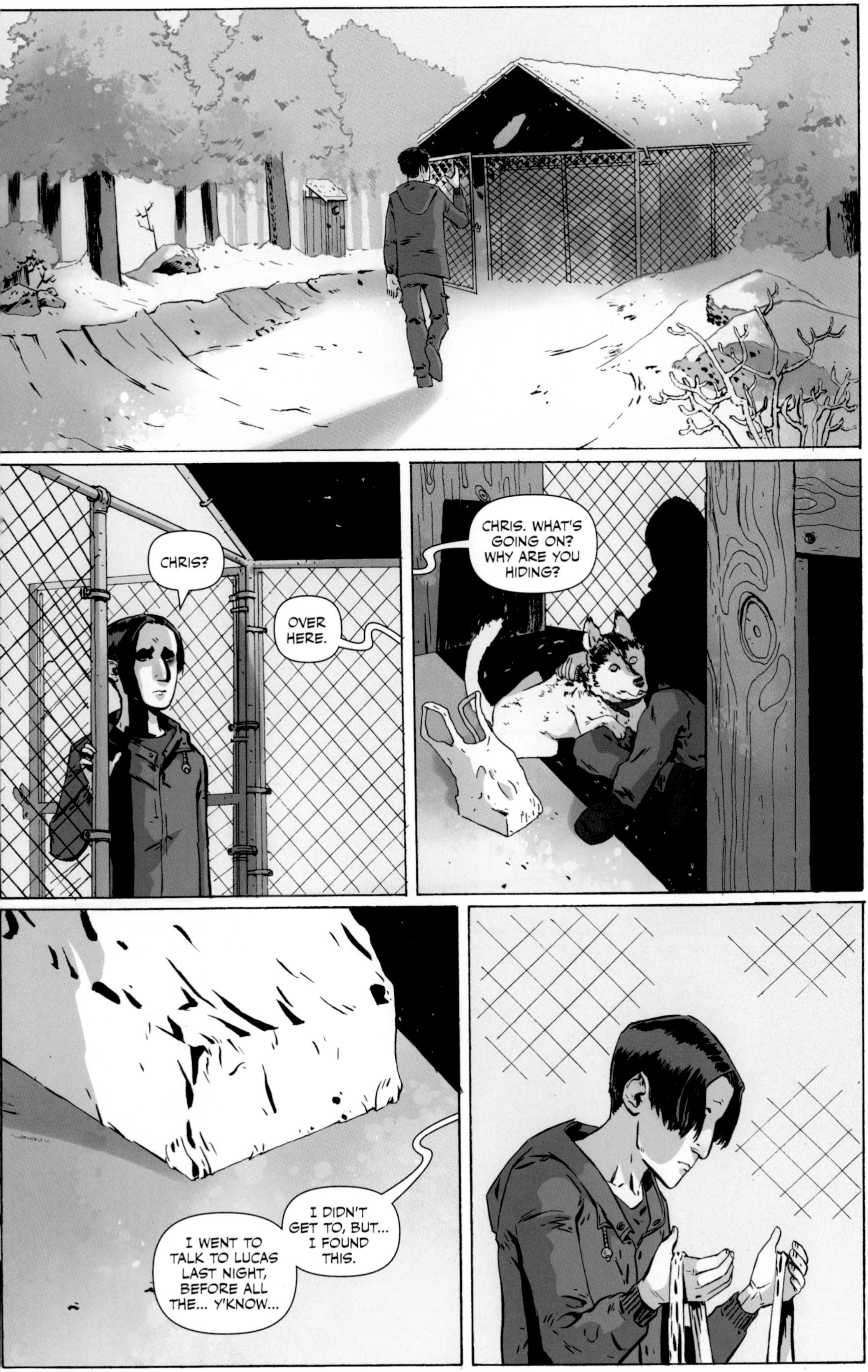
CHRIS?
OVER HERE.
CHRIS. WHAT'S GOING ON? WHY ARE YOU HIDING?
I WENT TO TALK TO LUCAS LAST NIGHT, BEFORE ALL THE... Y'KNOW...
I DIDN'T GET TO, BUT... I FOUND THIS.

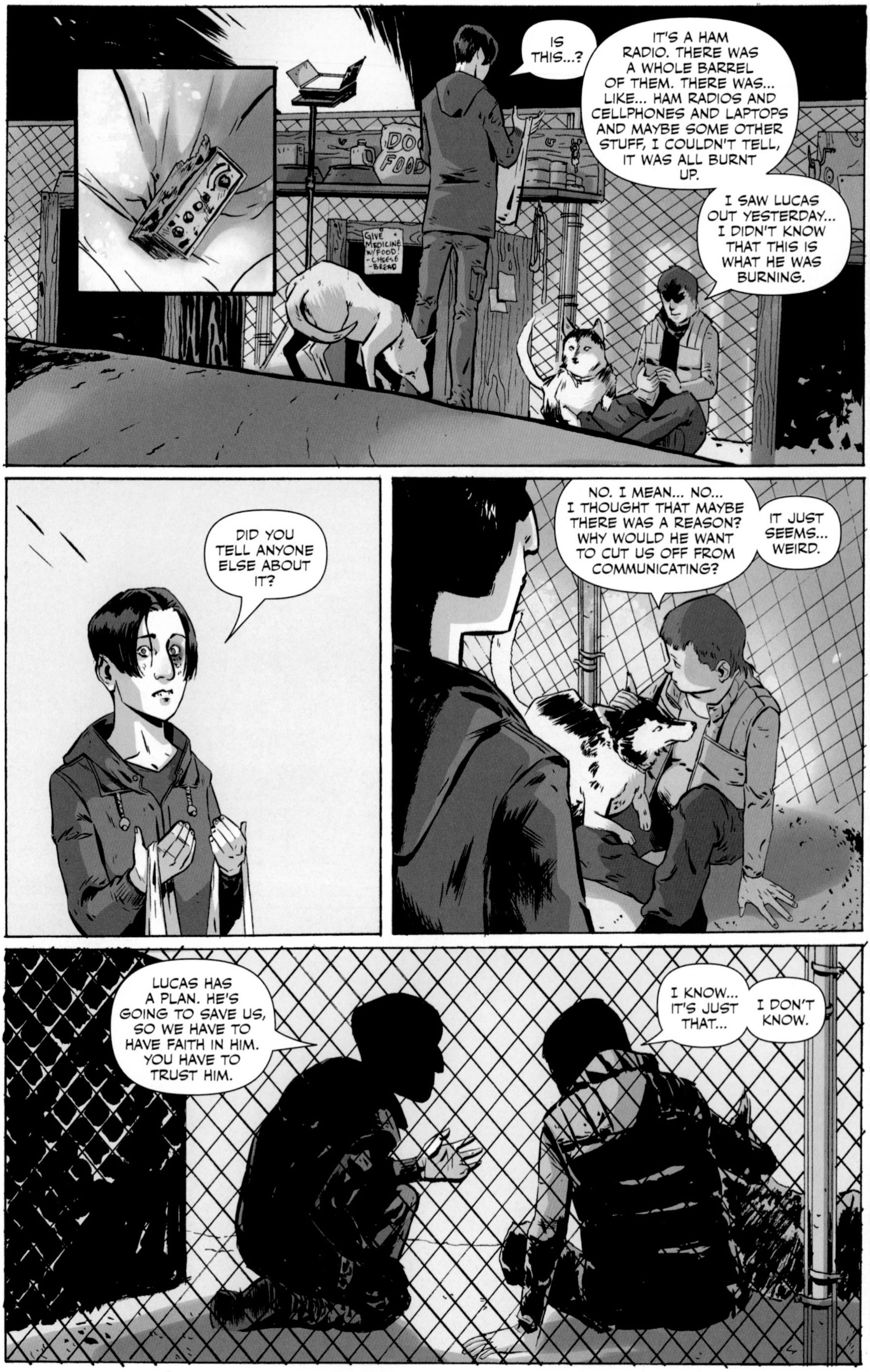
IS THIS...?
IT'S A HAM RADIO. THERE WAS A WHOLE BARREL OF THEM. THERE WAS... LIKE... HAM RADIOS AND CELLPHONES AND LAPTOPS AND MAYBE SOME OTHER STUFF, I COULDN'T TELL, IT WAS ALL BURNT UP.
I SAW LUCAS OUT YESTERDAY... I DIDN'T KNOW THAT THIS IS WHAT HE WAS BURNING.
DID YOU TELL ANYONE ELSE ABOUT IT?
NO. I MEAN... NO... I THOUGHT THAT MAYBE THERE WAS A REASON? WHY WOULD HE WANT TO CUT US OFF FROM COMMUNICATING?
IT JUST SEEMS... WEIRD.
LUCAS HAS A PLAN. HE'S GOING TO SAVE US, SO WE HAVE TO HAVE FAITH IN HIM. YOU HAVE TO TRUST HIM.
I KNOW... IT'S JUST THAT...
I DON'T KNOW.

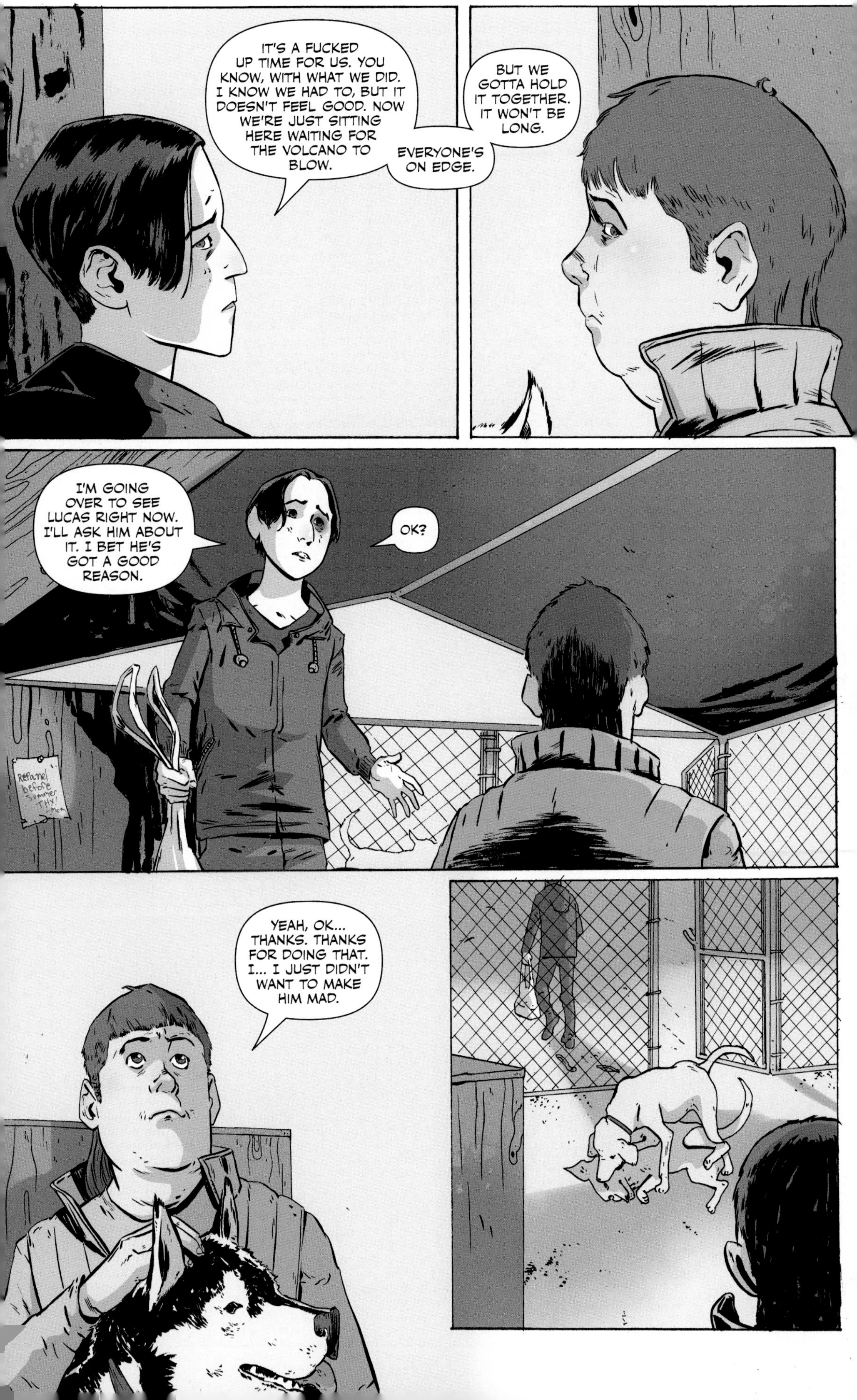
IT'S A FUCKED UP TIME FOR US. YOU KNOW, WITH WHAT WE DID. I KNOW WE HAD TO, BUT IT DOESN'T FEEL GOOD. NOW WE'RE JUST SITTING HERE WAITING FOR THE VOLCANO TO BLOW.
EVERYONE'S ON EDGE.
BUT WE GOTTA HOLD IT TOGETHER. IT WON'T BE LONG.
I'M GOING OVER TO SEE LUCAS RIGHT NOW. I'LL ASK HIM ABOUT IT. I BET HE'S GOT A GOOD REASON.
OK?
Repanel before Summer THX! —Mom
YEAH, OK... THANKS. THANKS FOR DOING THAT. I... I JUST DIDN'T WANT TO MAKE HIM MAD.

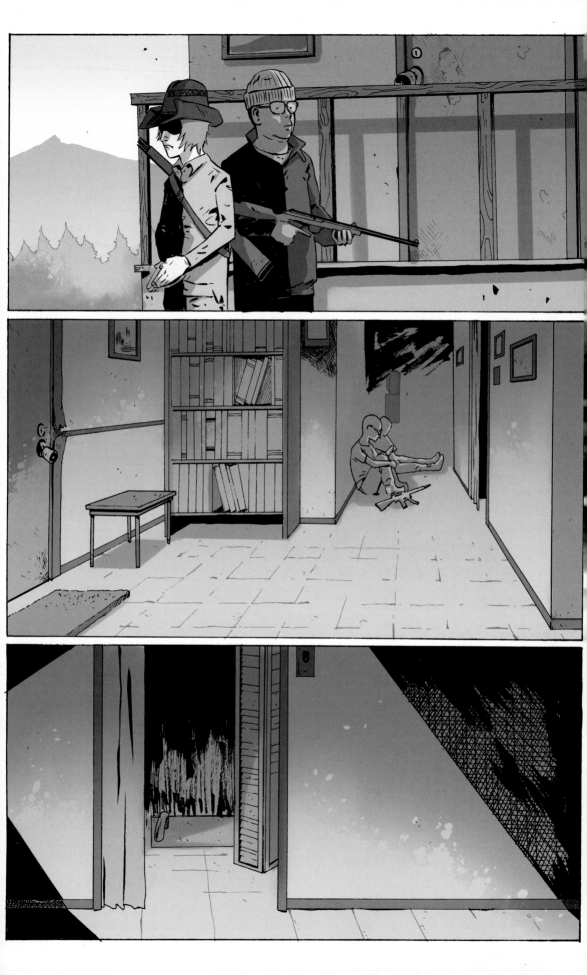

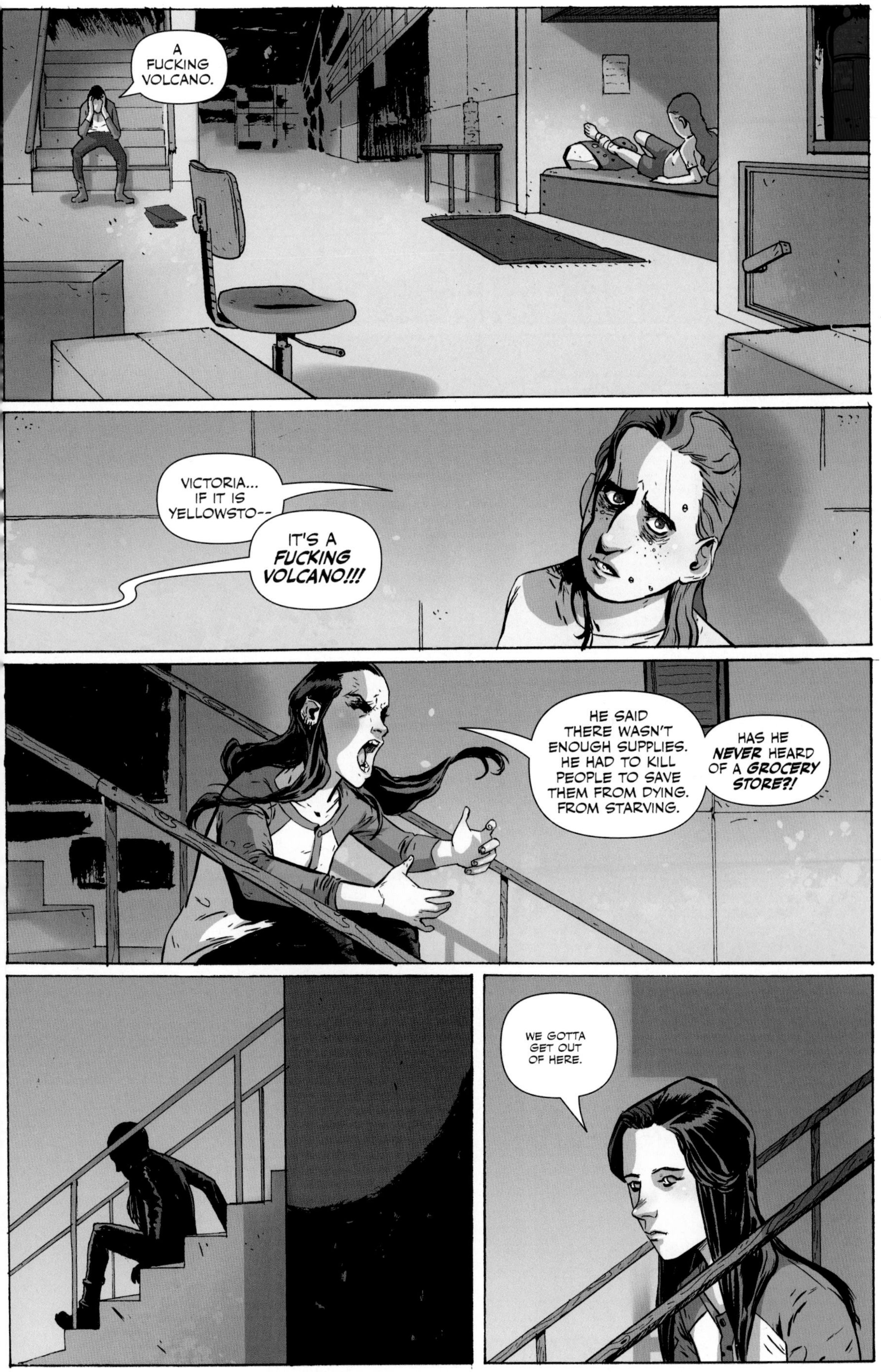
A FUCKING VOLCANO.
VICTORIA... IF IT IS YELLOWSTO--
IT'S A FUCKING VOLCANO!!!
HE SAID THERE WASN'T ENOUGH SUPPLIES. HE HAD TO KILL PEOPLE TO SAVE THEM FROM DYING. FROM STARVING.
HAS HE NEVER HEARD OF A GROCERY STORE?!
WE GOTTA GET OUT OF HERE.

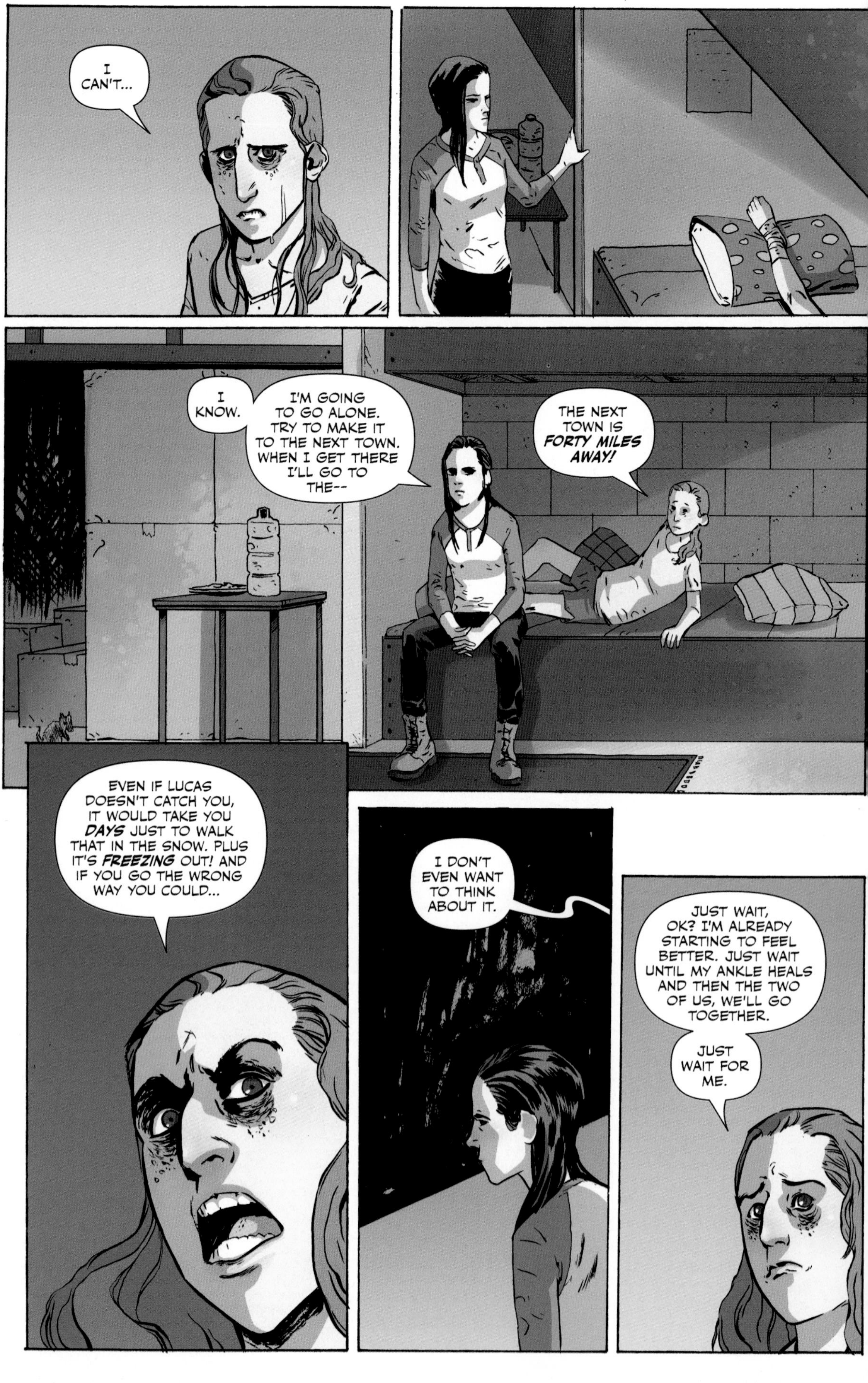
I CAN'T...
I KNOW.
I'M GOING TO GO ALONE. TRY TO MAKE IT TO THE NEXT TOWN. WHEN I GET THERE I'LL GO TO THE--
THE NEXT TOWN IS *FORTY MILES AWAY!*
EVEN IF LUCAS DOESN'T CATCH YOU, IT WOULD TAKE YOU *DAYS* JUST TO WALK THAT IN THE SNOW. PLUS IT'S *FREEZING* OUT! AND IF YOU GO THE WRONG WAY YOU COULD...
I DON'T EVEN WANT TO THINK ABOUT IT.
JUST WAIT, OK? I'M ALREADY STARTING TO FEEL BETTER. JUST WAIT UNTIL MY ANKLE HEALS AND THEN THE TWO OF US, WE'LL GO TOGETHER.
JUST WAIT FOR ME.

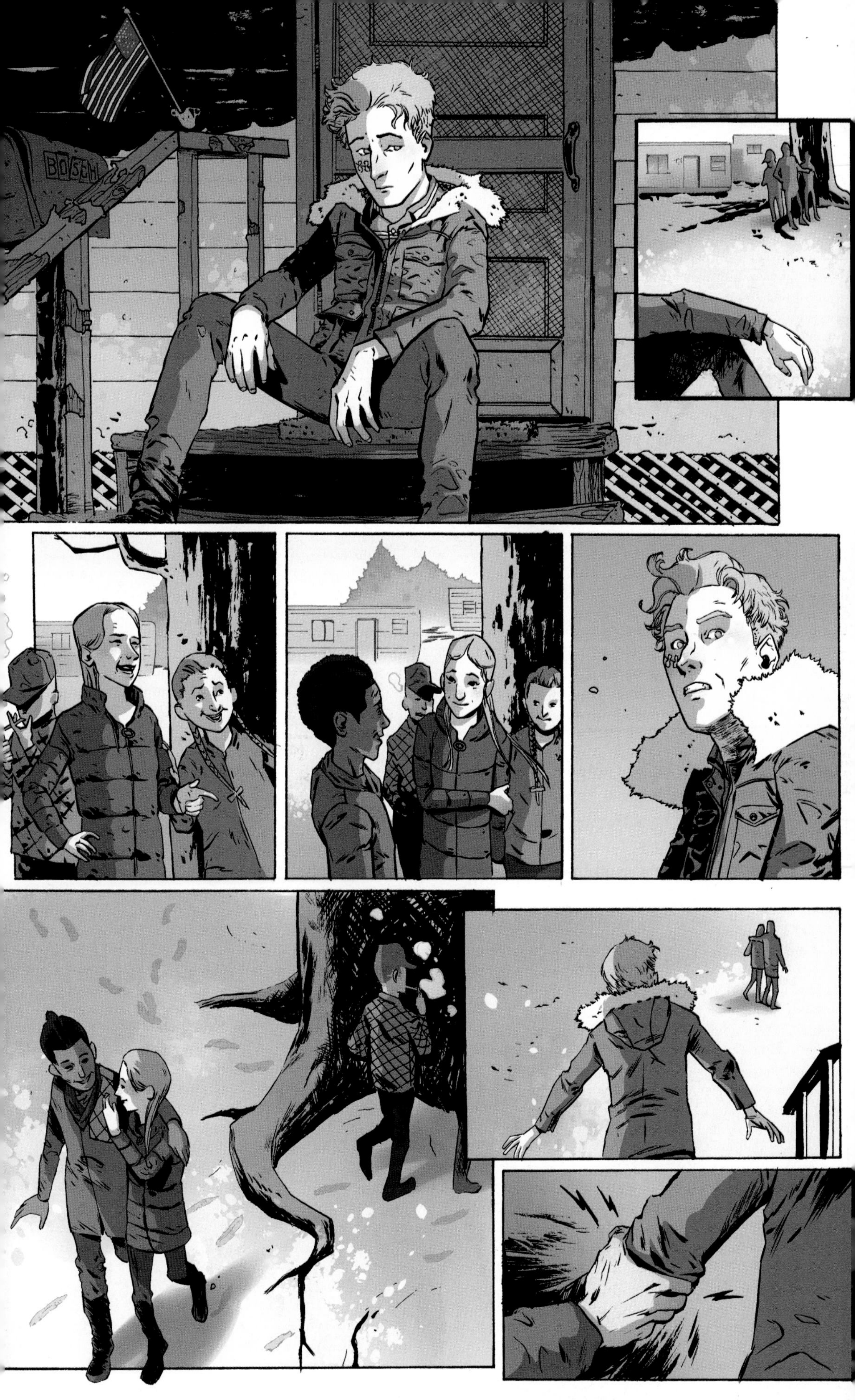
BOSCH

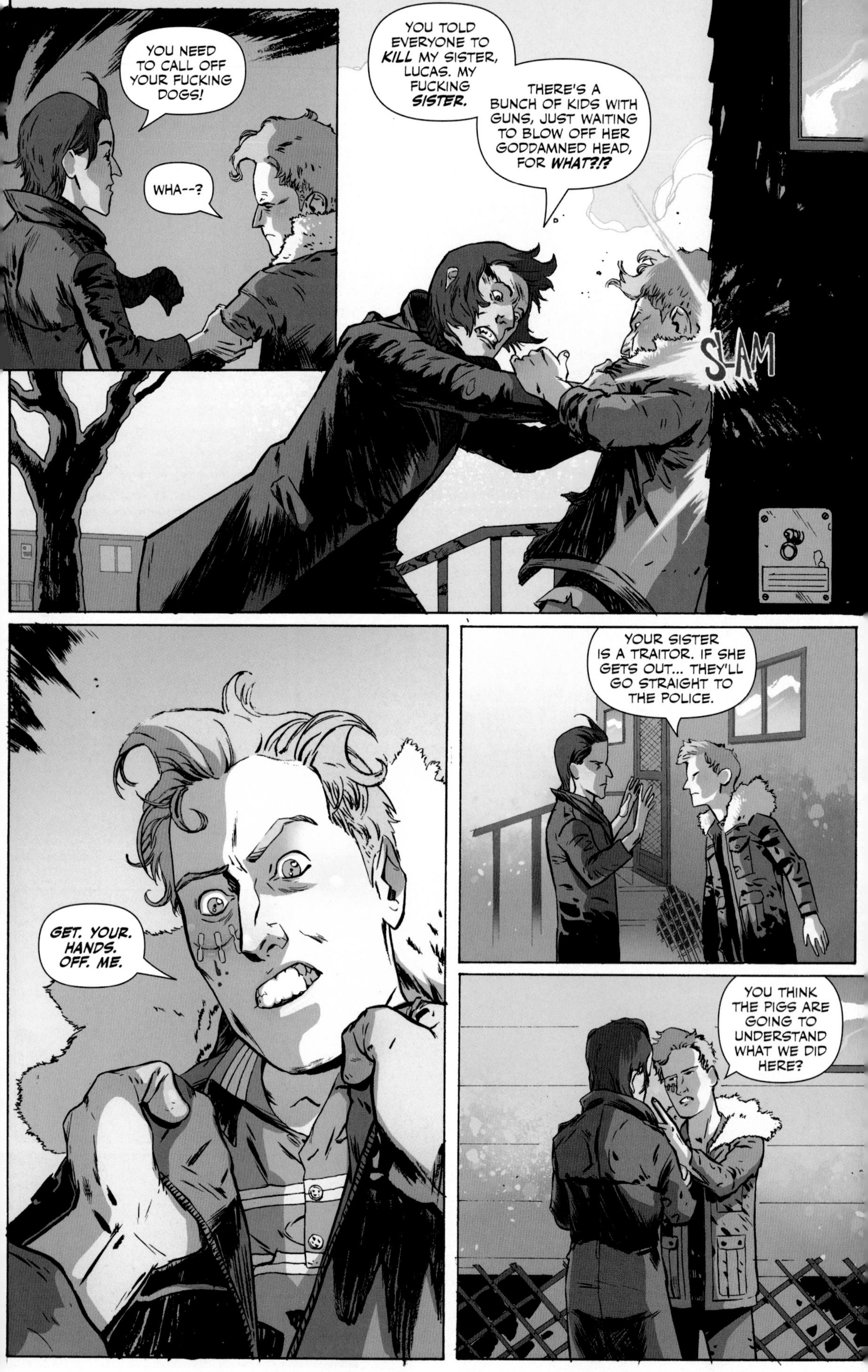
YOU NEED TO CALL OFF YOUR FUCKING DOGS!
WHA--?
YOU TOLD EVERYONE TO KILL MY SISTER, LUCAS. MY FUCKING SISTER.
THERE'S A BUNCH OF KIDS WITH GUNS, JUST WAITING TO BLOW OFF HER GODDAMNED HEAD, FOR WHAT?!?
SLAM
GET. YOUR. HANDS. OFF. ME.
YOUR SISTER IS A TRAITOR. IF SHE GETS OUT... THEY'LL GO STRAIGHT TO THE POLICE.
YOU THINK THE PIGS ARE GOING TO UNDERSTAND WHAT WE DID HERE?

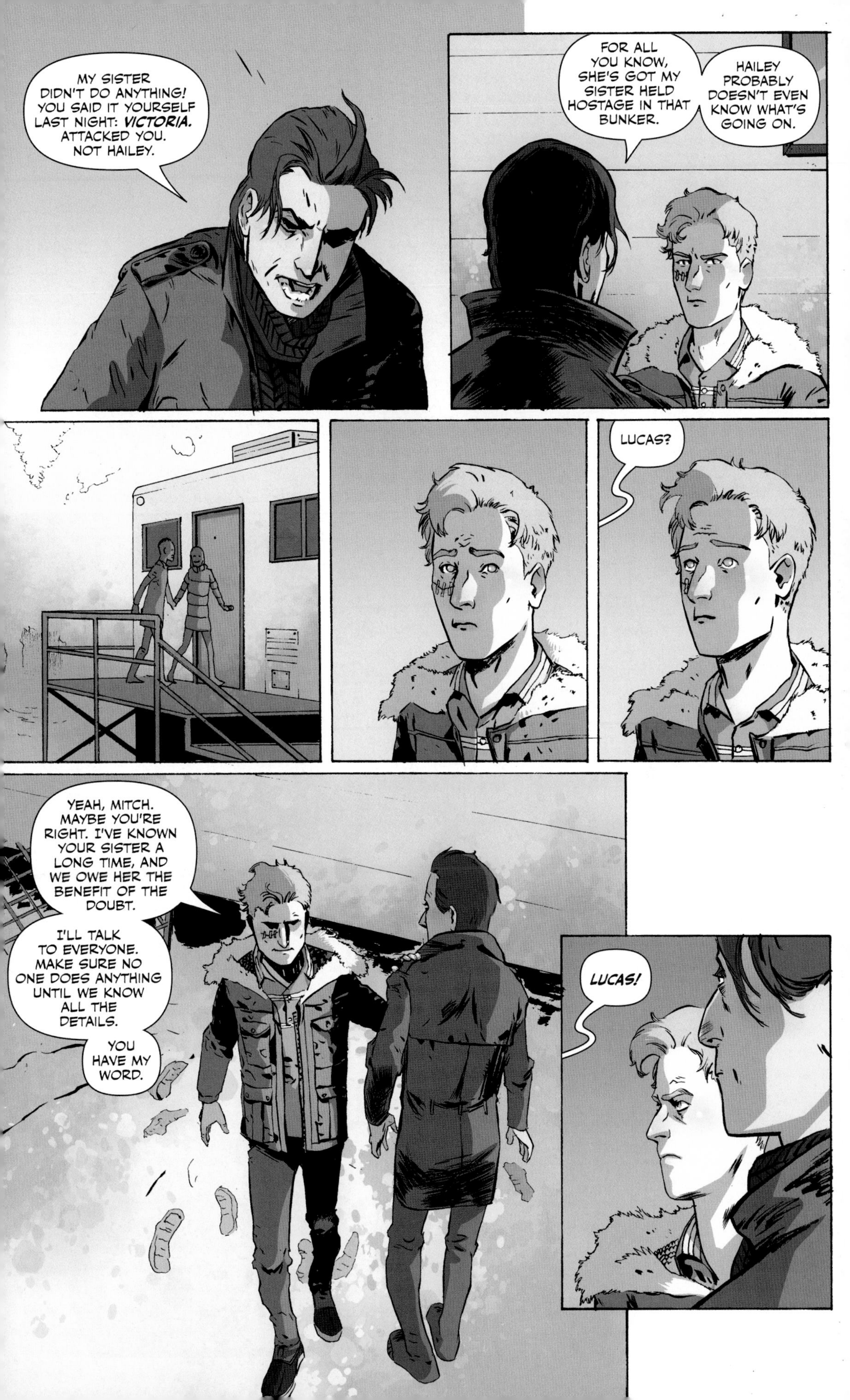
MY SISTER DIDN'T DO ANYTHING! YOU SAID IT YOURSELF LAST NIGHT: *VICTORIA.* ATTACKED YOU. NOT HAILEY.
FOR ALL YOU KNOW, SHE'S GOT MY SISTER HELD HOSTAGE IN THAT BUNKER.
HAILEY PROBABLY DOESN'T EVEN KNOW WHAT'S GOING ON.
LUCAS?
YEAH, MITCH. MAYBE YOU'RE RIGHT. I'VE KNOWN YOUR SISTER A LONG TIME, AND WE OWE HER THE BENEFIT OF THE DOUBT.
I'LL TALK TO EVERYONE. MAKE SURE NO ONE DOES ANYTHING UNTIL WE KNOW ALL THE DETAILS.
YOU HAVE MY WORD.
LUCAS!

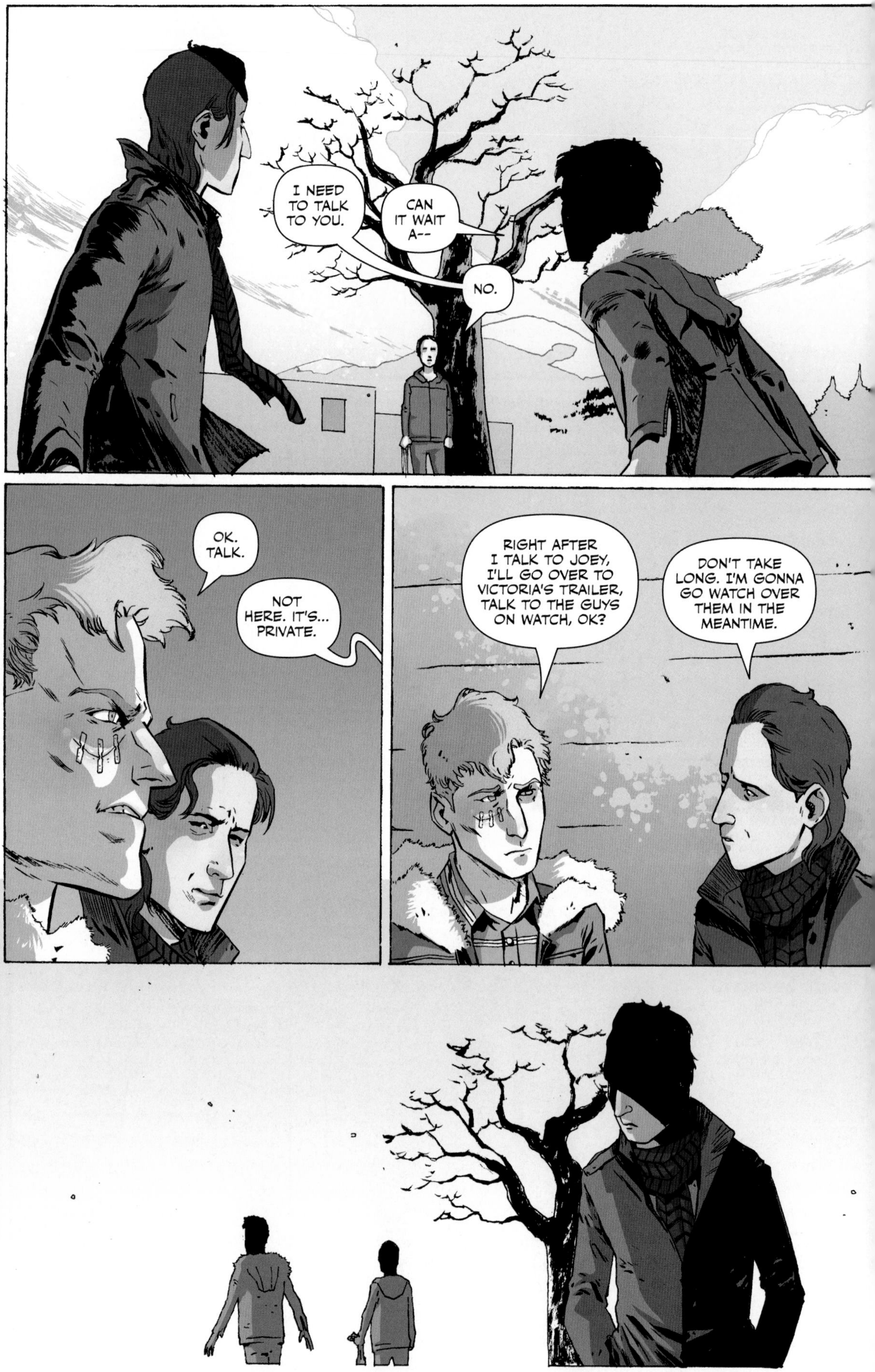
I NEED TO TALK TO YOU.
CAN IT WAIT A--
NO.
OK. TALK.
NOT HERE. IT'S... PRIVATE.
RIGHT AFTER I TALK TO JOEY, I'LL GO OVER TO VICTORIA'S TRAILER, TALK TO THE GUYS ON WATCH, OK?
DON'T TAKE LONG. I'M GONNA GO WATCH OVER THEM IN THE MEANTIME.

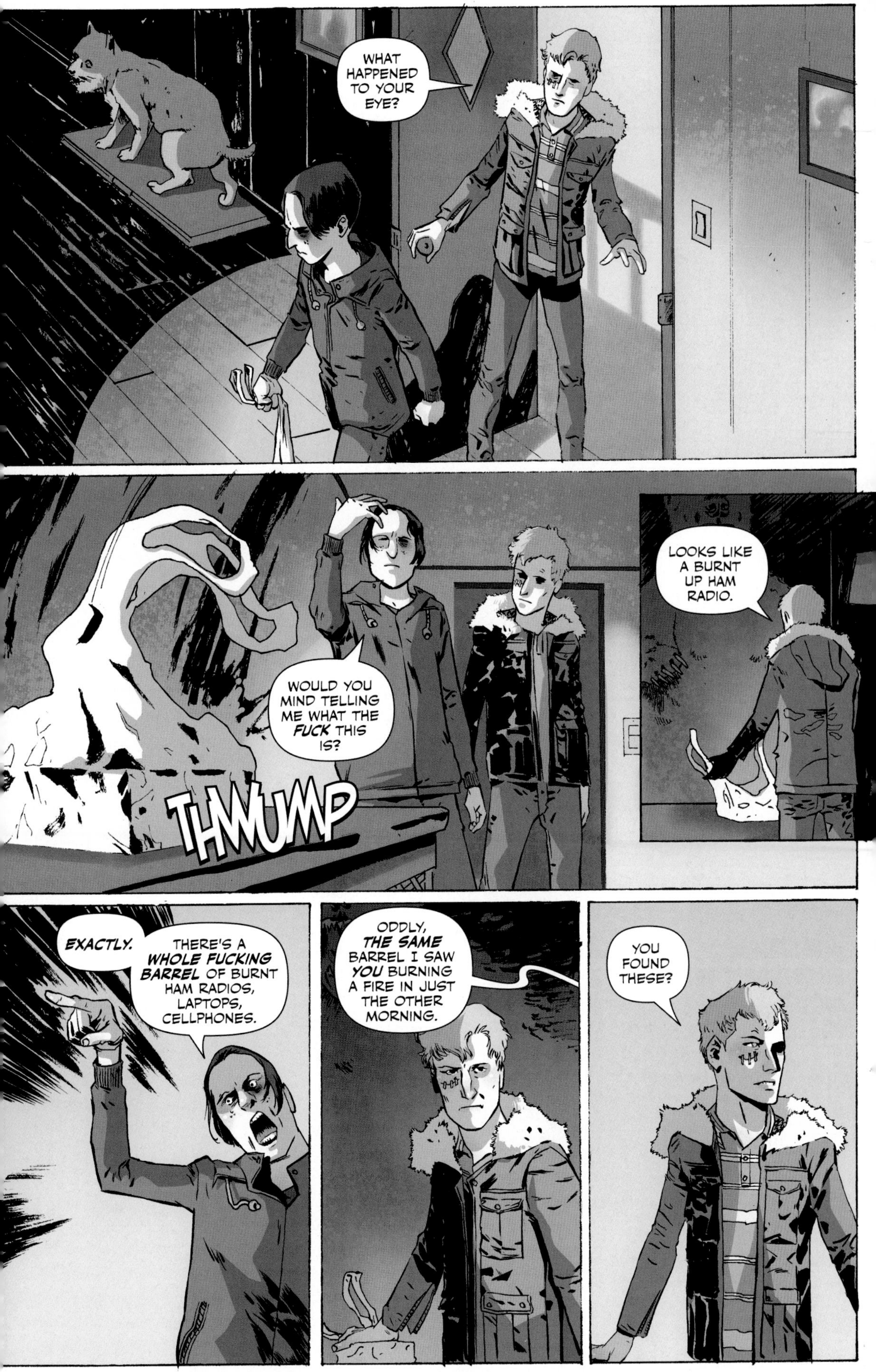
WHAT HAPPENED TO YOUR EYE?
WOULD YOU MIND TELLING ME WHAT THE FUCK THIS IS?
THWUMP
LOOKS LIKE A BURNT UP HAM RADIO.
EXACTLY.
THERE'S A WHOLE FUCKING BARREL OF BURNT HAM RADIOS, LAPTOPS, CELLPHONES.
ODDLY, THE SAME BARREL I SAW YOU BURNING A FIRE IN JUST THE OTHER MORNING.
YOU FOUND THESE?

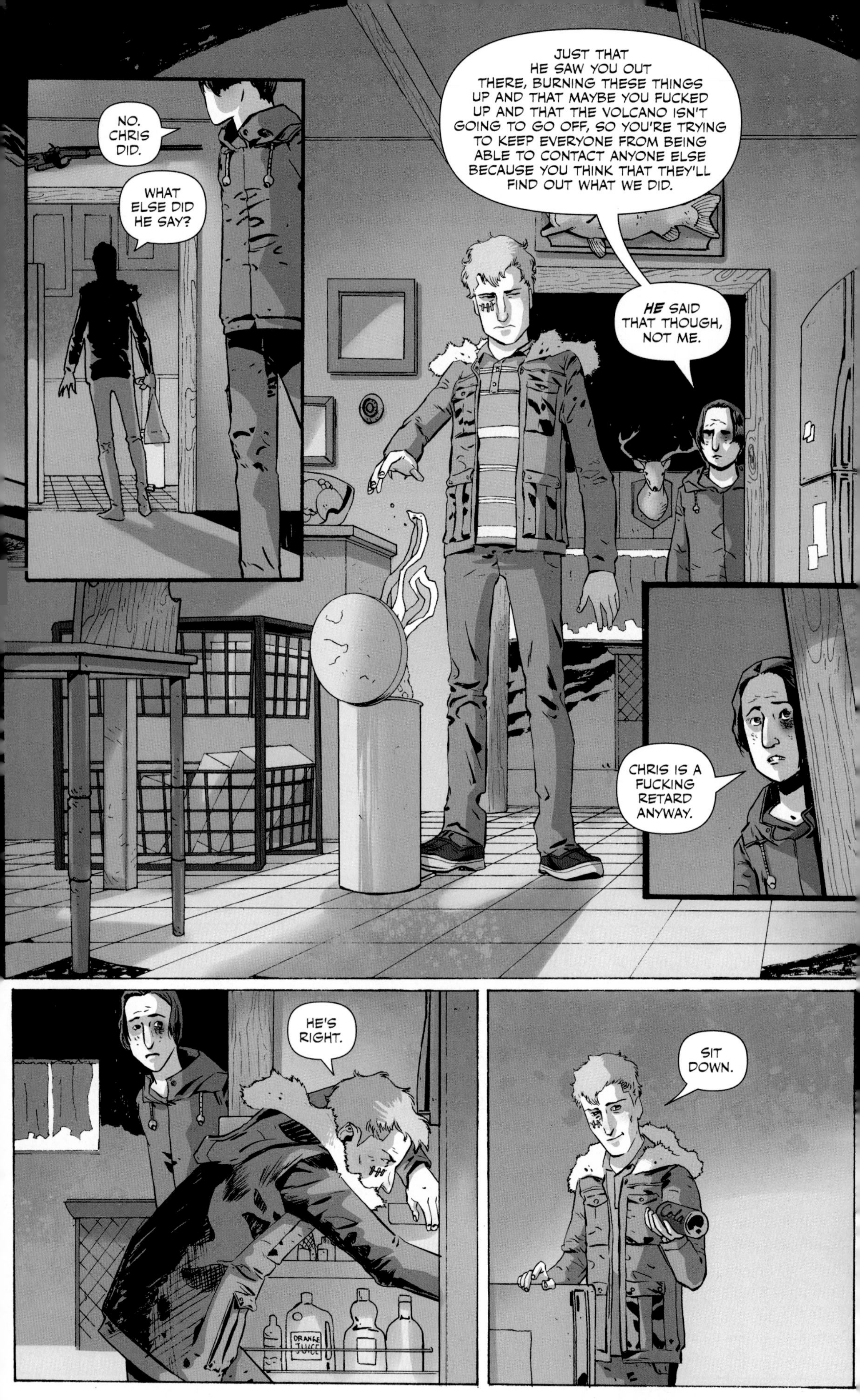
NO. CHRIS DID.
WHAT ELSE DID HE SAY?
JUST THAT HE SAW YOU OUT THERE, BURNING THESE THINGS UP AND THAT MAYBE YOU FUCKED UP AND THAT THE VOLCANO ISN'T GOING TO GO OFF, SO YOU'RE TRYING TO KEEP EVERYONE FROM BEING ABLE TO CONTACT ANYONE ELSE BECAUSE YOU THINK THAT THEY'LL FIND OUT WHAT WE DID.
HE SAID THAT THOUGH, NOT ME.
CHRIS IS A FUCKING RETARD ANYWAY.
HE'S RIGHT.
ORANGE JUICE
SIT DOWN.
Cola

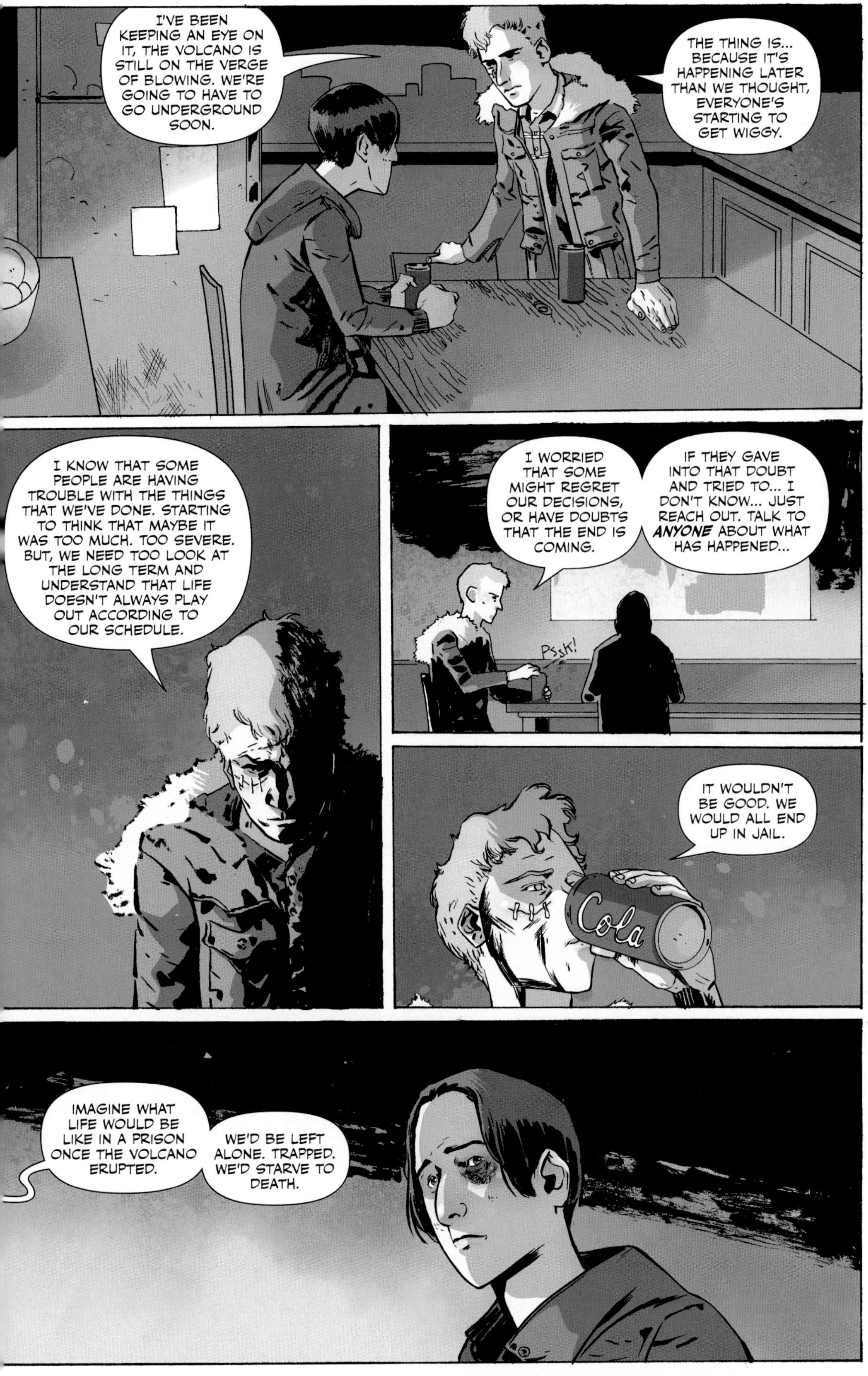
I'VE BEEN KEEPING AN EYE ON IT, THE VOLCANO IS STILL ON THE VERGE OF BLOWING. WE'RE GOING TO HAVE TO GO UNDERGROUND SOON.
THE THING IS... BECAUSE IT'S HAPPENING LATER THAN WE THOUGHT, EVERYONE'S STARTING TO GET WIGGY.
I KNOW THAT SOME PEOPLE ARE HAVING TROUBLE WITH THE THINGS THAT WE'VE DONE. STARTING TO THINK THAT MAYBE IT WAS TOO MUCH. TOO SEVERE. BUT, WE NEED TOO LOOK AT THE LONG TERM AND UNDERSTAND THAT LIFE DOESN'T ALWAYS PLAY OUT ACCORDING TO OUR SCHEDULE.
I WORRIED THAT SOME MIGHT REGRET OUR DECISIONS, OR HAVE DOUBTS THAT THE END IS COMING.
IF THEY GAVE INTO THAT DOUBT AND TRIED TO... I DON'T KNOW... JUST REACH OUT. TALK TO *ANYONE* ABOUT WHAT HAS HAPPENED...
Pssk!
IT WOULDN'T BE GOOD. WE WOULD ALL END UP IN JAIL.
Cola
IMAGINE WHAT LIFE WOULD BE LIKE IN A PRISON ONCE THE VOLCANO ERUPTED.
WE'D BE LEFT ALONE. TRAPPED. WE'D STARVE TO DEATH.

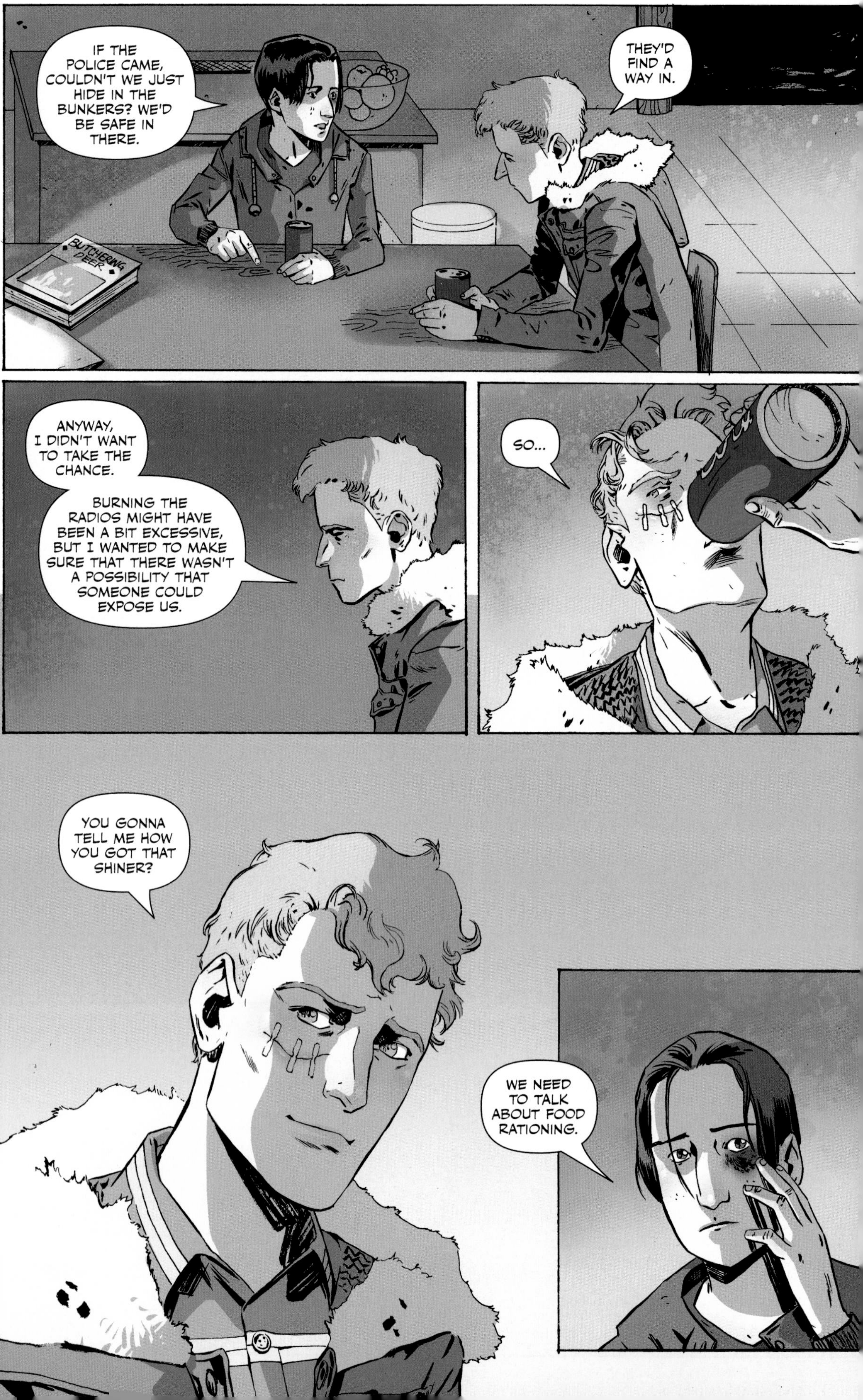
IF THE POLICE CAME, COULDN'T WE JUST HIDE IN THE BUNKERS? WE'D BE SAFE IN THERE.
THEY'D FIND A WAY IN.
BUTCHERING DEER
ANYWAY, I DIDN'T WANT TO TAKE THE CHANCE.
BURNING THE RADIOS MIGHT HAVE BEEN A BIT EXCESSIVE, BUT I WANTED TO MAKE SURE THAT THERE WASN'T A POSSIBILITY THAT SOMEONE COULD EXPOSE US.
SO...
YOU GONNA TELL ME HOW YOU GOT THAT SHINER?
WE NEED TO TALK ABOUT FOOD RATIONING.

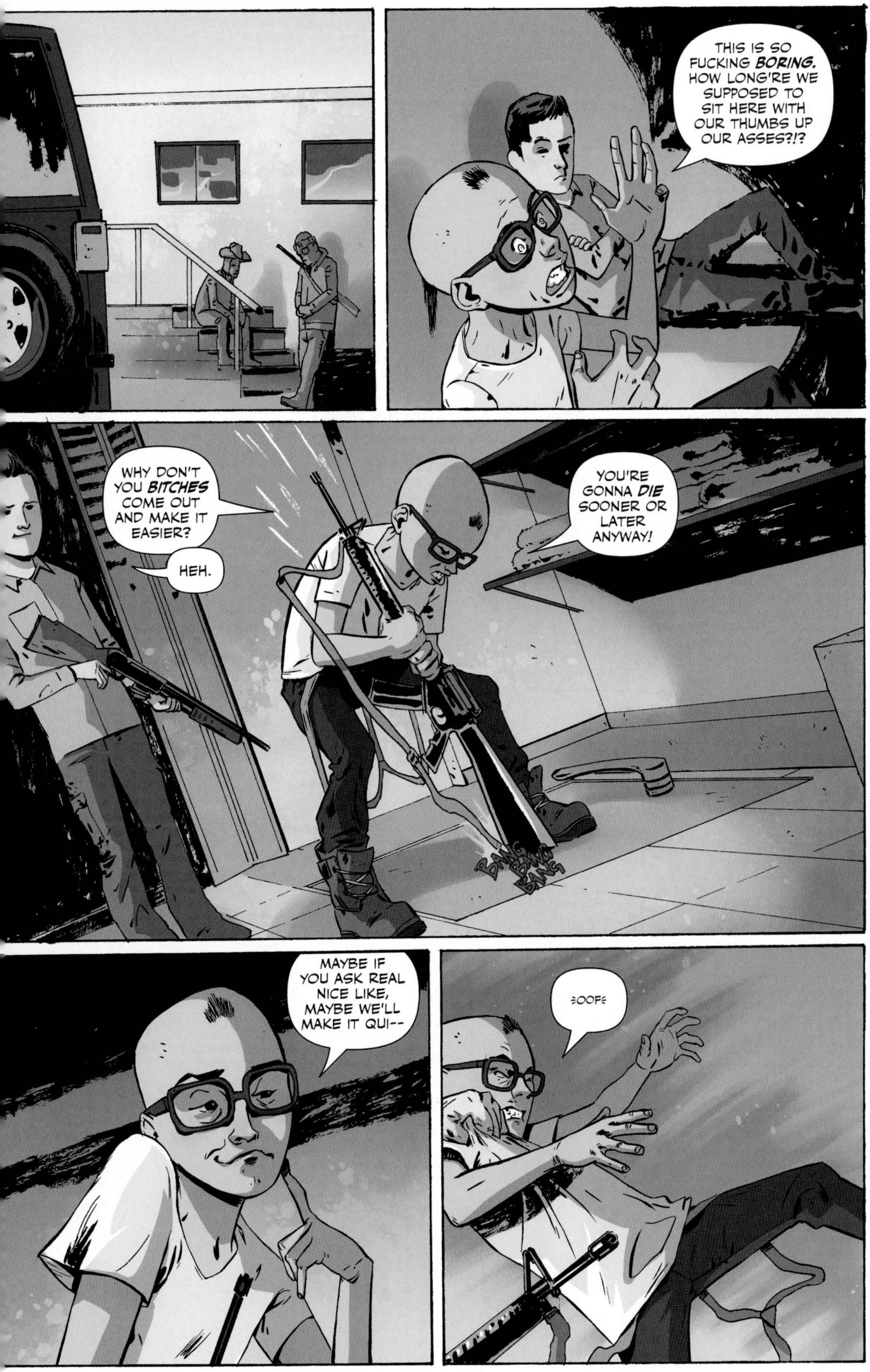
THIS IS SO FUCKING **BORING.** HOW LONG'RE WE SUPPOSED TO SIT HERE WITH OUR THUMBS UP OUR ASSES?!?
WHY DON'T YOU ***BITCHES*** COME OUT AND MAKE IT EASIER?
HEH.
YOU'RE GONNA ***DIE*** SOONER OR LATER ANYWAY!
BANG BANG BANG
MAYBE IF YOU ASK REAL NICE LIKE, MAYBE WE'LL MAKE IT QUI--
OOF

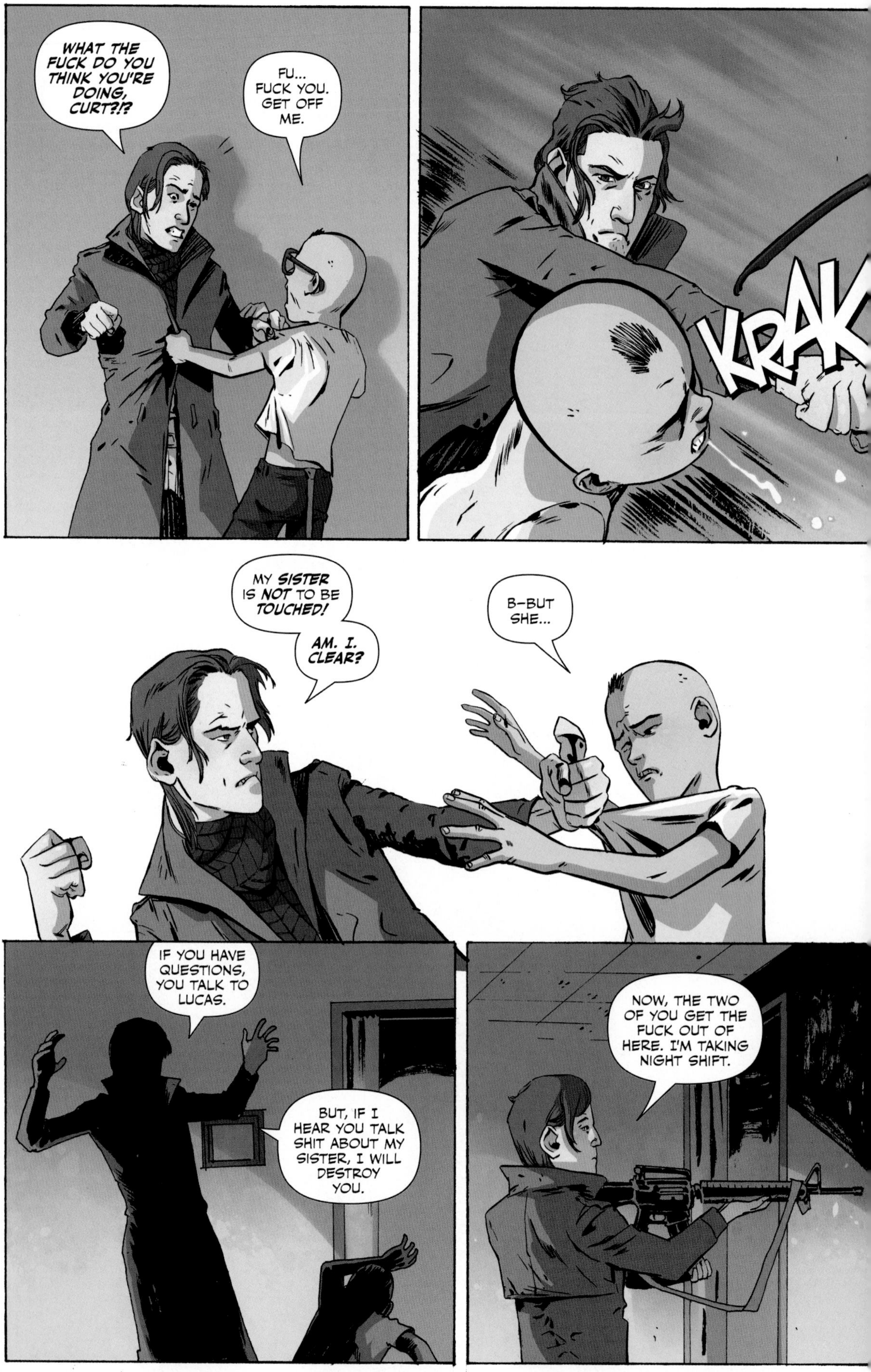
WHAT THE FUCK DO YOU THINK YOU'RE DOING, CURT?!?
FU... FUCK YOU. GET OFF ME.
KRAK
MY SISTER IS NOT TO BE TOUCHED!
AM. I. CLEAR?
B-BUT SHE...
IF YOU HAVE QUESTIONS, YOU TALK TO LUCAS.
BUT, IF I HEAR YOU TALK SHIT ABOUT MY SISTER, I WILL DESTROY YOU.
NOW, THE TWO OF YOU GET THE FUCK OUT OF HERE. I'M TAKING NIGHT SHIFT.

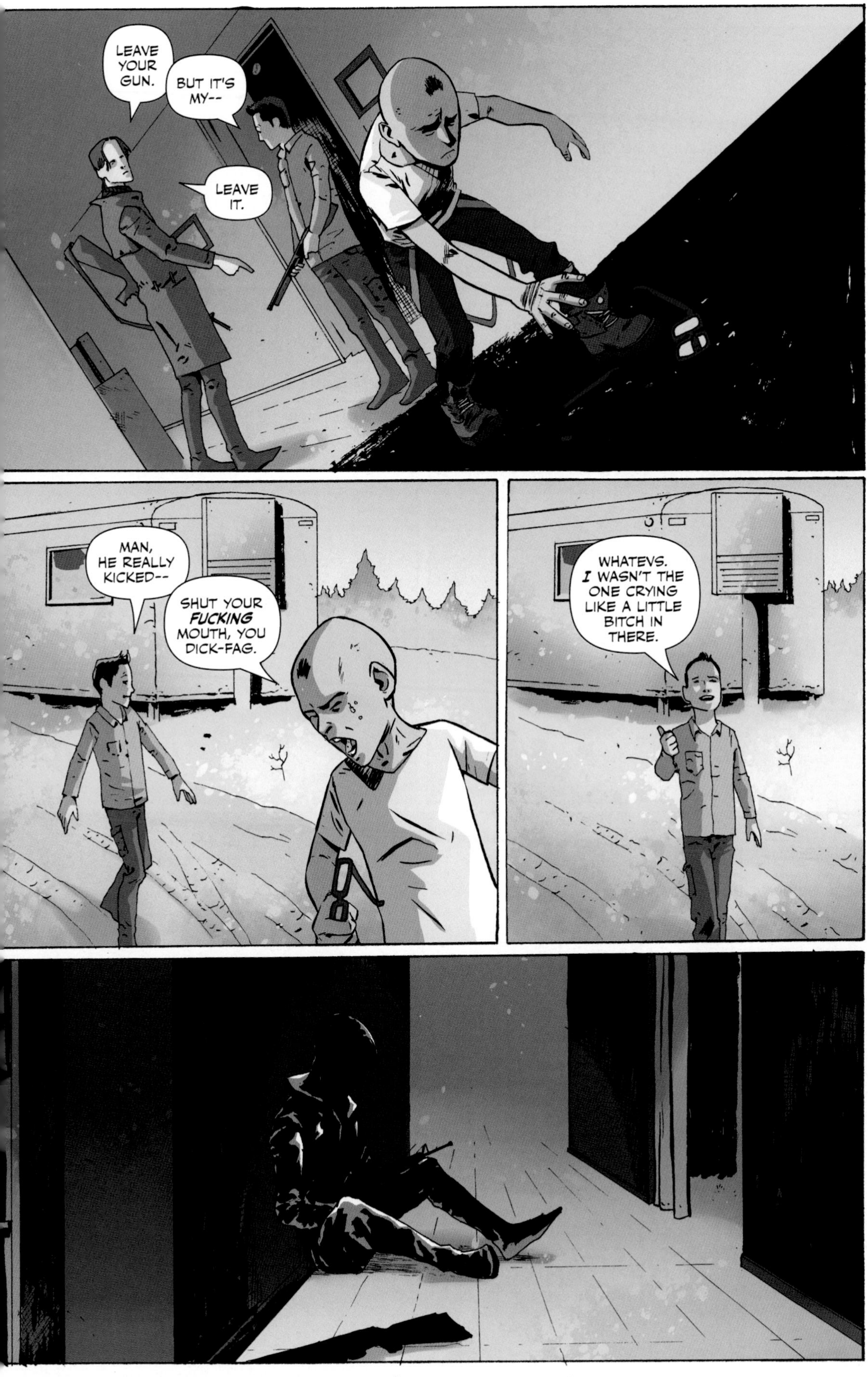
LEAVE YOUR GUN.
BUT IT'S MY--
LEAVE IT.
MAN, HE REALLY KICKED--
SHUT YOUR *FUCKING* MOUTH, YOU DICK-FAG.
WHATEVS. *I* WASN'T THE ONE CRYING LIKE A LITTLE BITCH IN THERE.

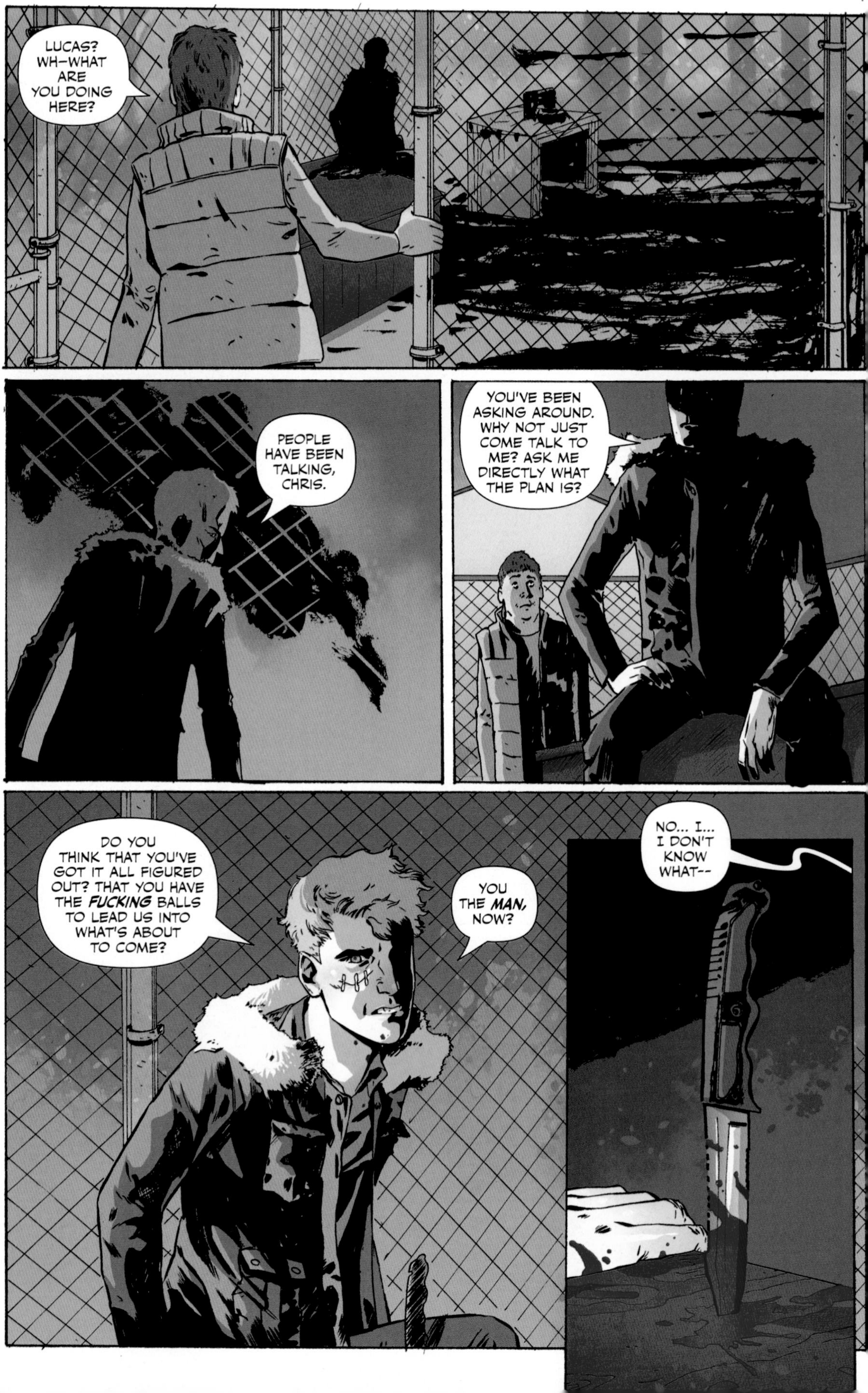
LUCAS? WH-WHAT ARE YOU DOING HERE?
PEOPLE HAVE BEEN TALKING, CHRIS.
YOU'VE BEEN ASKING AROUND. WHY NOT JUST COME TALK TO ME? ASK ME DIRECTLY WHAT THE PLAN IS?
DO YOU THINK THAT YOU'VE GOT IT ALL FIGURED OUT? THAT YOU HAVE THE *FUCKING* BALLS TO LEAD US INTO WHAT'S ABOUT TO COME?
YOU THE *MAN,* NOW?
NO... I... I DON'T KNOW WHAT--

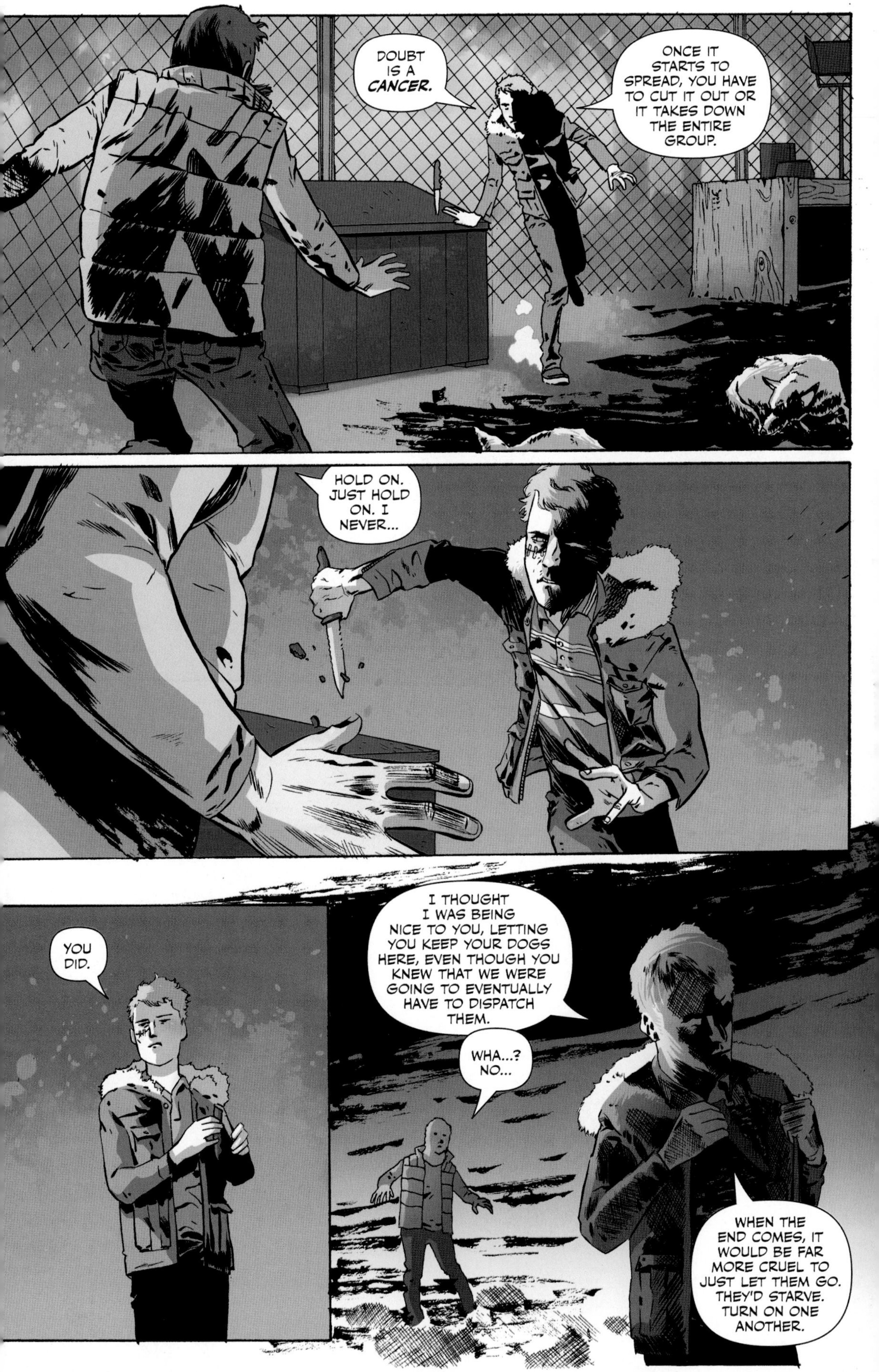
DOUBT IS A *CANCER.*
ONCE IT STARTS TO SPREAD, YOU HAVE TO CUT IT OUT OR IT TAKES DOWN THE ENTIRE GROUP.
HOLD ON. JUST HOLD ON. I NEVER...
YOU DID.
I THOUGHT I WAS BEING NICE TO YOU, LETTING YOU KEEP YOUR DOGS HERE, EVEN THOUGH YOU KNEW THAT WE WERE GOING TO EVENTUALLY HAVE TO DISPATCH THEM.
WHA...? NO...
WHEN THE END COMES, IT WOULD BE FAR MORE CRUEL TO JUST LET THEM GO. THEY'D STARVE. TURN ON ONE ANOTHER.

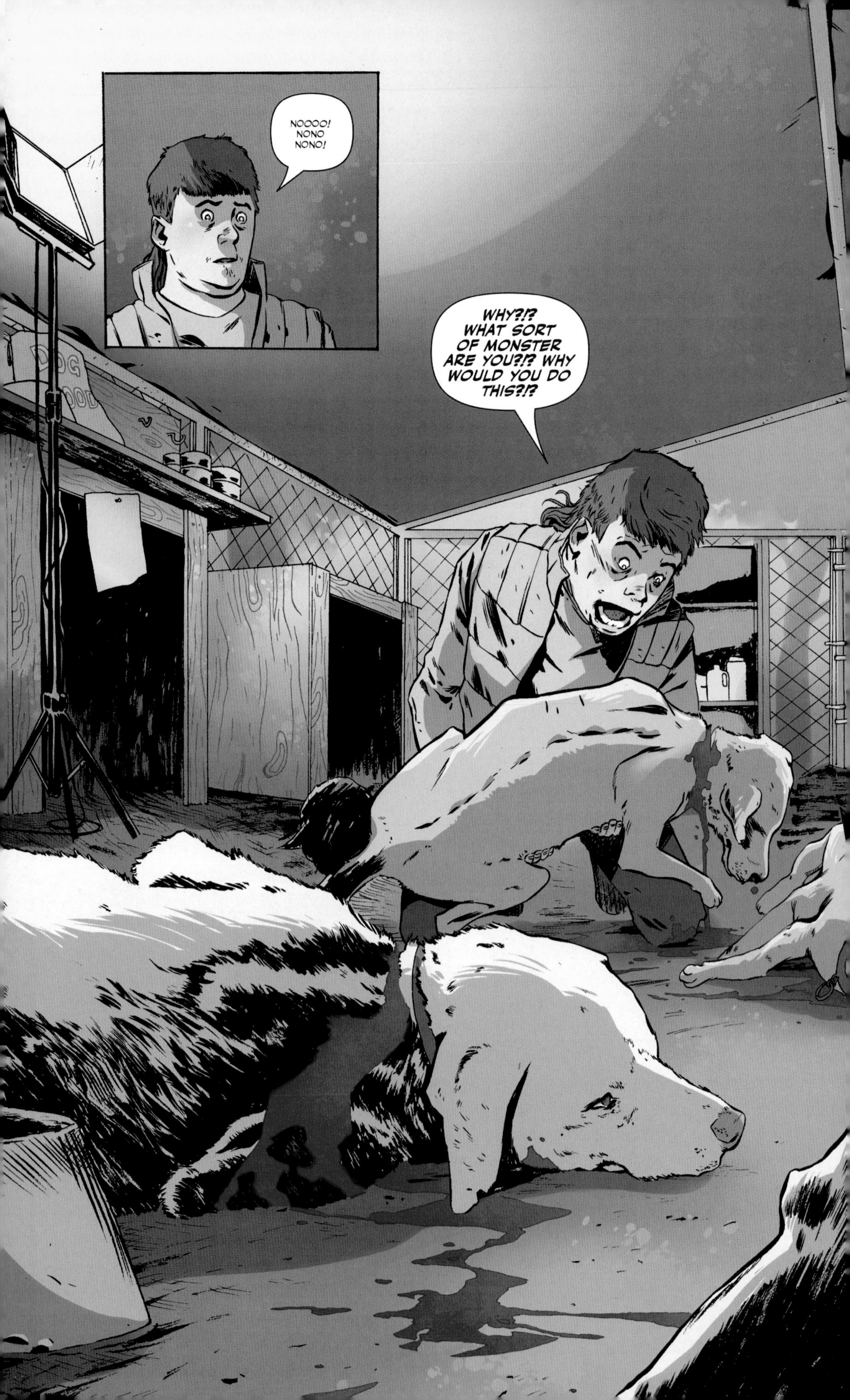
NOOOO! NONO NONO!
WHY?!? WHAT SORT OF MONSTER ARE YOU?!? WHY WOULD YOU DO THIS?!?
DOG

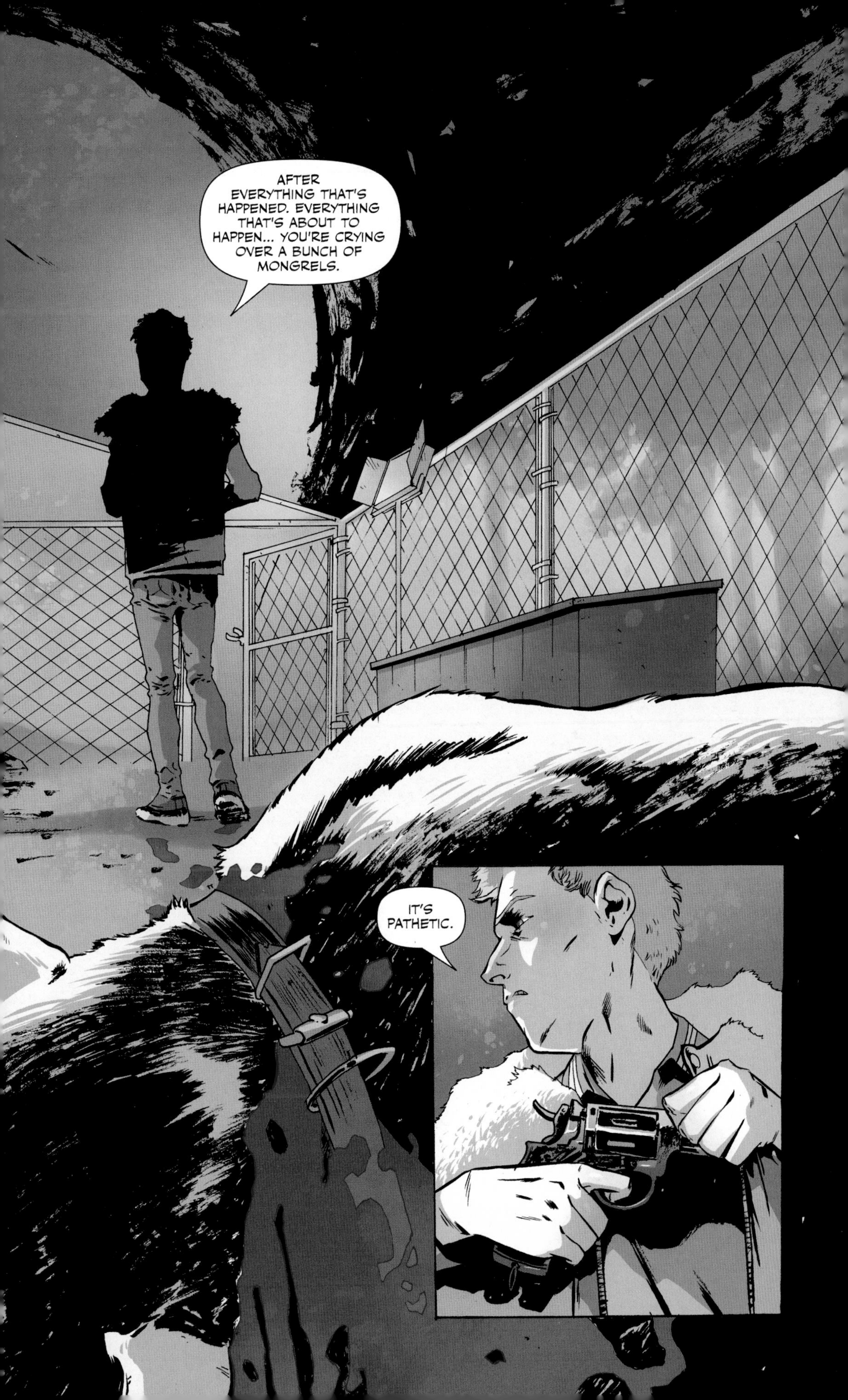
AFTER EVERYTHING THAT'S HAPPENED. EVERYTHING THAT'S ABOUT TO HAPPEN... YOU'RE CRYING OVER A BUNCH OF MONGRELS.
IT'S PATHETIC.

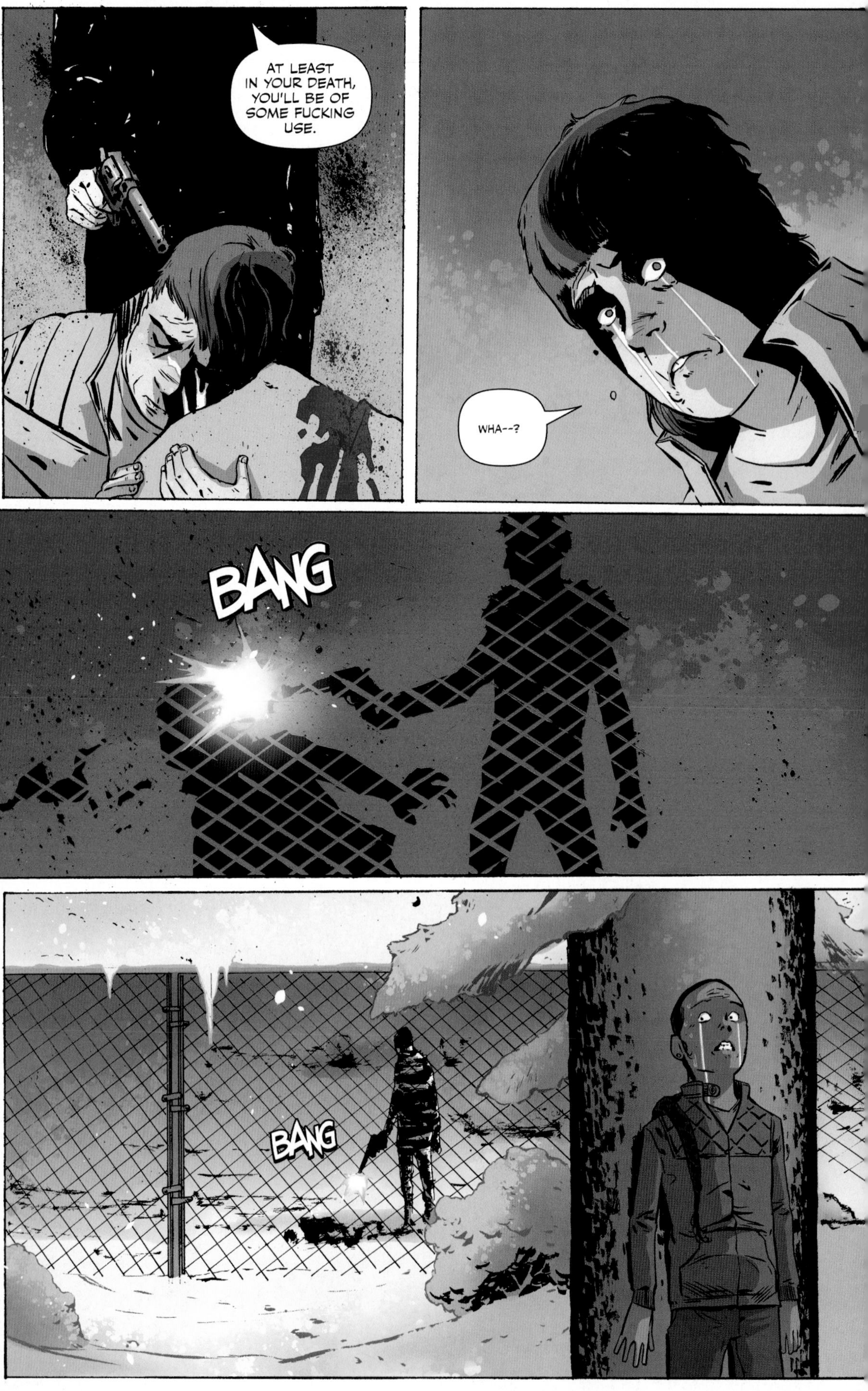
AT LEAST IN YOUR DEATH, YOU'LL BE OF SOME FUCKING USE.
WHA--?
BANG
BANG

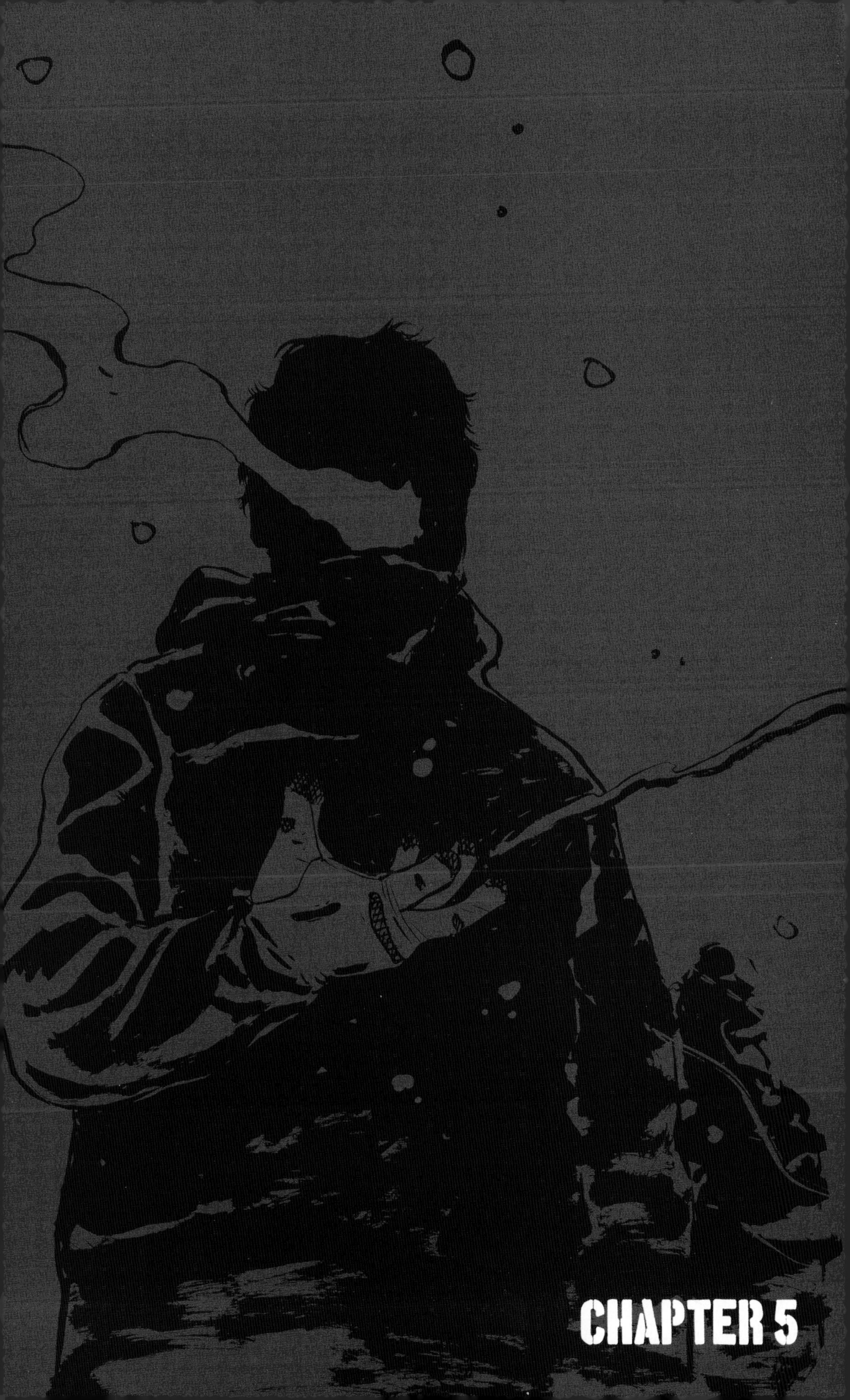
CHAPTER 5

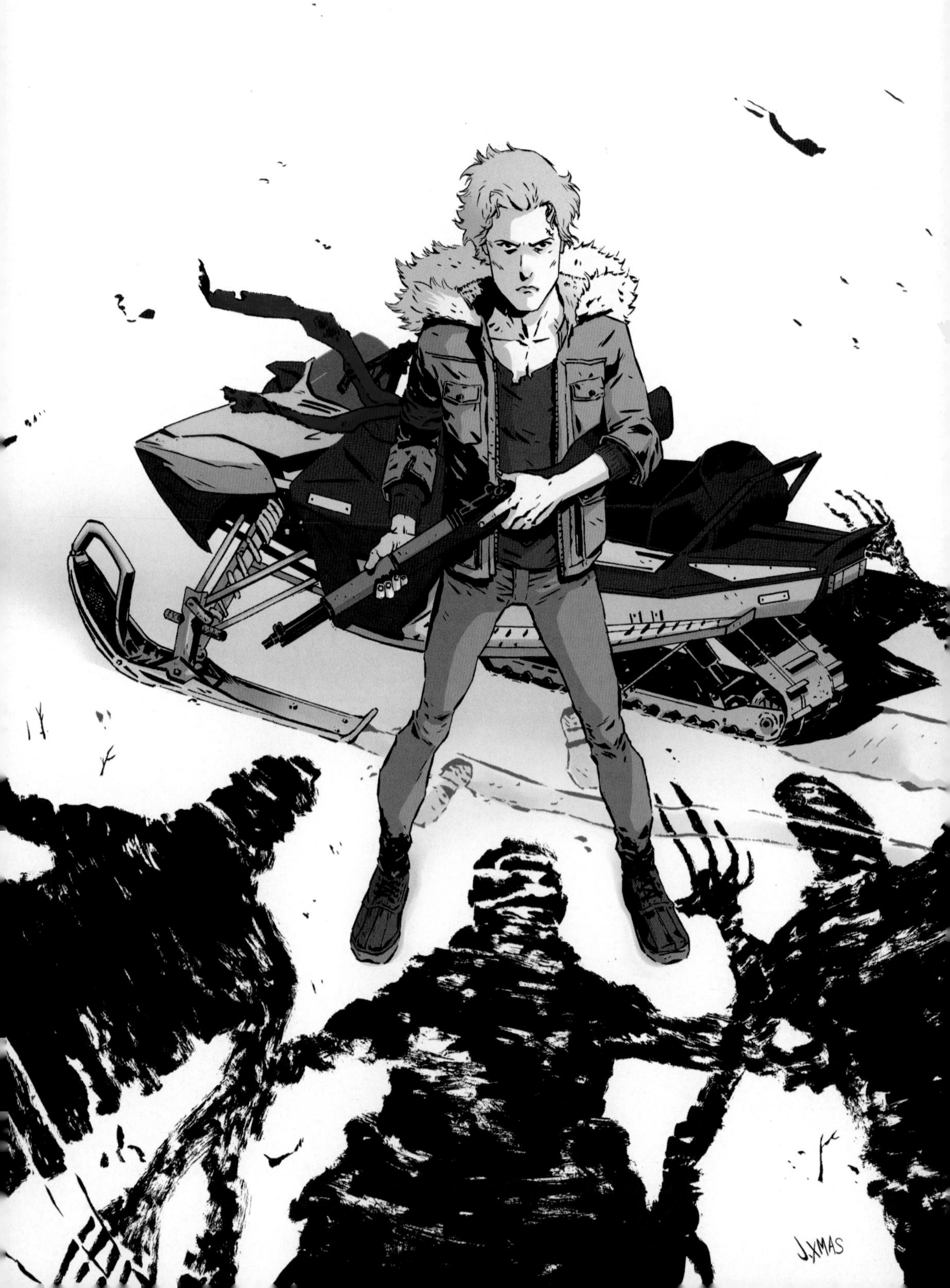
J.XMAS

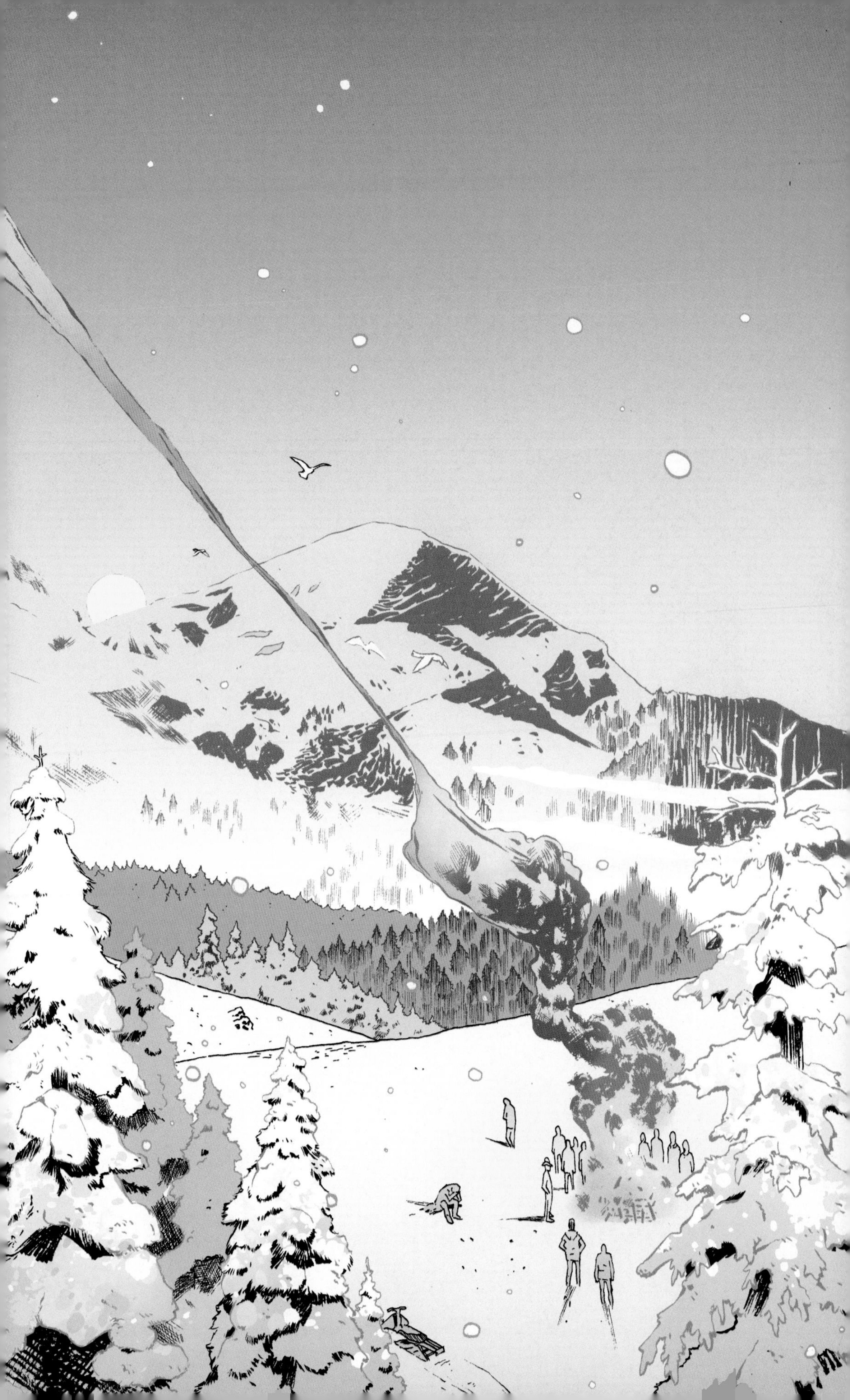

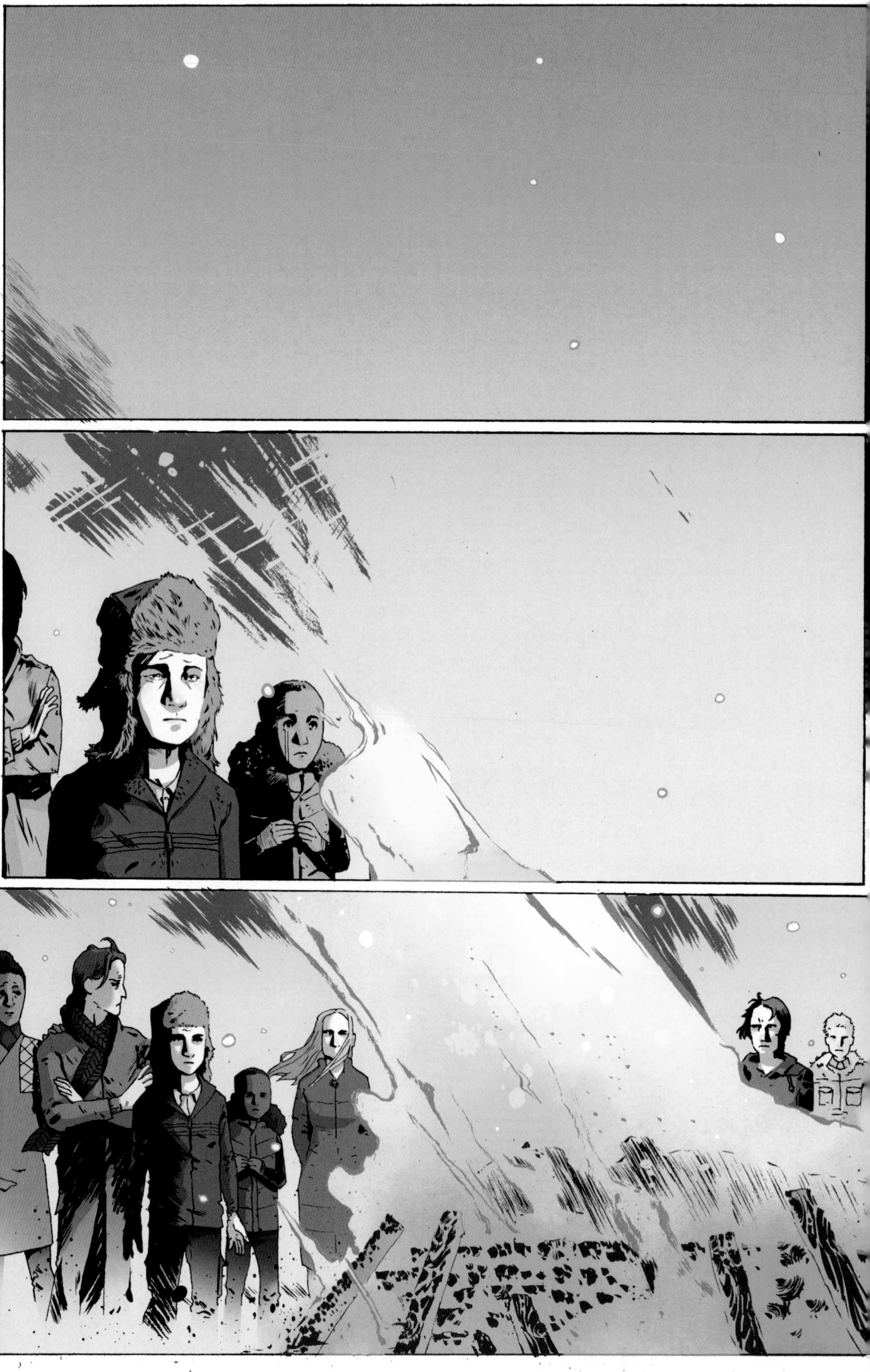

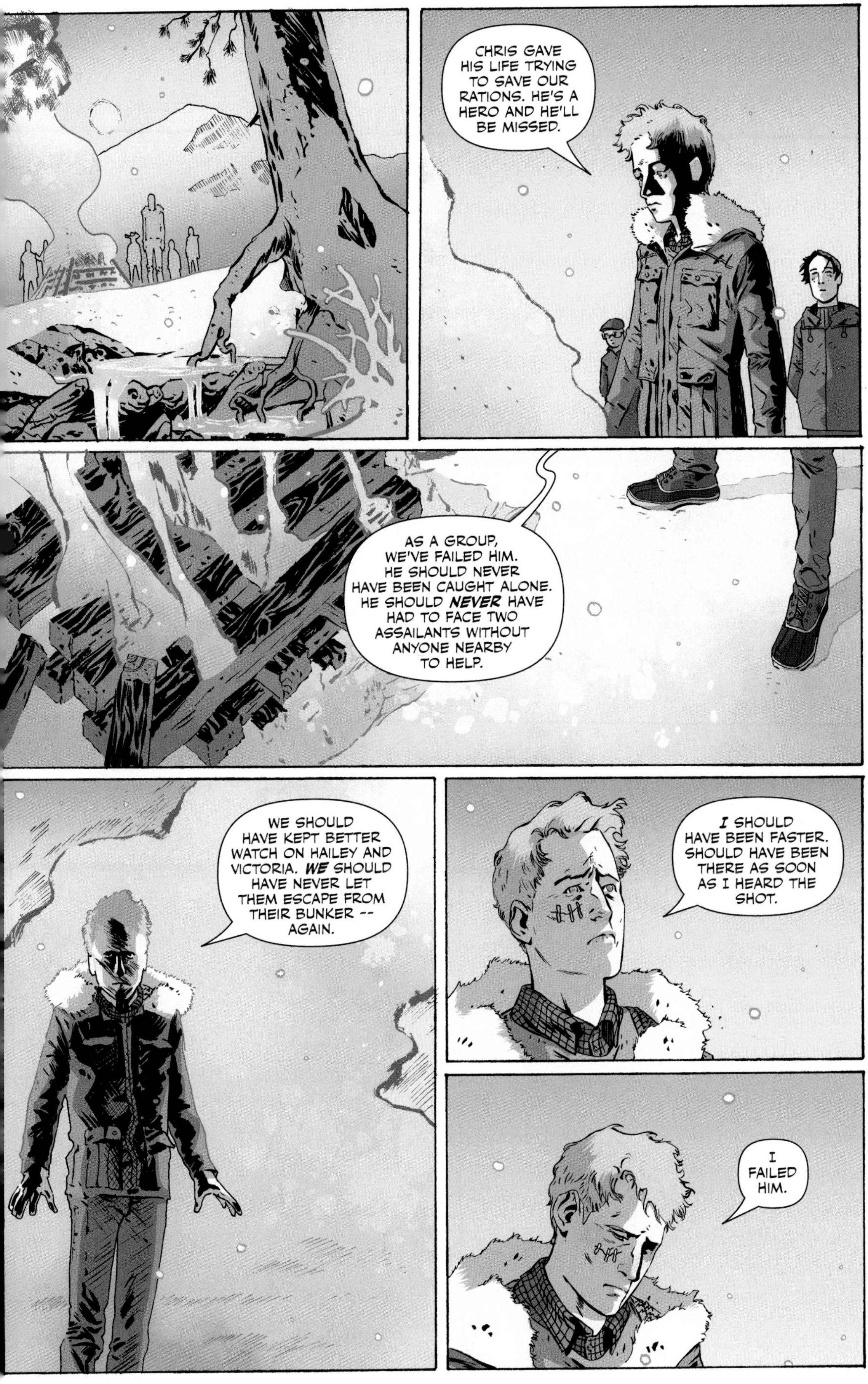

CHRIS GAVE HIS LIFE TRYING TO SAVE OUR RATIONS. HE'S A HERO AND HE'LL BE MISSED.
AS A GROUP, WE'VE FAILED HIM. HE SHOULD NEVER HAVE BEEN CAUGHT ALONE. HE SHOULD NEVER HAVE HAD TO FACE TWO ASSAILANTS WITHOUT ANYONE NEARBY TO HELP.
WE SHOULD HAVE KEPT BETTER WATCH ON HAILEY AND VICTORIA. WE SHOULD HAVE NEVER LET THEM ESCAPE FROM THEIR BUNKER -- AGAIN.
I SHOULD HAVE BEEN FASTER. SHOULD HAVE BEEN THERE AS SOON AS I HEARD THE SHOT.
I FAILED HIM.

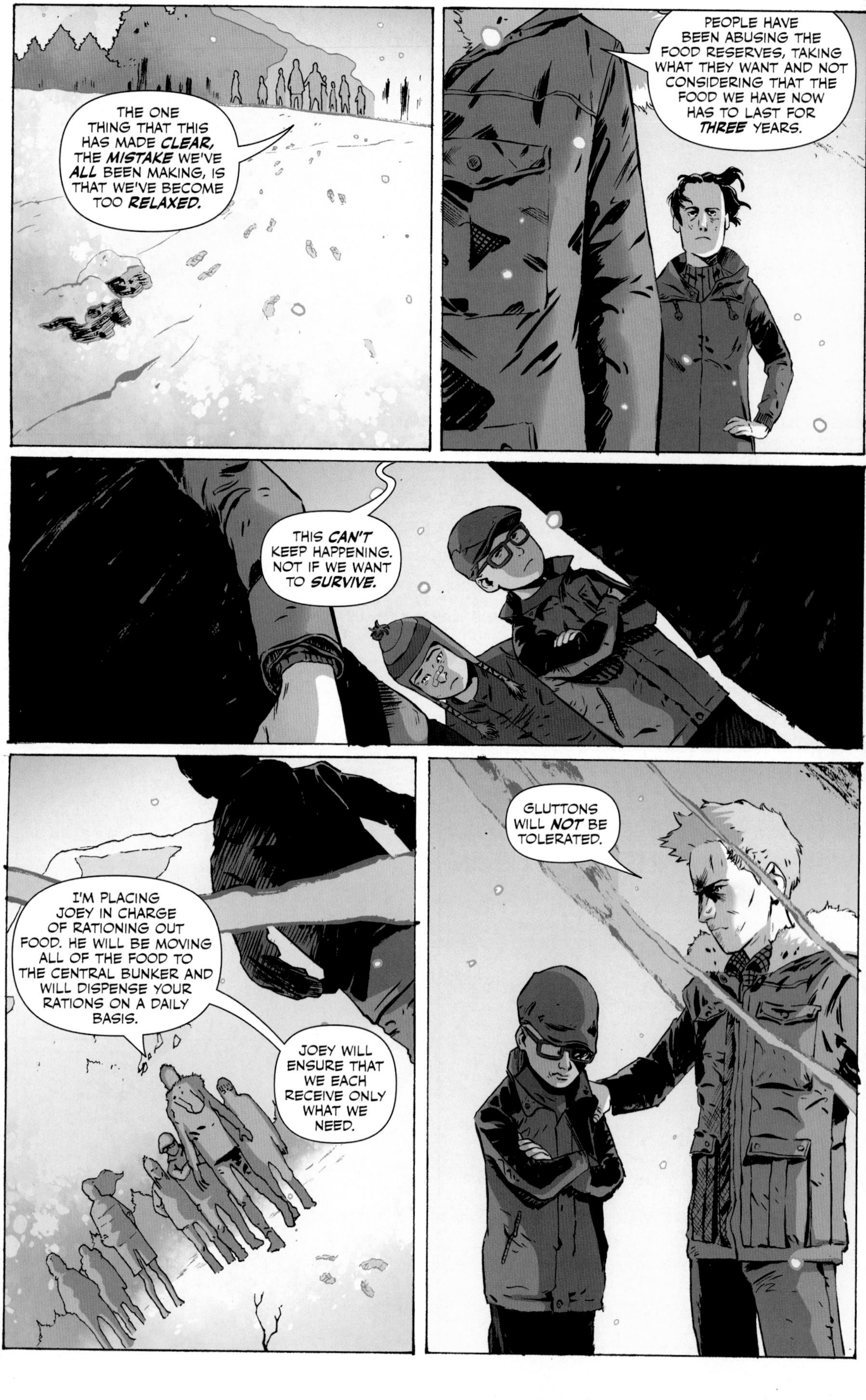
THE ONE THING THAT THIS HAS MADE CLEAR, THE MISTAKE WE'VE ALL BEEN MAKING, IS THAT WE'VE BECOME TOO RELAXED.
PEOPLE HAVE BEEN ABUSING THE FOOD RESERVES, TAKING WHAT THEY WANT AND NOT CONSIDERING THAT THE FOOD WE HAVE NOW HAS TO LAST FOR THREE YEARS.
THIS CAN'T KEEP HAPPENING. NOT IF WE WANT TO SURVIVE.
I'M PLACING JOEY IN CHARGE OF RATIONING OUT FOOD. HE WILL BE MOVING ALL OF THE FOOD TO THE CENTRAL BUNKER AND WILL DISPENSE YOUR RATIONS ON A DAILY BASIS.
JOEY WILL ENSURE THAT WE EACH RECEIVE ONLY WHAT WE NEED.
GLUTTONS WILL NOT BE TOLERATED.

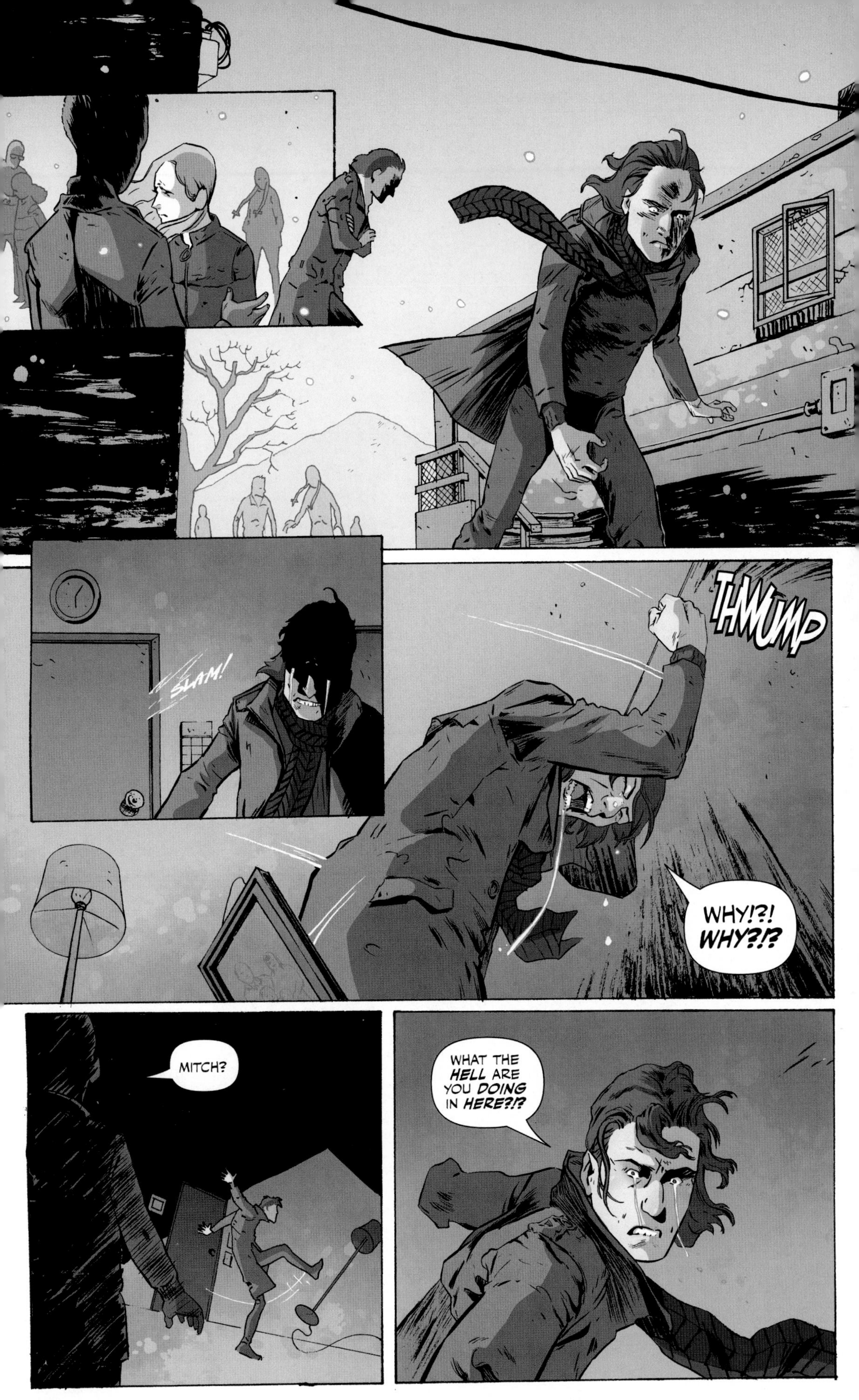

SLAM!
THWUMP
WHY!?! WHY?!?
MITCH?
WHAT THE HELL ARE YOU DOING IN HERE?!?

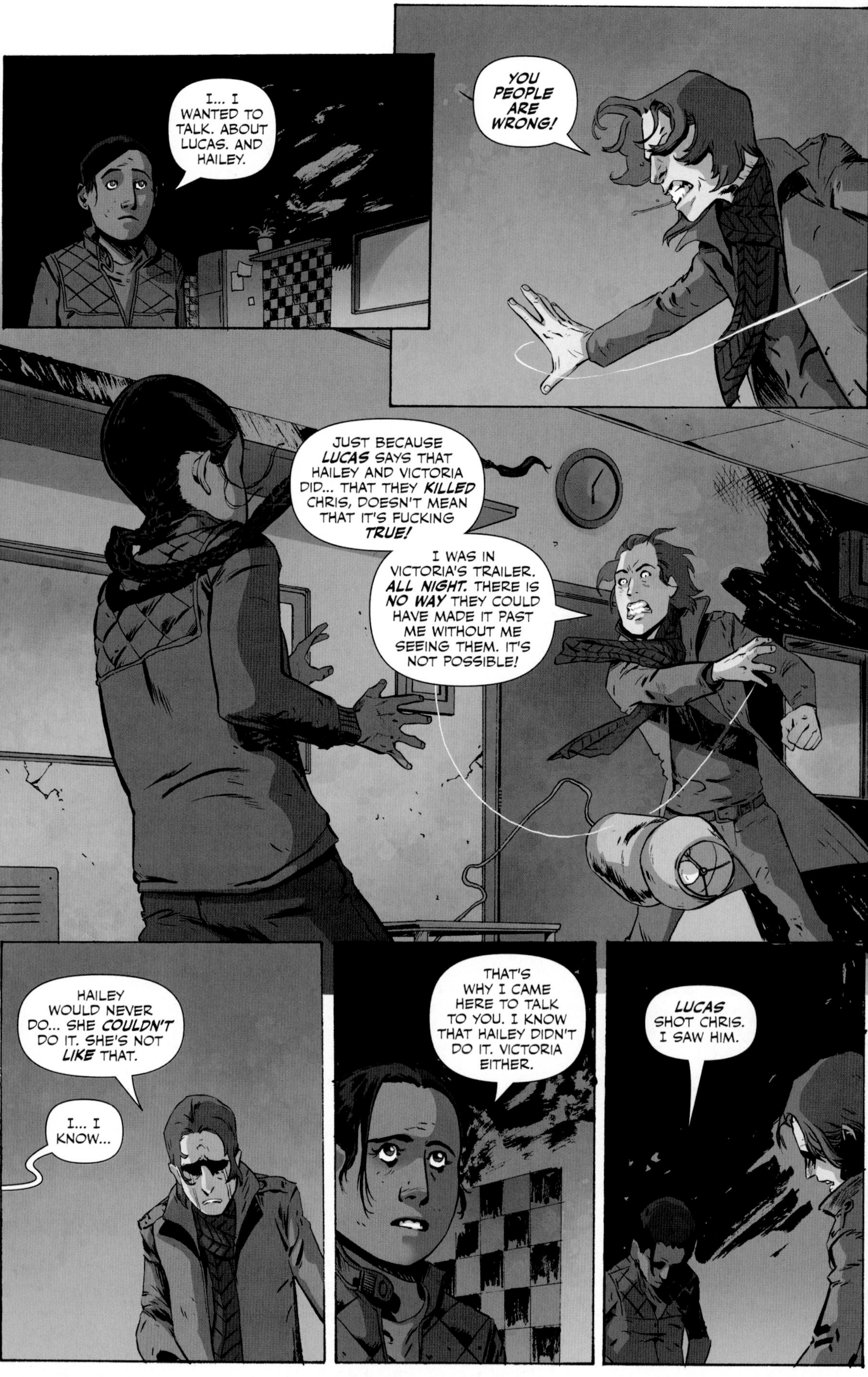
I... I WANTED TO TALK. ABOUT LUCAS. AND HAILEY.
YOU PEOPLE ARE WRONG!
JUST BECAUSE LUCAS SAYS THAT HAILEY AND VICTORIA DID... THAT THEY KILLED CHRIS, DOESN'T MEAN THAT IT'S FUCKING TRUE!
I WAS IN VICTORIA'S TRAILER. ALL NIGHT. THERE IS NO WAY THEY COULD HAVE MADE IT PAST ME WITHOUT ME SEEING THEM. IT'S NOT POSSIBLE!
HAILEY WOULD NEVER DO... SHE COULDN'T DO IT. SHE'S NOT LIKE THAT.
I... I KNOW...
THAT'S WHY I CAME HERE TO TALK TO YOU. I KNOW THAT HAILEY DIDN'T DO IT. VICTORIA EITHER.
LUCAS SHOT CHRIS. I SAW HIM.

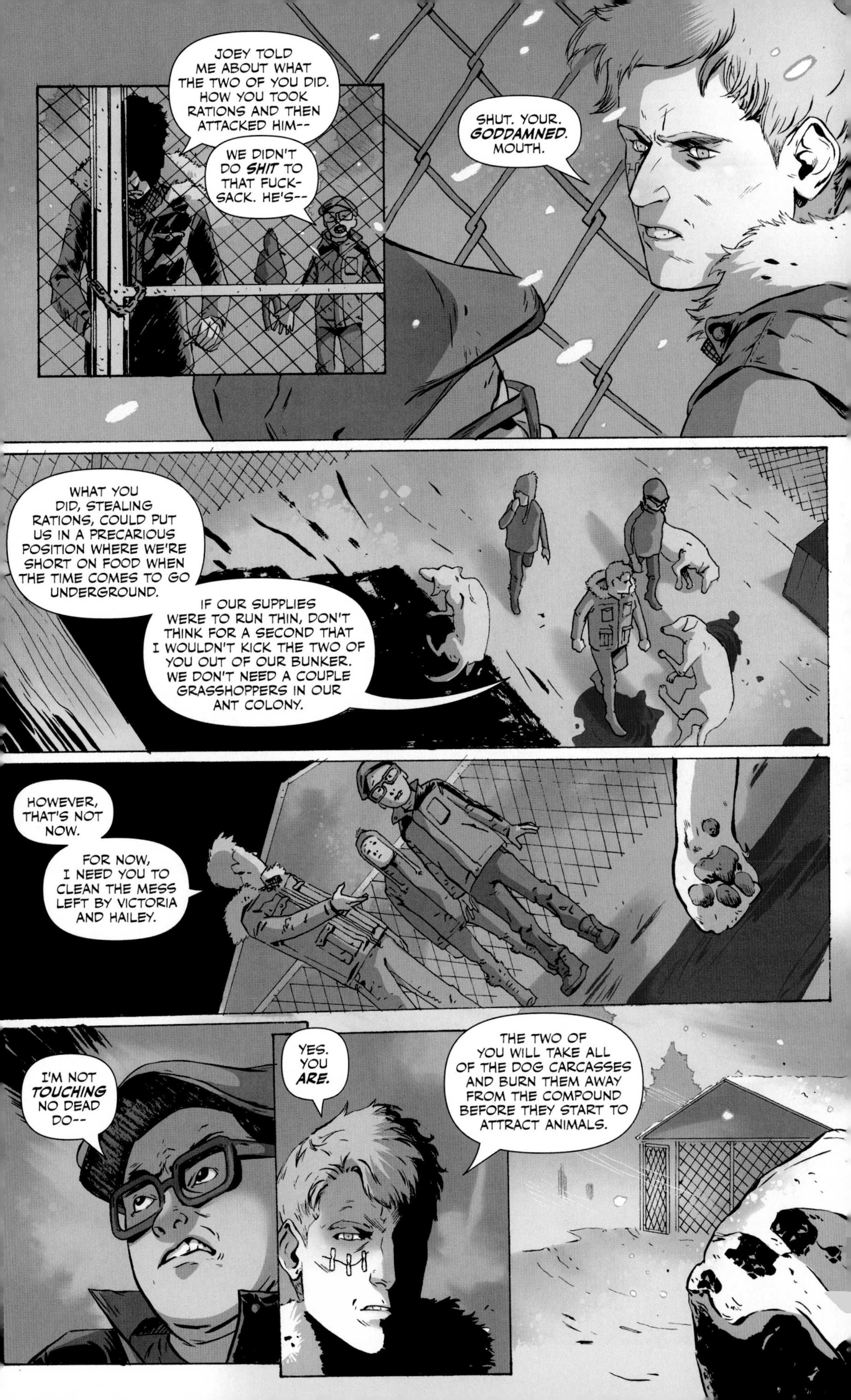
JOEY TOLD ME ABOUT WHAT THE TWO OF YOU DID. HOW YOU TOOK RATIONS AND THEN ATTACKED HIM--
WE DIDN'T DO *SHIT* TO THAT FUCK-SACK. HE'S--
SHUT. YOUR. *GODDAMNED.* MOUTH.
WHAT YOU DID, STEALING RATIONS, COULD PUT US IN A PRECARIOUS POSITION WHERE WE'RE SHORT ON FOOD WHEN THE TIME COMES TO GO UNDERGROUND.
IF OUR SUPPLIES WERE TO RUN THIN, DON'T THINK FOR A SECOND THAT I WOULDN'T KICK THE TWO OF YOU OUT OF OUR BUNKER. WE DON'T NEED A COUPLE GRASSHOPPERS IN OUR ANT COLONY.
HOWEVER, THAT'S NOT NOW.
FOR NOW, I NEED YOU TO CLEAN THE MESS LEFT BY VICTORIA AND HAILEY.
I'M NOT *TOUCHING* NO DEAD DO--
YES. YOU *ARE.*
THE TWO OF YOU WILL TAKE ALL OF THE DOG CARCASSES AND BURN THEM AWAY FROM THE COMPOUND BEFORE THEY START TO ATTRACT ANIMALS.

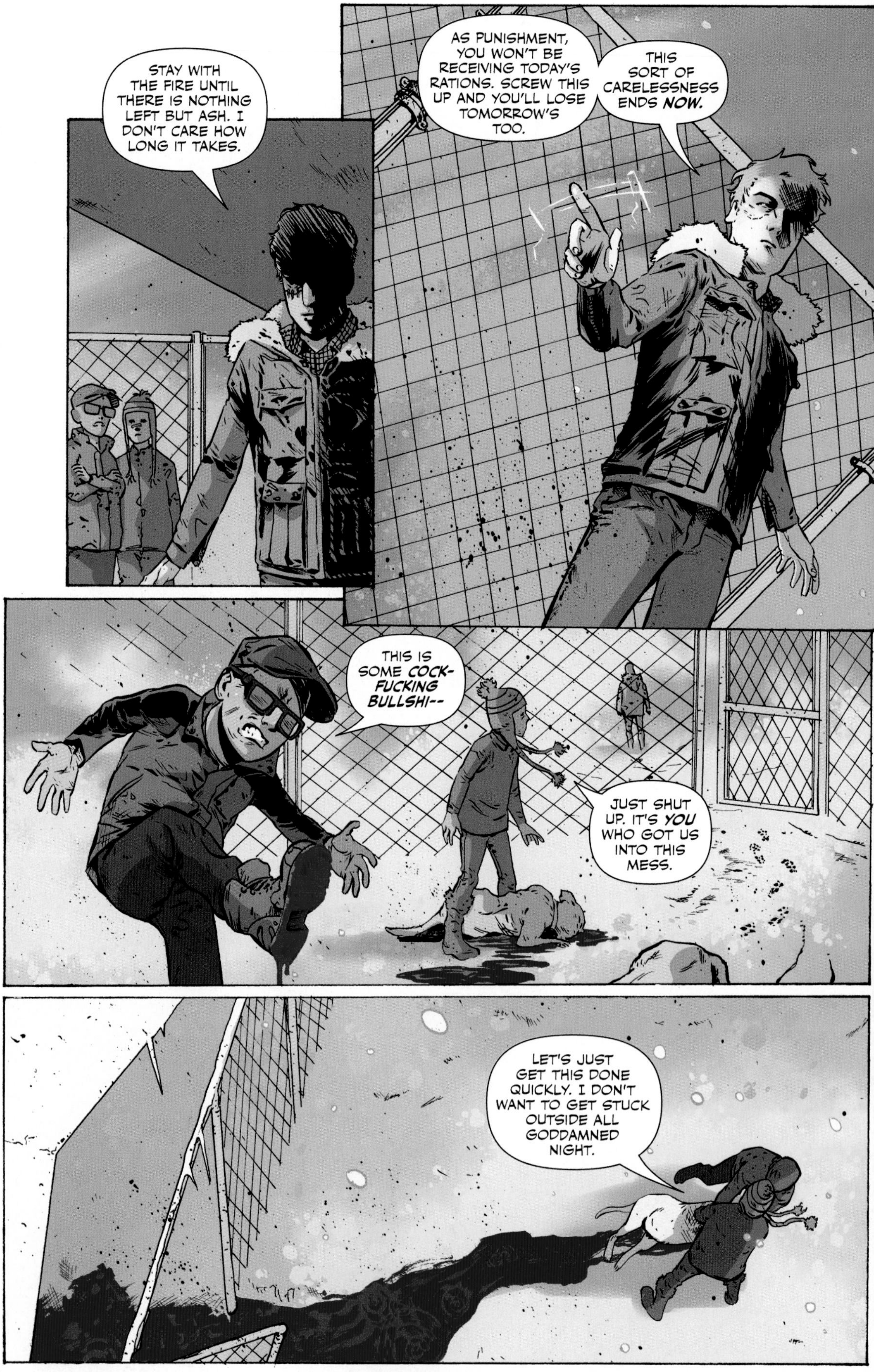
STAY WITH THE FIRE UNTIL THERE IS NOTHING LEFT BUT ASH. I DON'T CARE HOW LONG IT TAKES.
AS PUNISHMENT, YOU WON'T BE RECEIVING TODAY'S RATIONS. SCREW THIS UP AND YOU'LL LOSE TOMORROW'S TOO.
THIS SORT OF CARELESSNESS ENDS *NOW.*
THIS IS SOME *COCK-FUCKING* BULLSHI--
JUST SHUT UP. IT'S *YOU* WHO GOT US INTO THIS MESS.
LET'S JUST GET THIS DONE QUICKLY. I DON'T WANT TO GET STUCK OUTSIDE ALL GODDAMNED NIGHT.

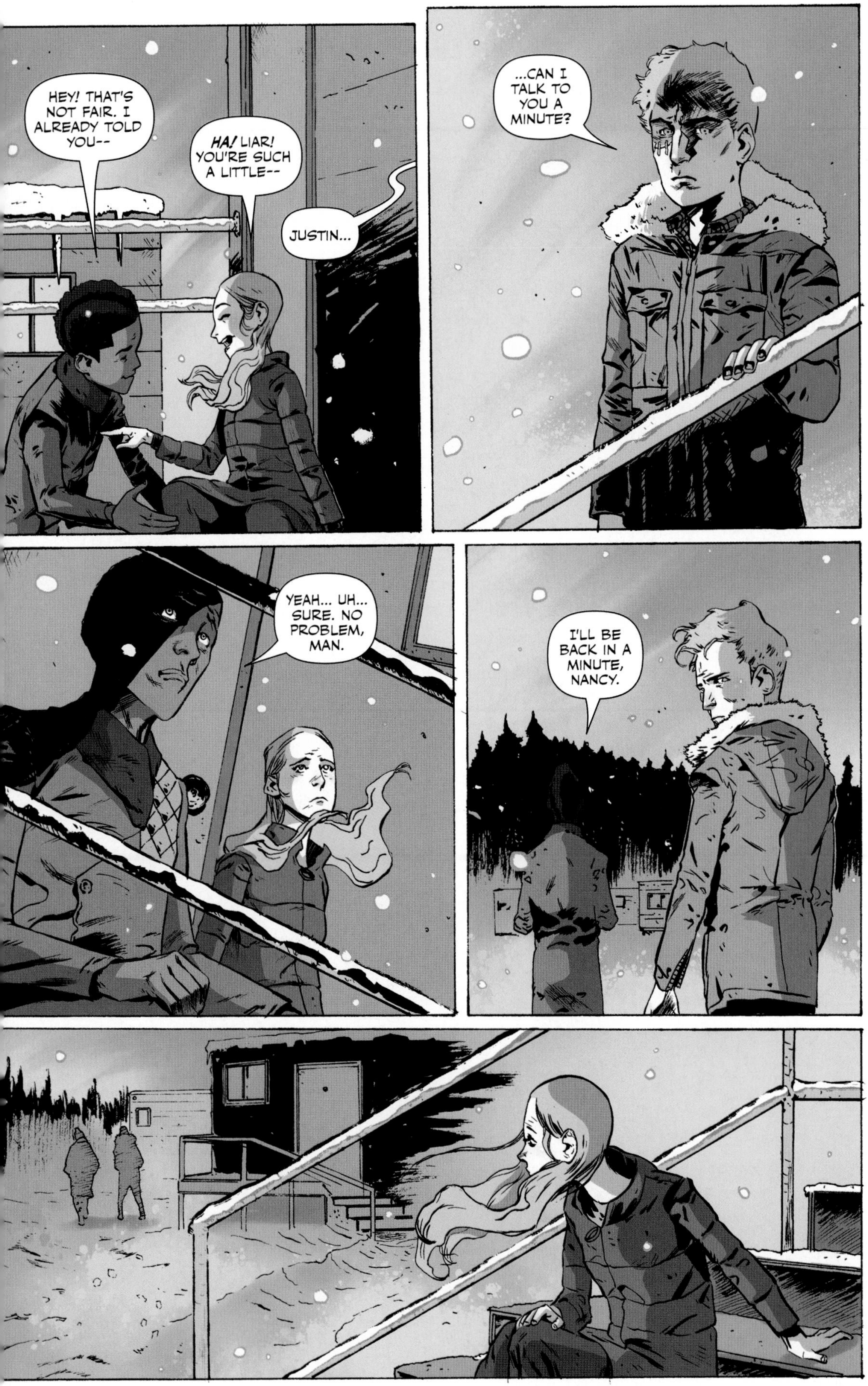
HEY! THAT'S NOT FAIR. I ALREADY TOLD YOU--
HA! LIAR! YOU'RE SUCH A LITTLE--
JUSTIN...
...CAN I TALK TO YOU A MINUTE?
YEAH... UH... SURE. NO PROBLEM, MAN.
I'LL BE BACK IN A MINUTE, NANCY.

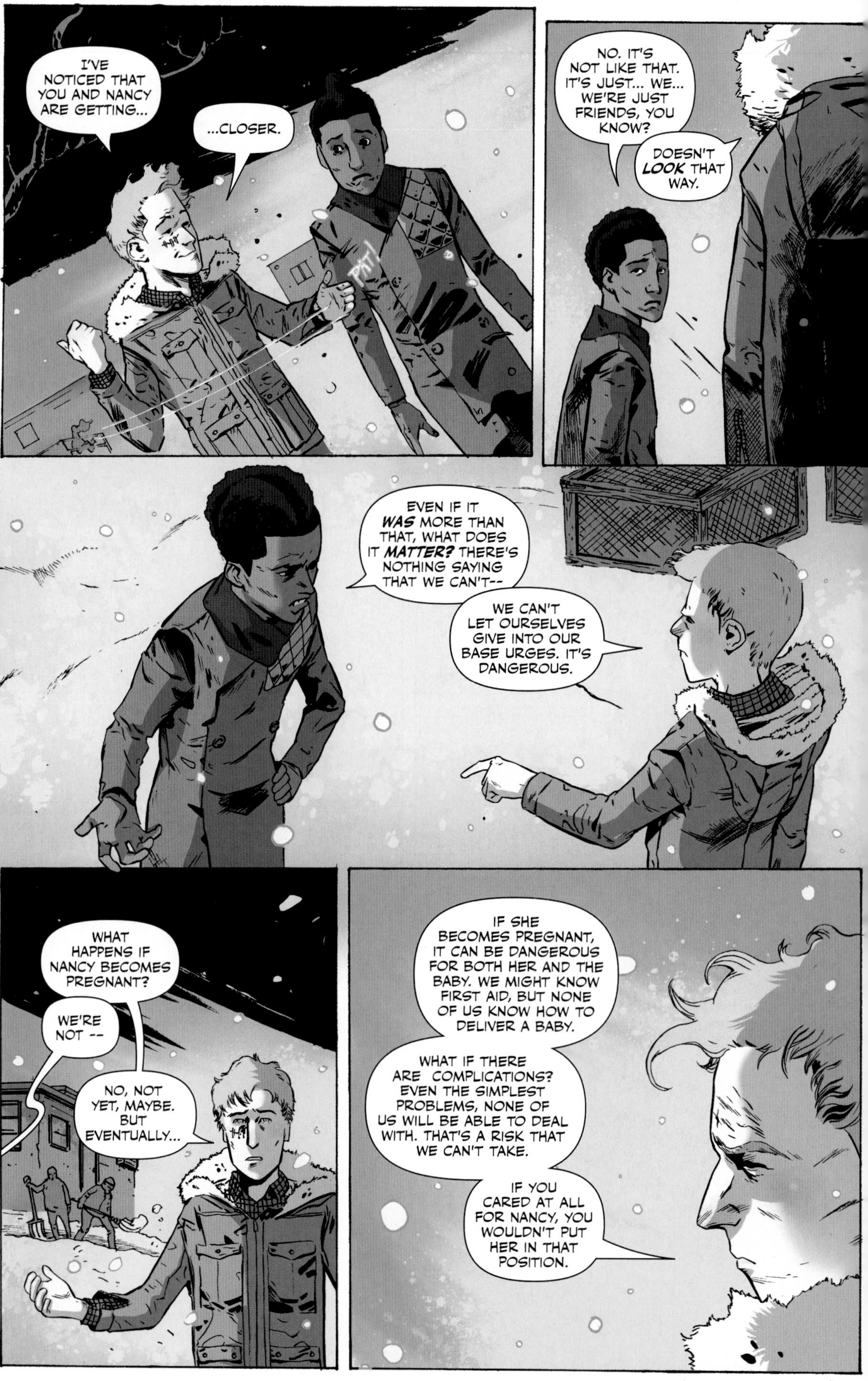
I'VE NOTICED THAT YOU AND NANCY ARE GETTING...
...CLOSER.
PAT!
NO. IT'S NOT LIKE THAT. IT'S JUST... WE... WE'RE JUST FRIENDS, YOU KNOW?
DOESN'T LOOK THAT WAY.
EVEN IF IT WAS MORE THAN THAT, WHAT DOES IT MATTER? THERE'S NOTHING SAYING THAT WE CAN'T--
WE CAN'T LET OURSELVES GIVE INTO OUR BASE URGES. IT'S DANGEROUS.
WHAT HAPPENS IF NANCY BECOMES PREGNANT?
WE'RE NOT --
NO, NOT YET, MAYBE. BUT EVENTUALLY...
IF SHE BECOMES PREGNANT, IT CAN BE DANGEROUS FOR BOTH HER AND THE BABY. WE MIGHT KNOW FIRST AID, BUT NONE OF US KNOW HOW TO DELIVER A BABY.
WHAT IF THERE ARE COMPLICATIONS? EVEN THE SIMPLEST PROBLEMS, NONE OF US WILL BE ABLE TO DEAL WITH. THAT'S A RISK THAT WE CAN'T TAKE.
IF YOU CARED AT ALL FOR NANCY, YOU WOULDN'T PUT HER IN THAT POSITION.

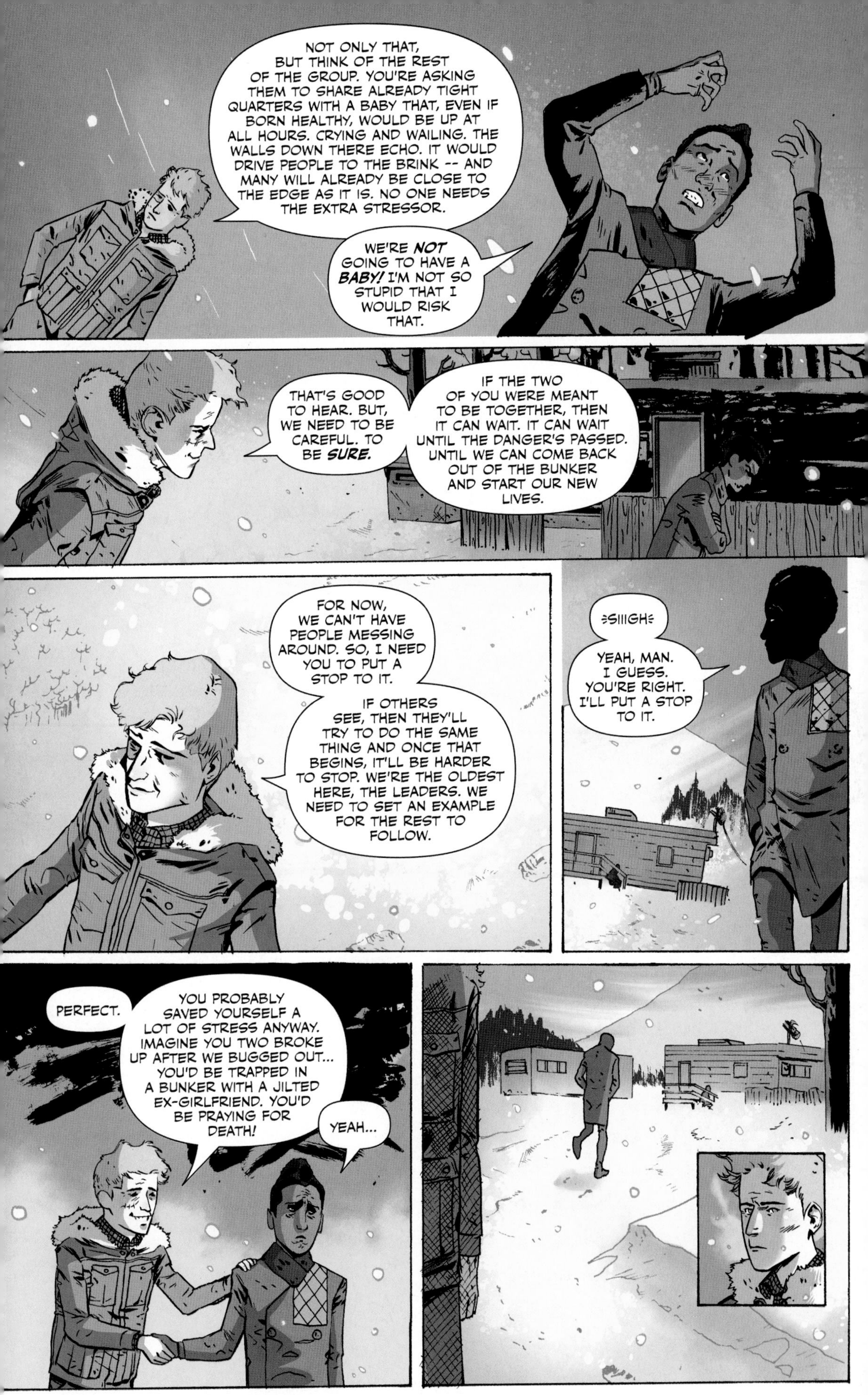
NOT ONLY THAT, BUT THINK OF THE REST OF THE GROUP. YOU'RE ASKING THEM TO SHARE ALREADY TIGHT QUARTERS WITH A BABY THAT, EVEN IF BORN HEALTHY, WOULD BE UP AT ALL HOURS. CRYING AND WAILING. THE WALLS DOWN THERE ECHO. IT WOULD DRIVE PEOPLE TO THE BRINK -- AND MANY WILL ALREADY BE CLOSE TO THE EDGE AS IT IS. NO ONE NEEDS THE EXTRA STRESSOR.
WE'RE ***NOT*** GOING TO HAVE A ***BABY!*** I'M NOT SO STUPID THAT I WOULD RISK THAT.
THAT'S GOOD TO HEAR. BUT, WE NEED TO BE CAREFUL. TO BE ***SURE.***
IF THE TWO OF YOU WERE MEANT TO BE TOGETHER, THEN IT CAN WAIT. IT CAN WAIT UNTIL THE DANGER'S PASSED. UNTIL WE CAN COME BACK OUT OF THE BUNKER AND START OUR NEW LIVES.
FOR NOW, WE CAN'T HAVE PEOPLE MESSING AROUND. SO, I NEED YOU TO PUT A STOP TO IT.
IF OTHERS SEE, THEN THEY'LL TRY TO DO THE SAME THING AND ONCE THAT BEGINS, IT'LL BE HARDER TO STOP. WE'RE THE OLDEST HERE, THE LEADERS. WE NEED TO SET AN EXAMPLE FOR THE REST TO FOLLOW.
SIIIGH
YEAH, MAN. I GUESS. YOU'RE RIGHT. I'LL PUT A STOP TO IT.
PERFECT.
YOU PROBABLY SAVED YOURSELF A LOT OF STRESS ANYWAY. IMAGINE YOU TWO BROKE UP AFTER WE BUGGED OUT... YOU'D BE TRAPPED IN A BUNKER WITH A JILTED EX-GIRLFRIEND. YOU'D BE PRAYING FOR DEATH!
YEAH...

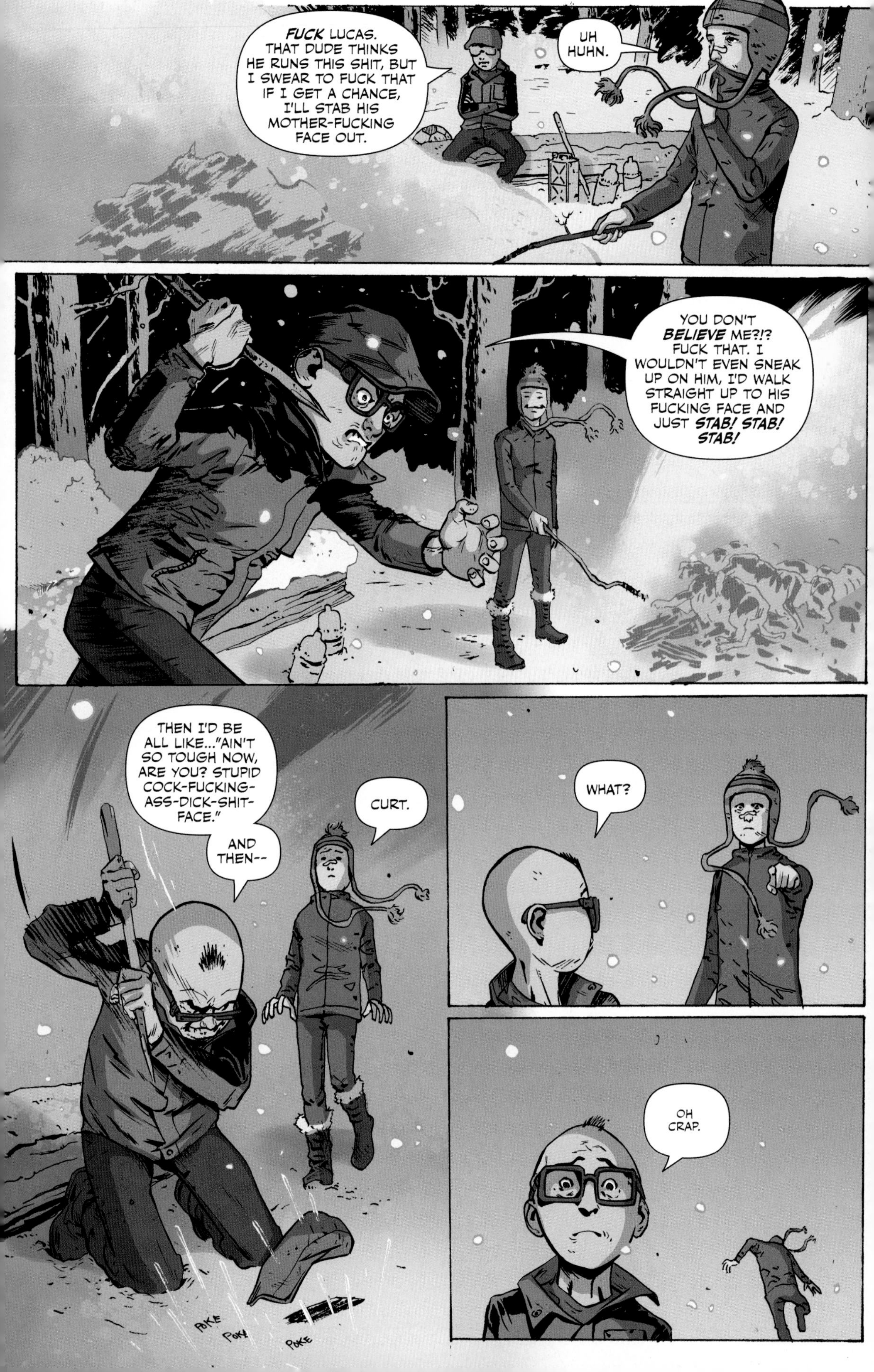
FUCK LUCAS. THAT DUDE THINKS HE RUNS THIS SHIT, BUT I SWEAR TO FUCK THAT IF I GET A CHANCE, I'LL STAB HIS MOTHER-FUCKING FACE OUT.
UH HUHN.
YOU DON'T BELIEVE ME?!? FUCK THAT. I WOULDN'T EVEN SNEAK UP ON HIM, I'D WALK STRAIGHT UP TO HIS FUCKING FACE AND JUST STAB! STAB! STAB!
THEN I'D BE ALL LIKE..."AIN'T SO TOUGH NOW, ARE YOU? STUPID COCK-FUCKING-ASS-DICK-SHIT-FACE."
AND THEN--
CURT.
POKE
POKE
POKE
WHAT?
OH CRAP.

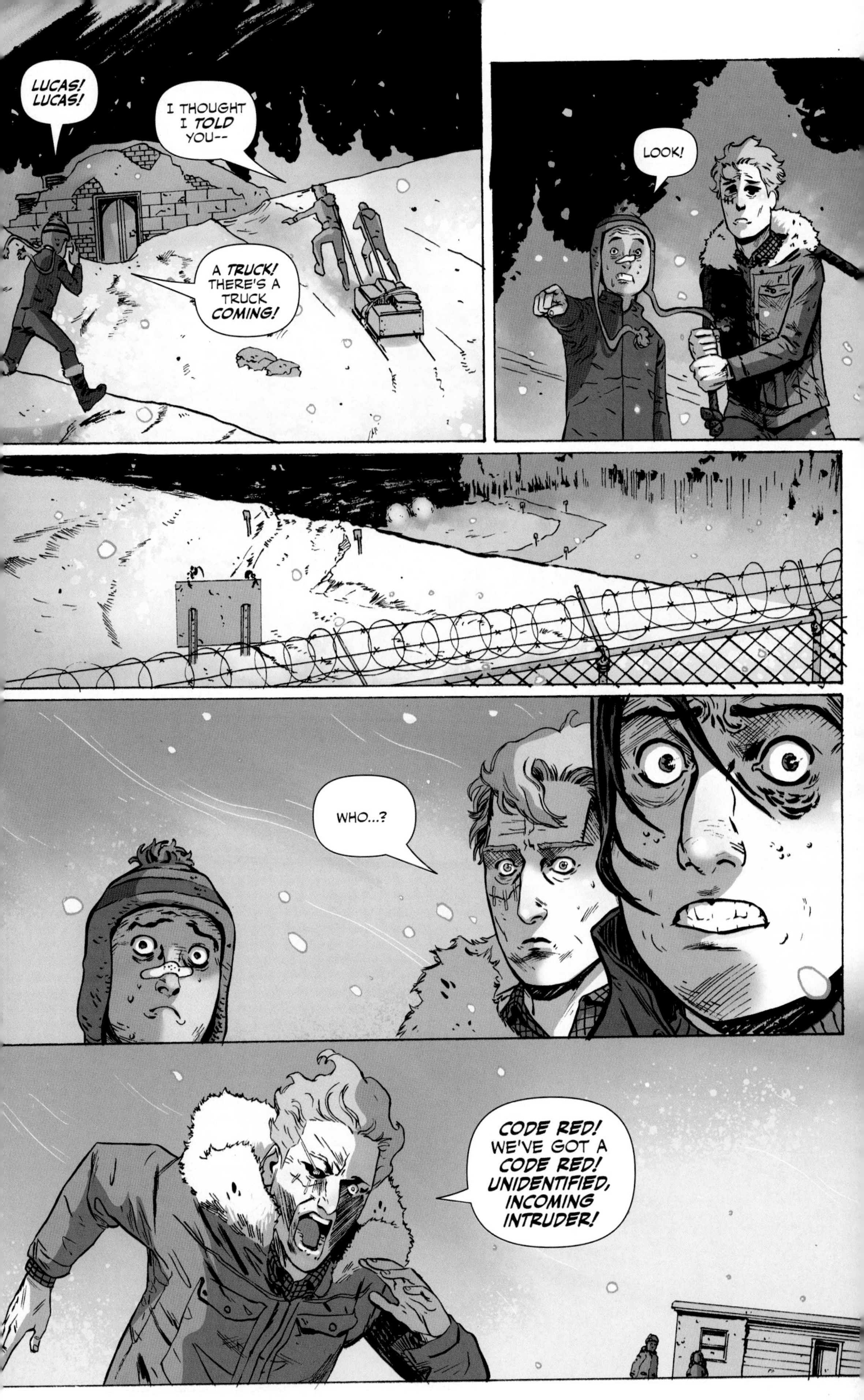
LUCAS! LUCAS!
I THOUGHT I TOLD YOU--
A TRUCK! THERE'S A TRUCK COMING!
LOOK!
WHO...?
CODE RED! WE'VE GOT A CODE RED! UNIDENTIFIED, INCOMING INTRUDER!

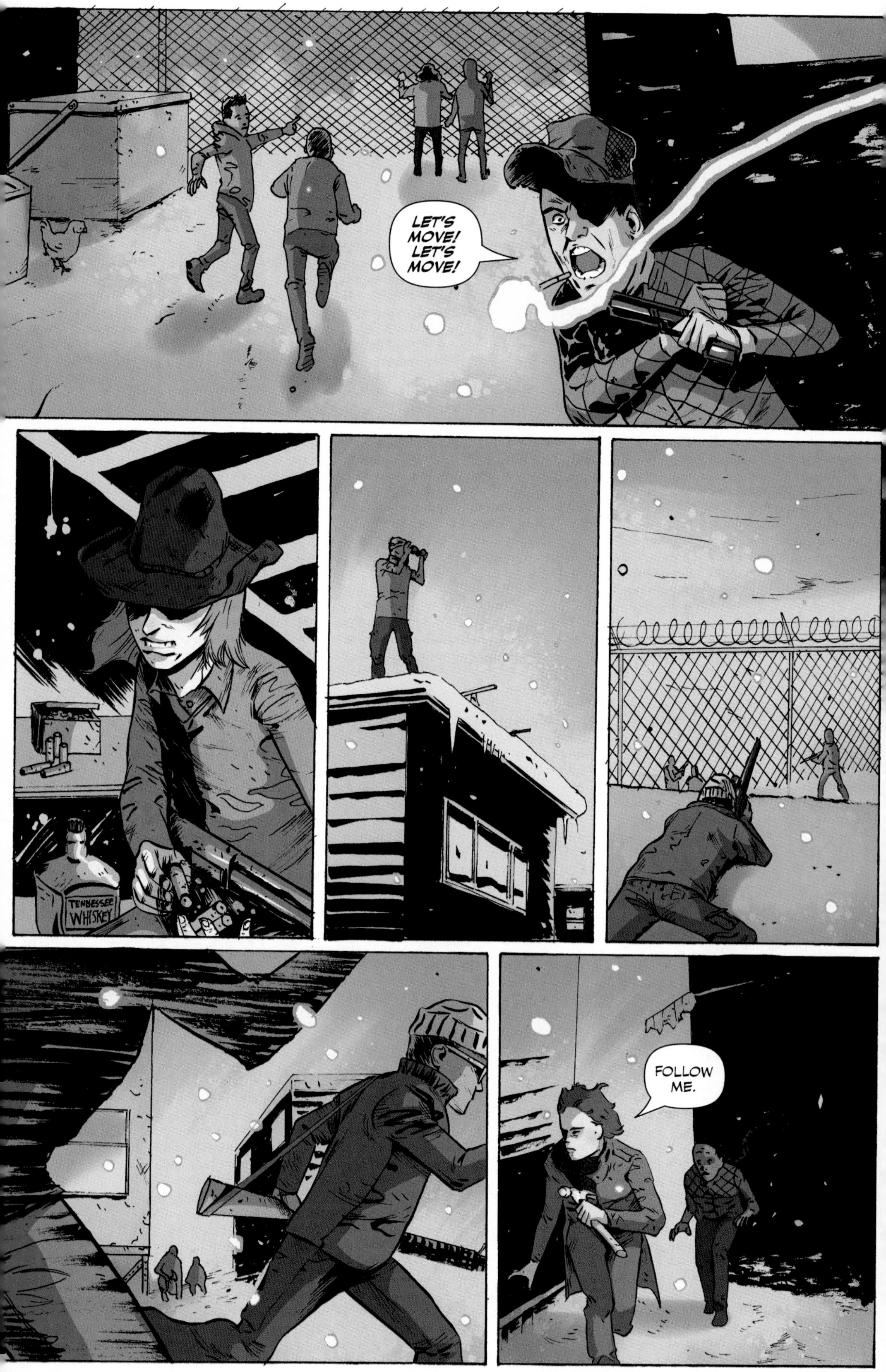

LET'S MOVE! LET'S MOVE!
TENNESSEE WHISKEY
FOLLOW ME.

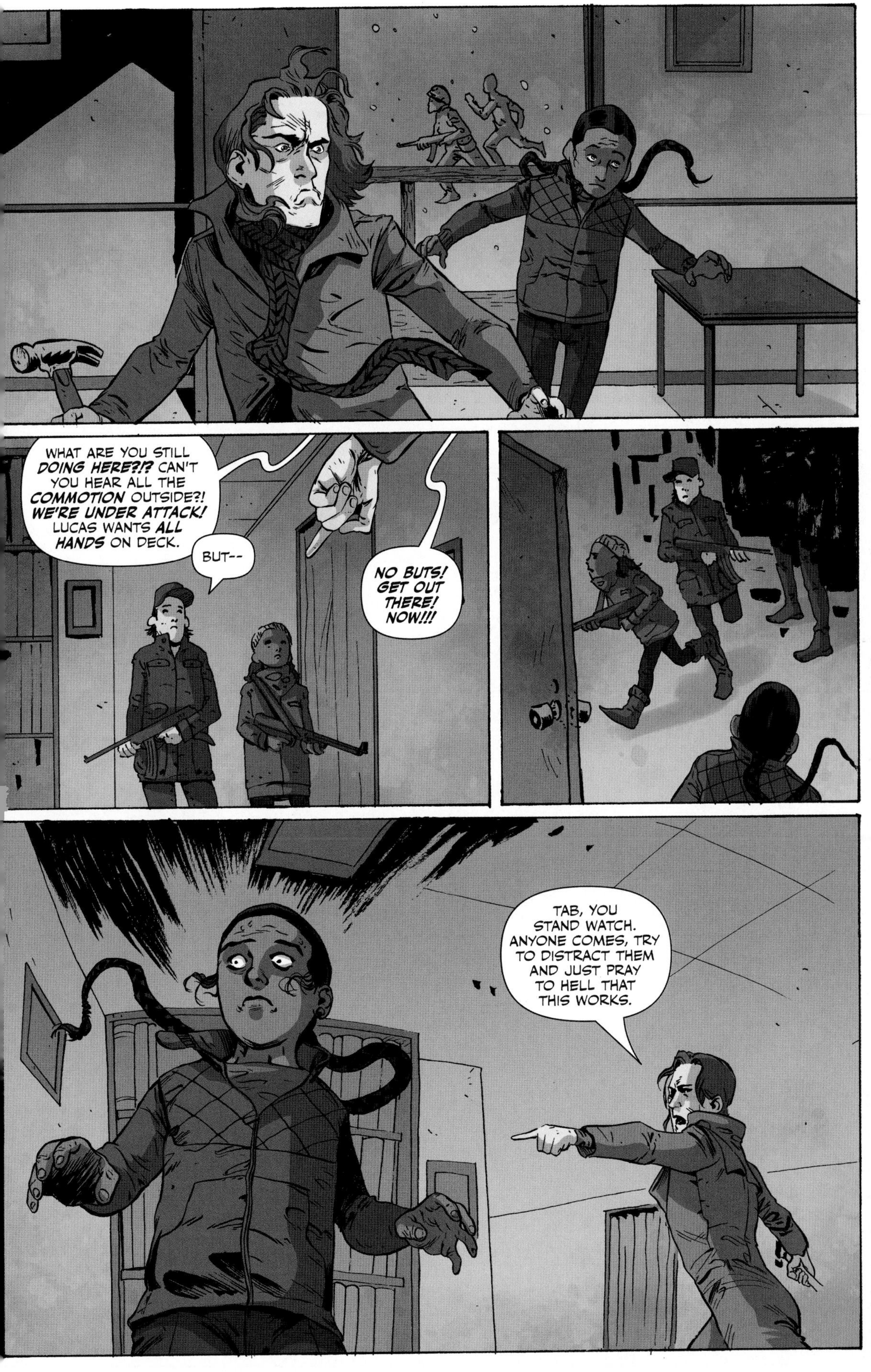
WHAT ARE YOU STILL DOING HERE?!? CAN'T YOU HEAR ALL THE COMMOTION OUTSIDE?! WE'RE UNDER ATTACK! LUCAS WANTS ALL HANDS ON DECK.
BUT--
NO BUTS! GET OUT THERE! NOW!!!
TAB, YOU STAND WATCH. ANYONE COMES, TRY TO DISTRACT THEM AND JUST PRAY TO HELL THAT THIS WORKS.

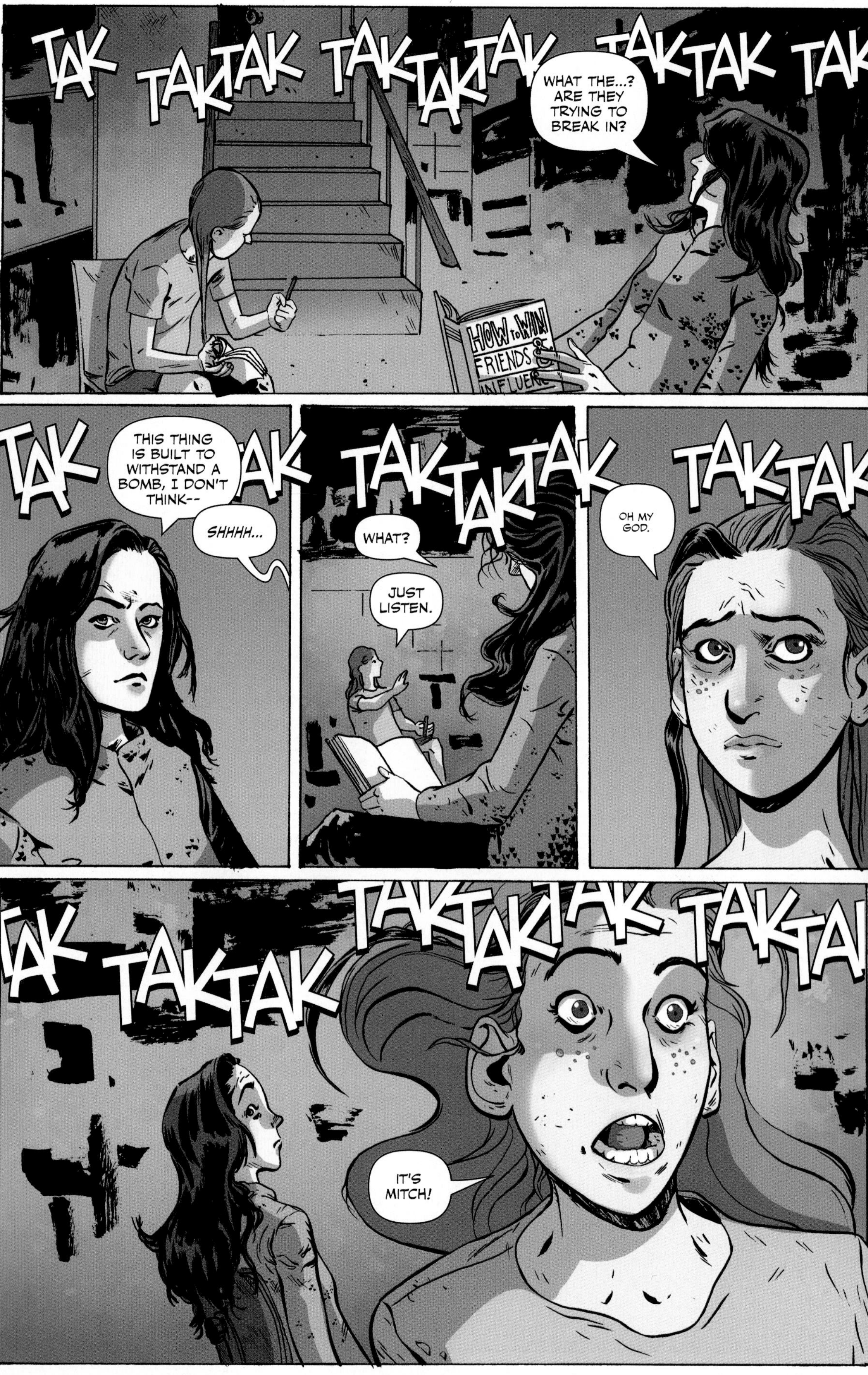
TAK TAKTAK TAKTAKTAK TAKTAK TAK
WHAT THE...? ARE THEY TRYING TO BREAK IN?
HOW TO WIN FRIENDS & INFLUENC
TAK TAK
THIS THING IS BUILT TO WITHSTAND A BOMB, I DON'T THINK--
SHHHH...
TAKTAKTAK
WHAT?
JUST LISTEN.
TAKTAK
OH MY GOD.
TAK TAKTAK TAKTAKTAK TAKTAK
IT'S MITCH!

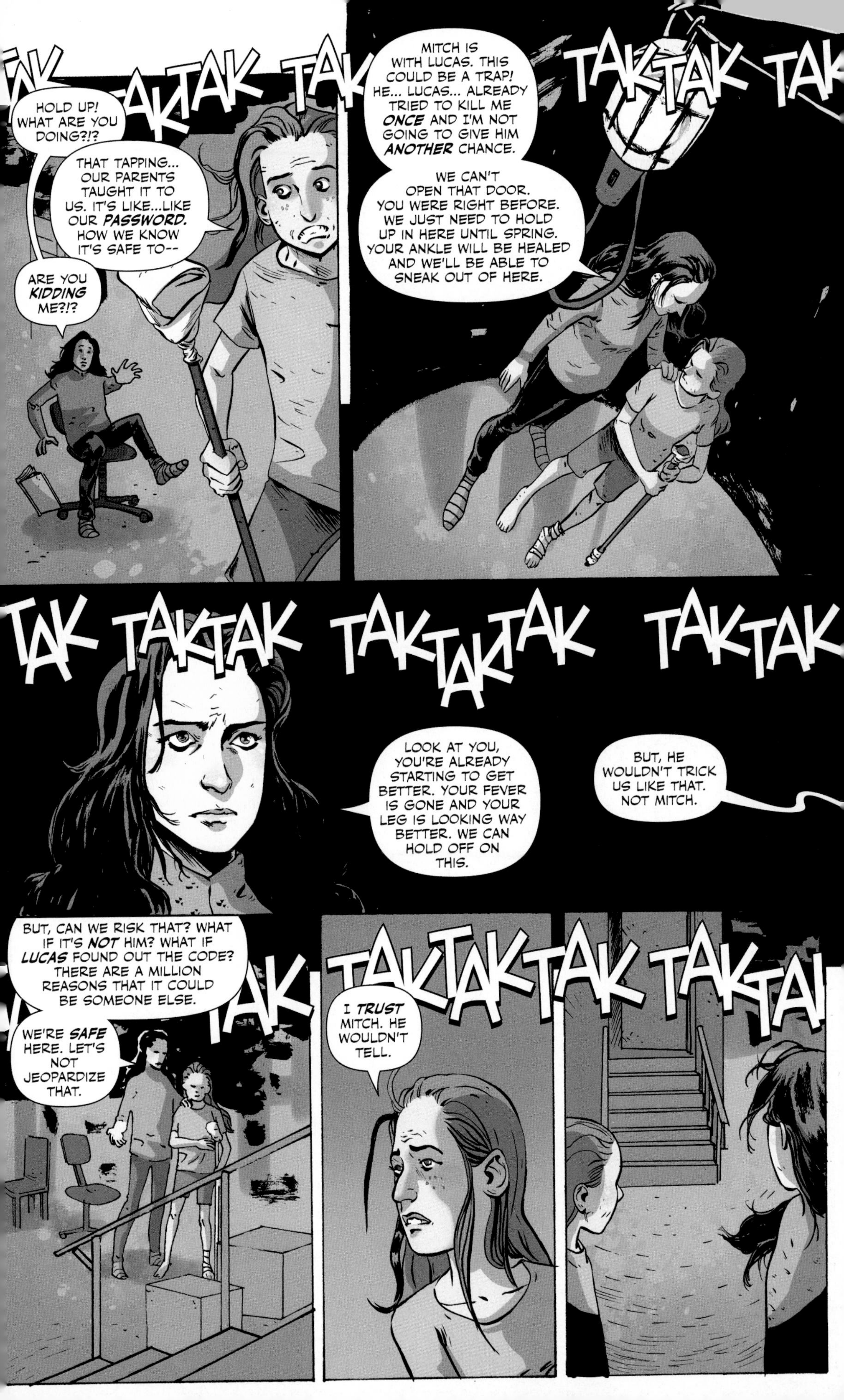
TAK TAKTAK TAK
HOLD UP! WHAT ARE YOU DOING?!?
THAT TAPPING... OUR PARENTS TAUGHT IT TO US. IT'S LIKE...LIKE OUR *PASSWORD.* HOW WE KNOW IT'S SAFE TO--
ARE YOU *KIDDING* ME?!?
MITCH IS WITH LUCAS. THIS COULD BE A TRAP! HE... LUCAS... ALREADY TRIED TO KILL ME *ONCE* AND I'M NOT GOING TO GIVE HIM *ANOTHER* CHANCE.
WE CAN'T OPEN THAT DOOR. YOU WERE RIGHT BEFORE. WE JUST NEED TO HOLD UP IN HERE UNTIL SPRING. YOUR ANKLE WILL BE HEALED AND WE'LL BE ABLE TO SNEAK OUT OF HERE.
TAKTAK TAK
TAK TAKTAK TAKTAKTAK TAKTAK
LOOK AT YOU, YOU'RE ALREADY STARTING TO GET BETTER. YOUR FEVER IS GONE AND YOUR LEG IS LOOKING WAY BETTER. WE CAN HOLD OFF ON THIS.
BUT, HE WOULDN'T TRICK US LIKE THAT. NOT MITCH.
BUT, CAN WE RISK THAT? WHAT IF IT'S *NOT* HIM? WHAT IF *LUCAS* FOUND OUT THE CODE? THERE ARE A MILLION REASONS THAT IT COULD BE SOMEONE ELSE.
WE'RE *SAFE* HERE. LET'S NOT JEOPARDIZE THAT.
I *TRUST* MITCH. HE WOULDN'T TELL.
TAKTAKTAK TAKTA

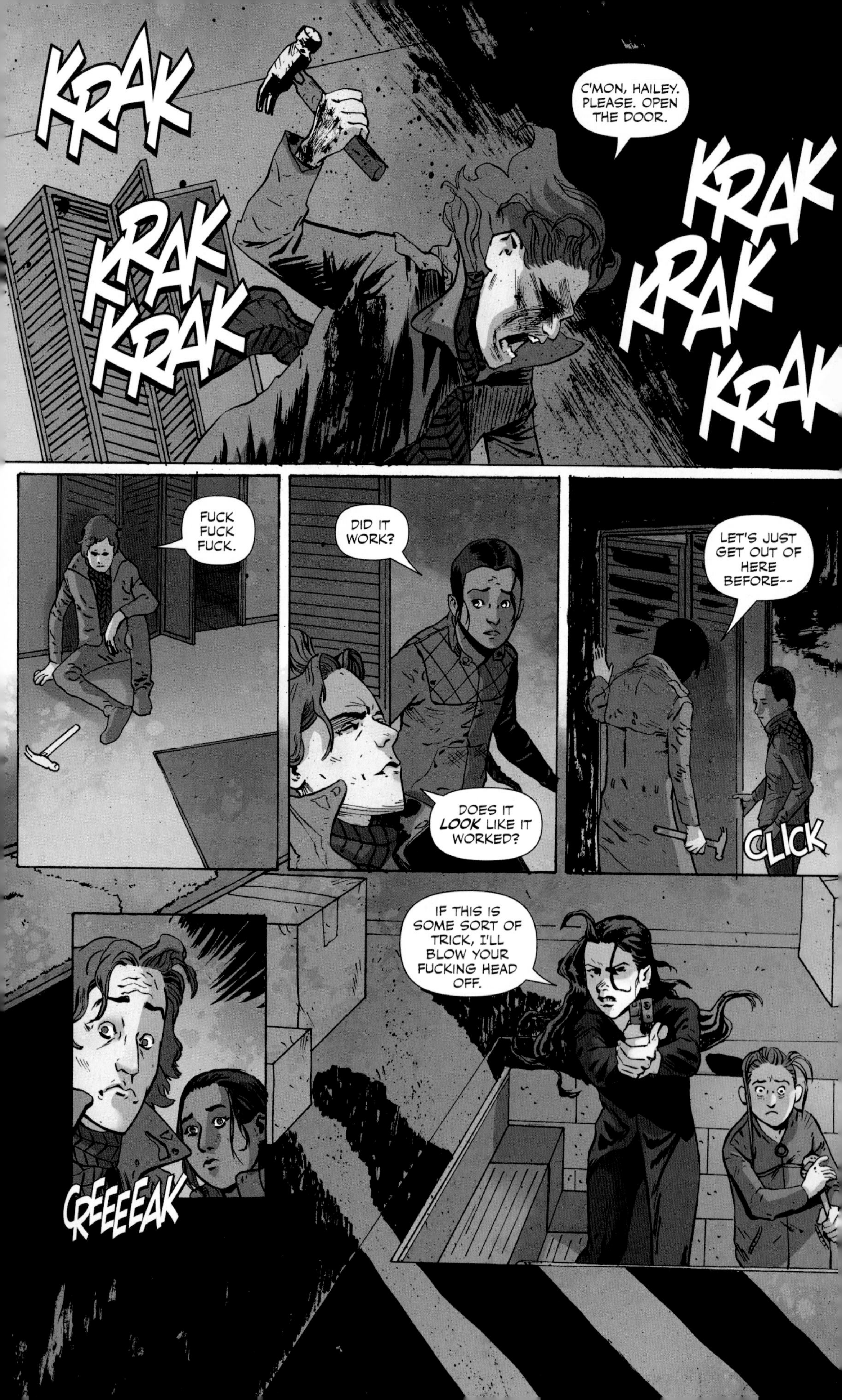
KRAK
C'MON, HAILEY. PLEASE. OPEN THE DOOR.
KRAK KRAK KRAK
KRAK KRAK KRAK
FUCK FUCK FUCK.
DID IT WORK?
DOES IT LOOK LIKE IT WORKED?
LET'S JUST GET OUT OF HERE BEFORE--
CLICK
CREEEEAK
IF THIS IS SOME SORT OF TRICK, I'LL BLOW YOUR FUCKING HEAD OFF.

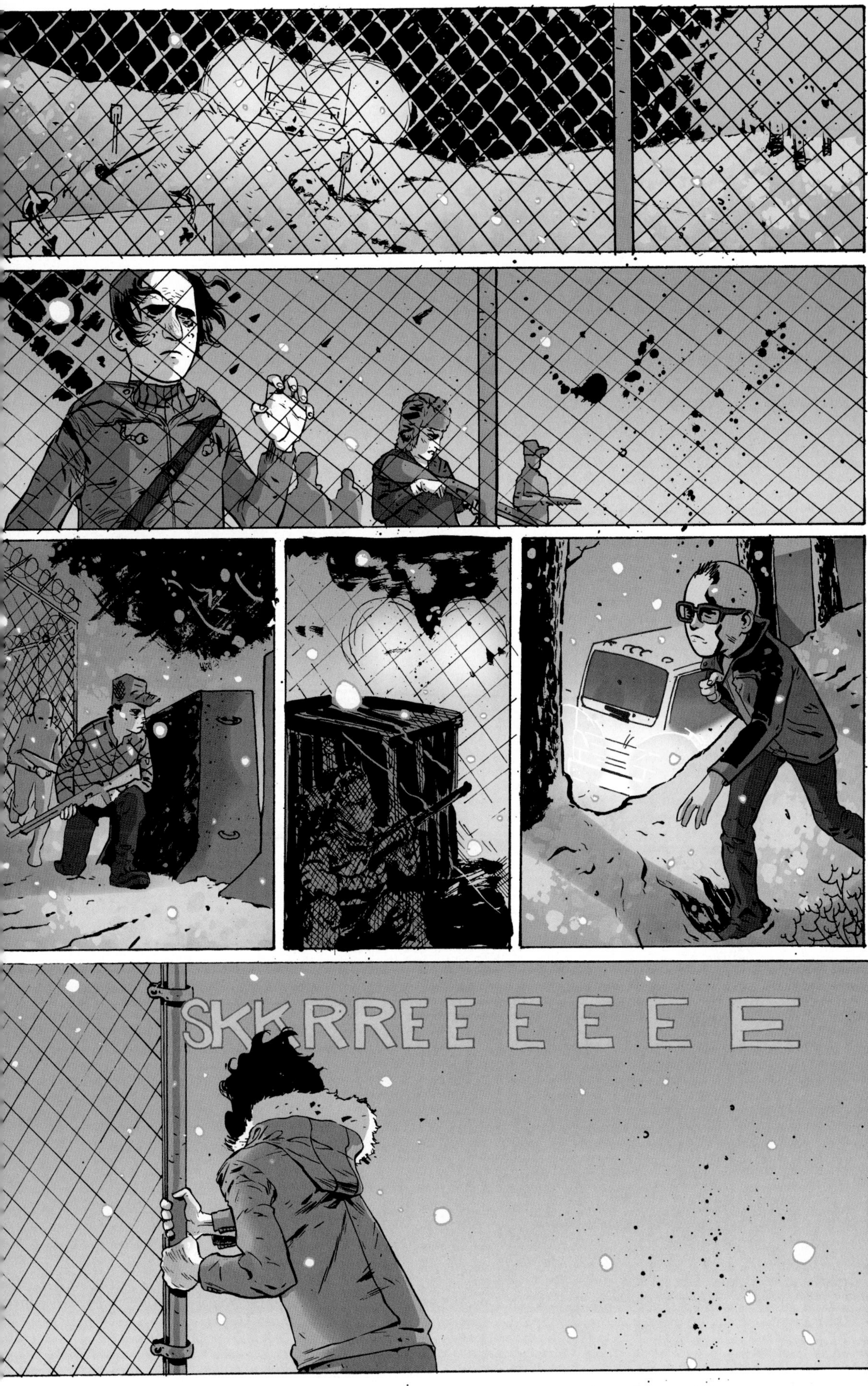
SKKRREEEEEE

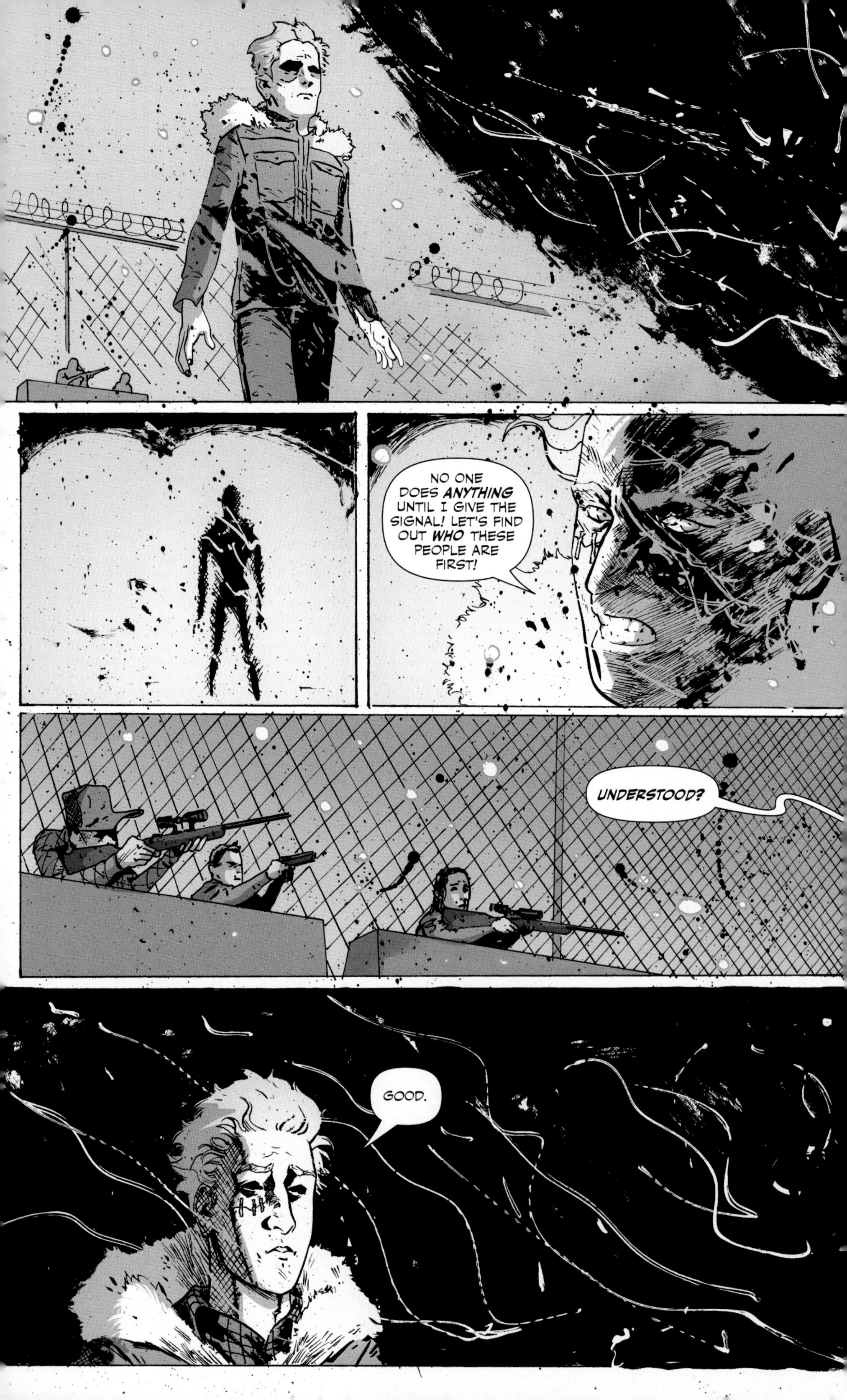

NO ONE DOES ANYTHING UNTIL I GIVE THE SIGNAL! LET'S FIND OUT WHO THESE PEOPLE ARE FIRST!
UNDERSTOOD?
GOOD.

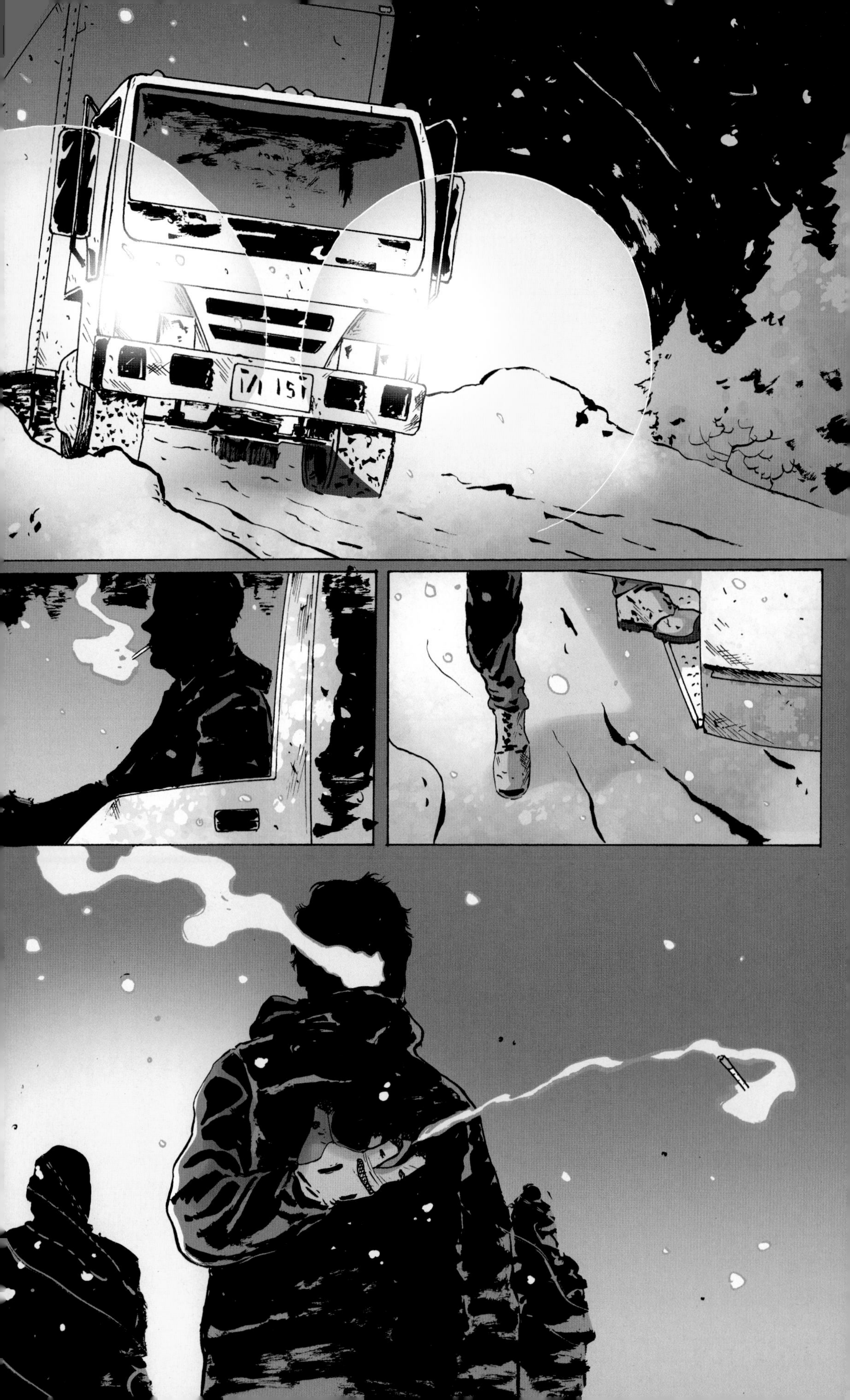

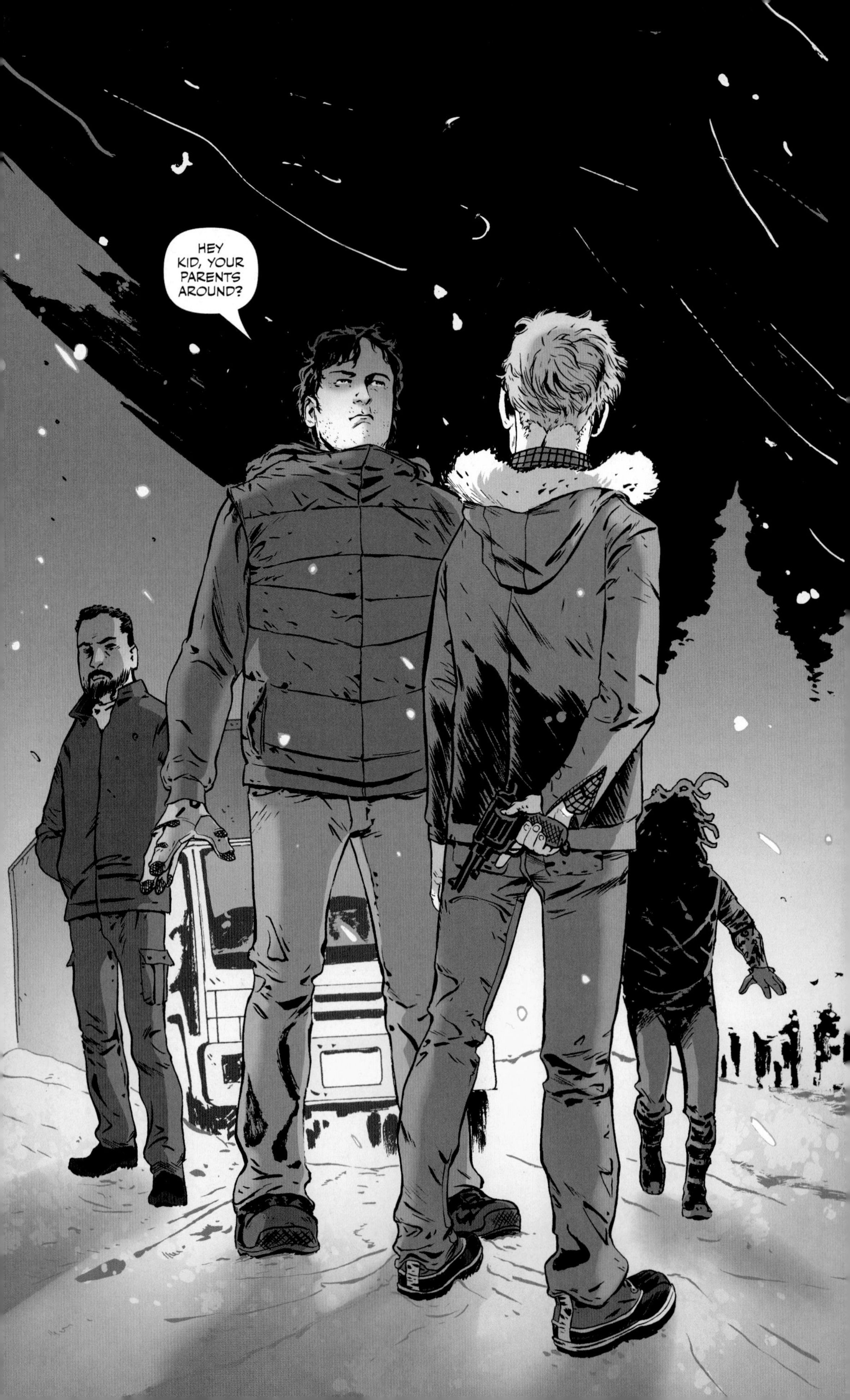
HEY KID, YOUR PARENTS AROUND?

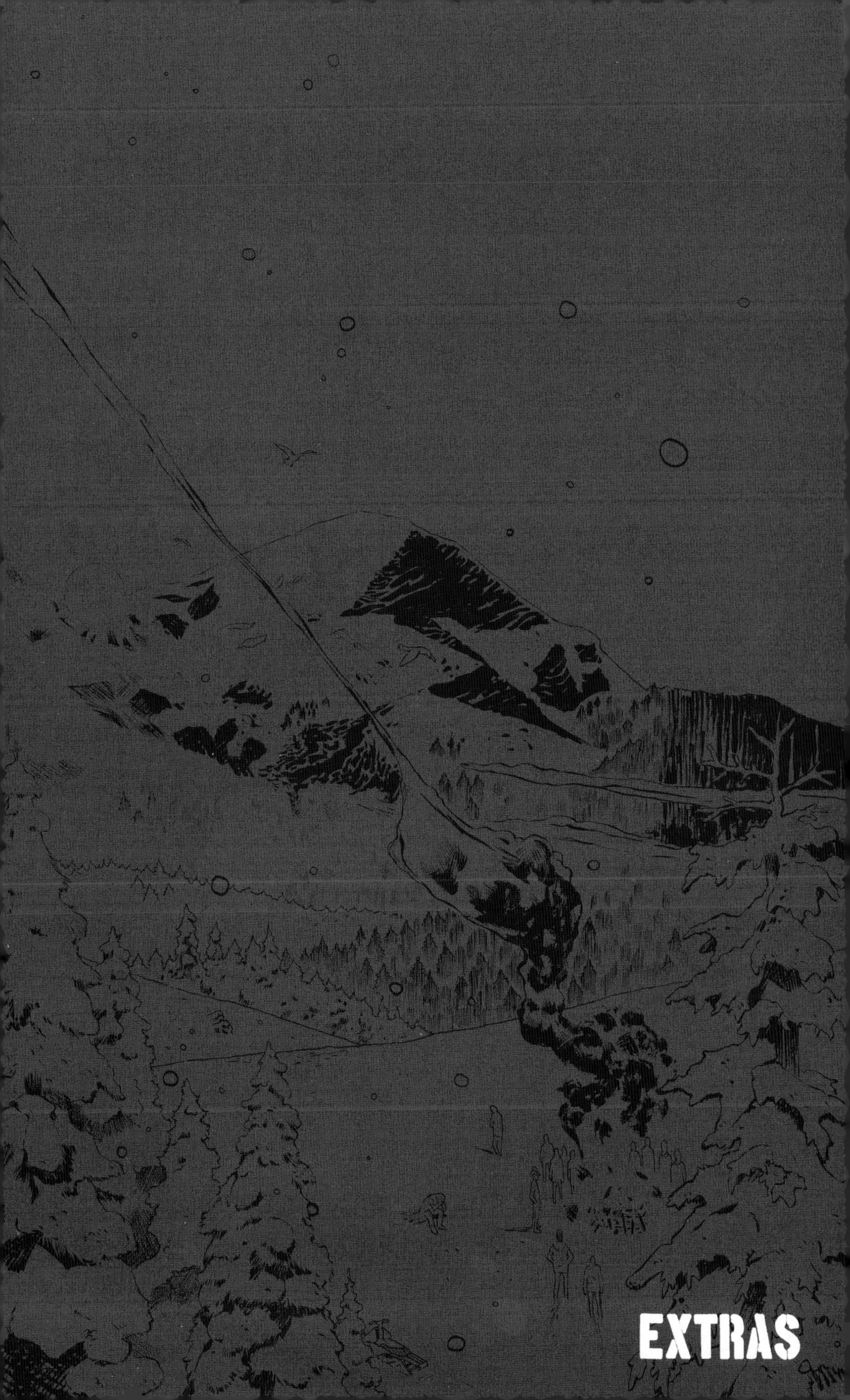

EXTRAS

JOHNNIE'S SKETCHBOOK

Opposites even in character design, I toyed around with a few ideas for Victoria's look before finding the one I liked. Whereas Lucas' look came together almost instantly.

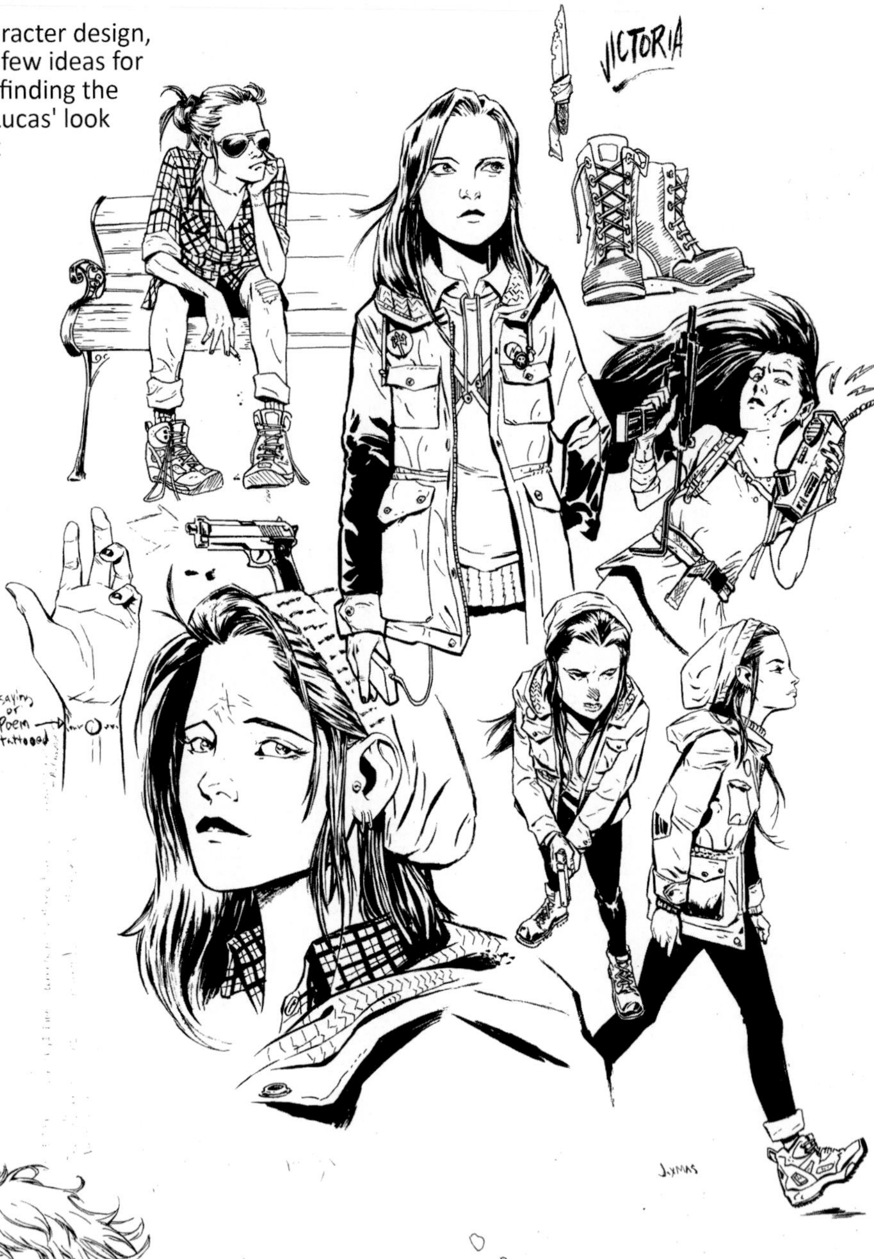
VICTORIA
saying or Poem tattooed

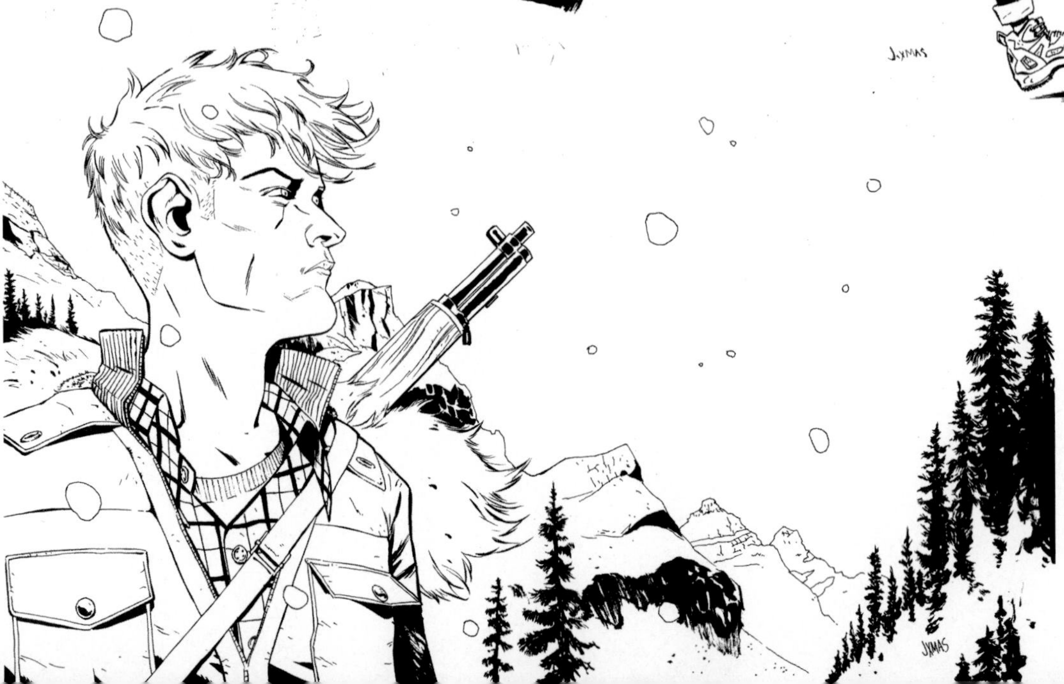

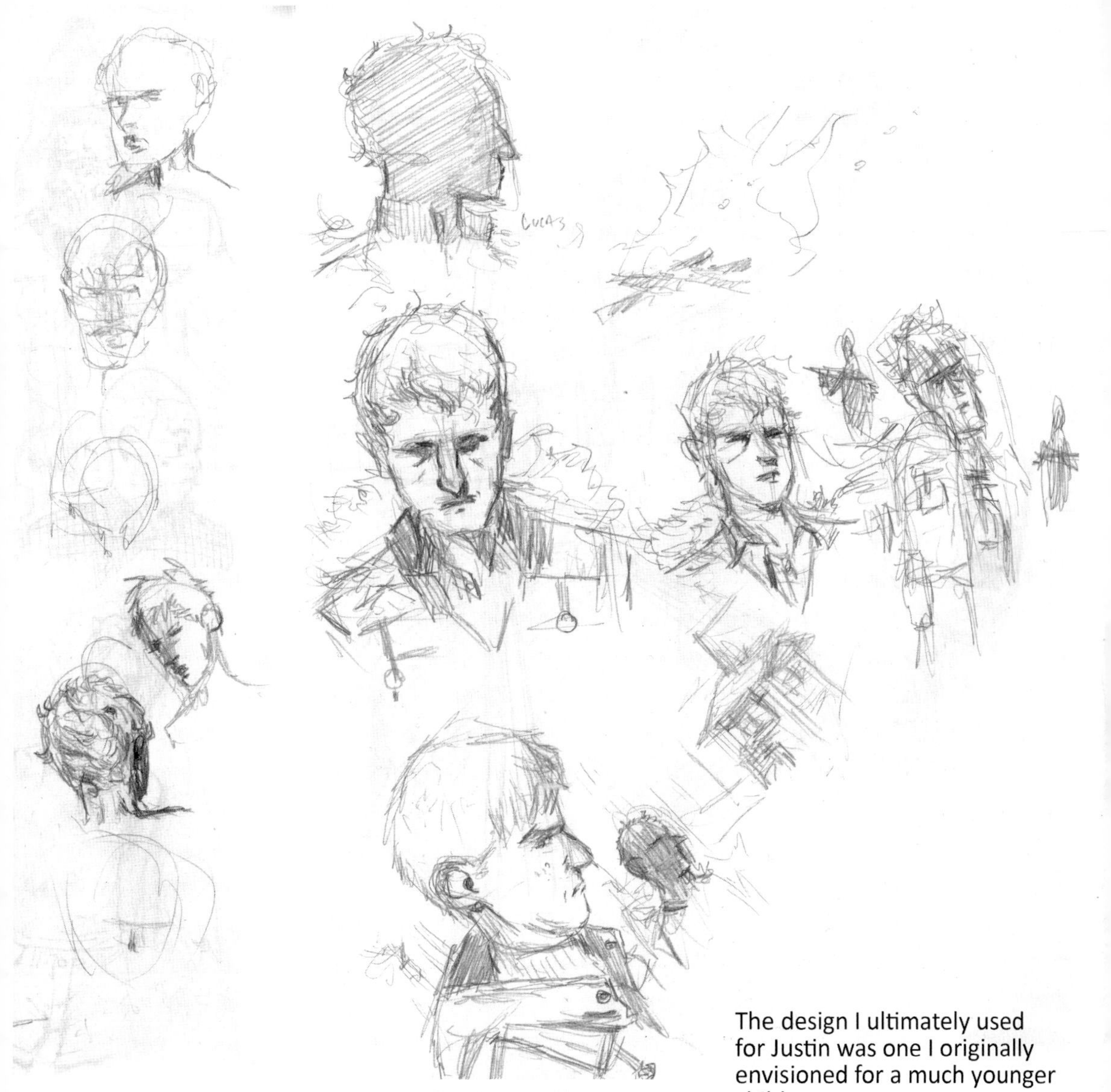
Lucas

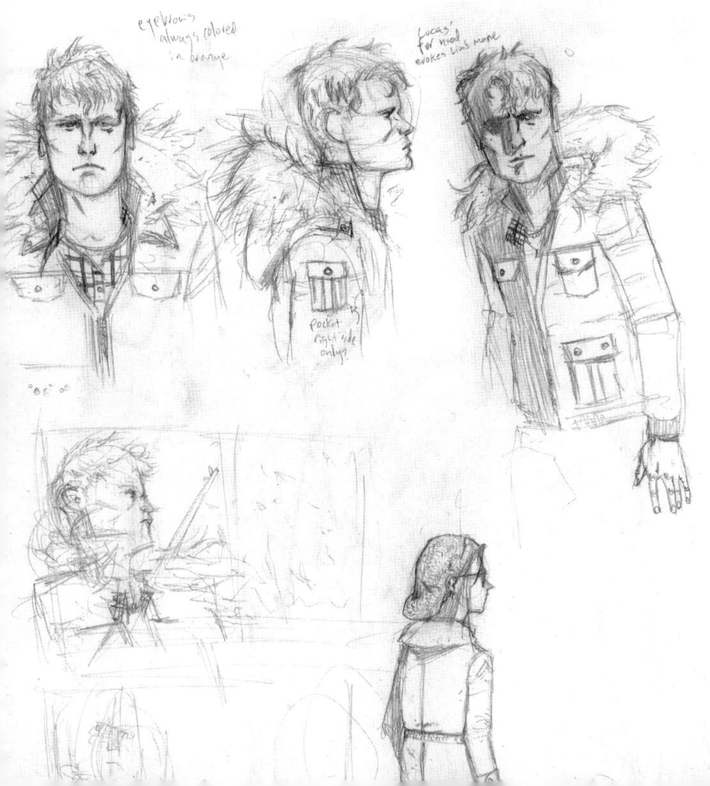
eyebrows always colored in orange
Lucas' fur hood evokes lion's mane
pocket right side only?

The design I ultimately used for Justin was one I originally envisioned for a much younger child.

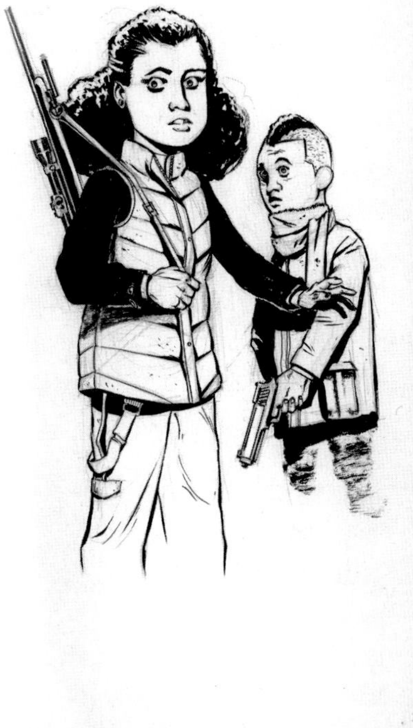

PROCESS: FROM SCRIPT TO FINAL

PAGE EIGHT

PANEL 1

Curt pushes Joey back. Shit is on.

CURT: You can't tell us what to do.

PANEL 2

Joey lands on his ass. Cookies and cereal flying everywhere.

JOEY: oof.

PANEL 3

Curt and Robin are on top of Joey. Joey throws his hands up to protect himself.

PANEL 4

They're raining blows down on poor, poor Joey. This should be an emotional, cathartic moment for the kids. There's a lot of pent up aggression coming out. Have some tears welling up in Curt's eyes.

CURT: YOU CAN'T TELL US WHAT TO DO!

PANEL 5

End this page on a nice shot of the cookies and cereal spilled all over the place in the foreground and the two kids beating the fuck out of Joey in the background.

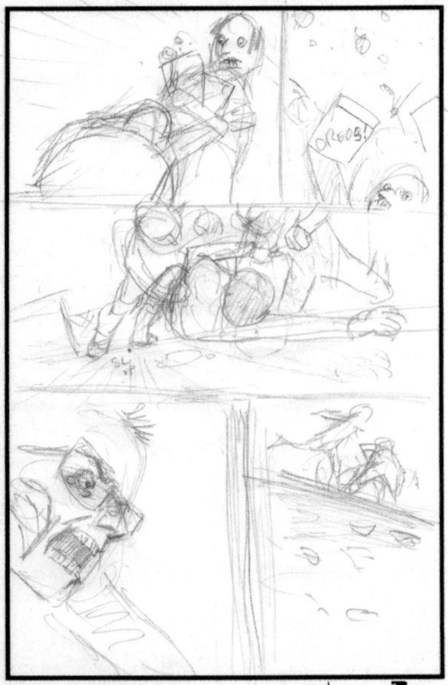

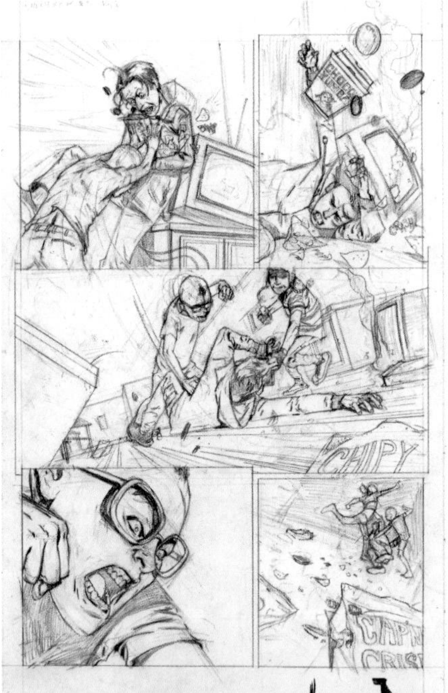
CHIPY

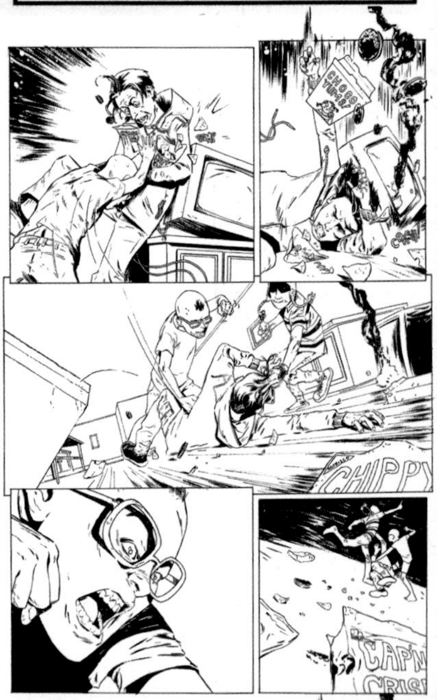
CHIPPY

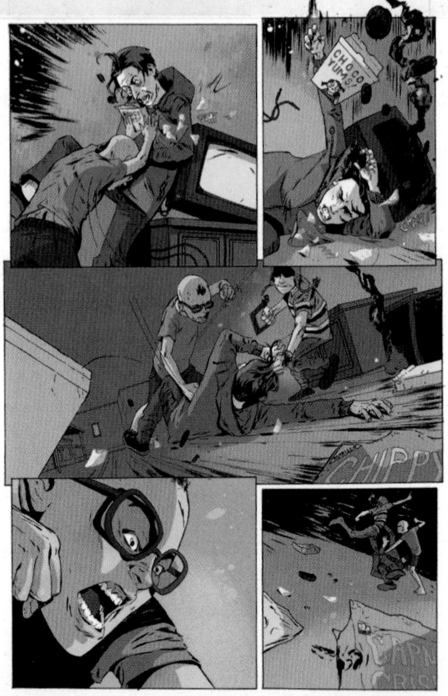

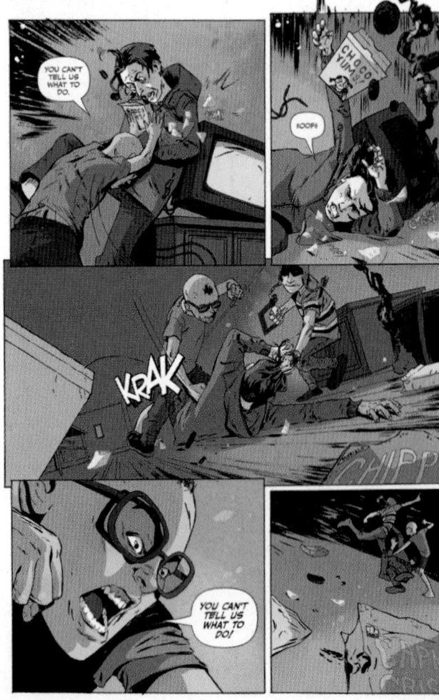
YOU CAN'T TELL US WHAT TO DO.
!OOF!
KRAK
YOU CAN'T TELL US WHAT TO DO!

AN OLD BEGINNING

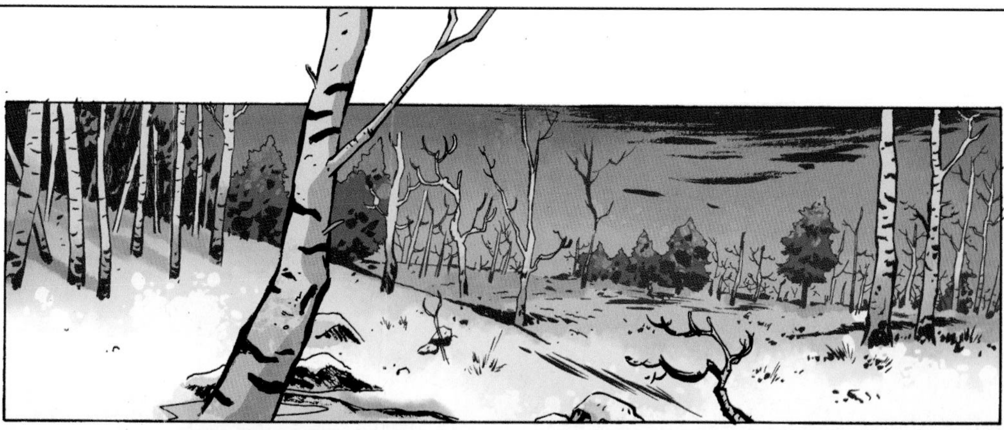

In the early stages of developing SHELTERED, we were initially going to have the killing of the adults of Safe Haven happen in the first few pages of the first issue and move the story forward from there. We later decided that we wanted to give a bit more information and set some things up first, so decided to move that scene to the end of the first issue.

This page was originally intended to be the very first page of the series, but was scrapped when we moved the death scene . As you can see, we were just going to drop the reader right into the thick of things.

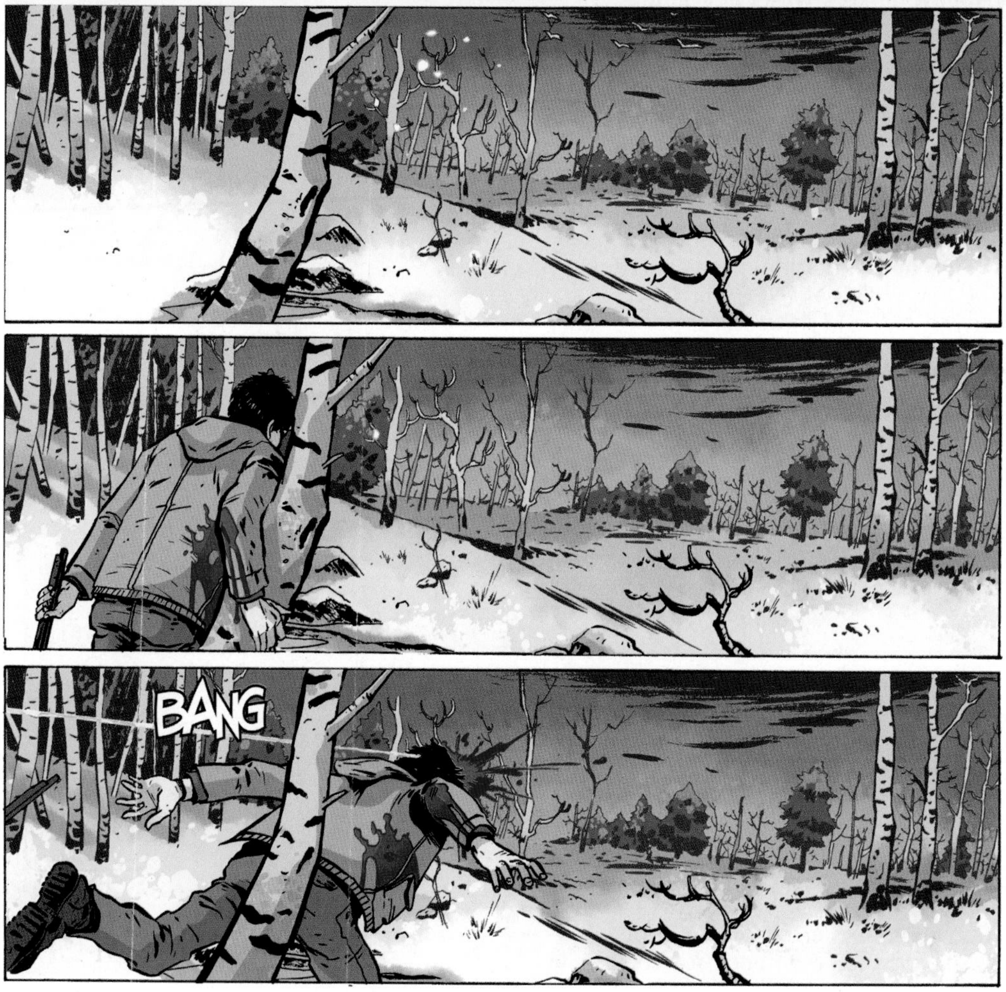
BANG

JOHNNIE

Johnnie Christmas has illustrated stories seen in CONTINUUM: THE WAR FILES, A Graphic Novel companion to the Syfy/Showcase series, MURDER BOOK, as well as self-penned stories appearing in the Cloudscape Society anthologies EXPLODED VIEW, 21 JOURNEYS and GIANTS OF MAIN STREET.

A graduate of the Pratt Institute in Brooklyn, NY, Johnnie lives in Vancouver, BC.

You can follow him on twitter at @j_xmas.

ED

Ed Brisson is the writer behind the creator-owned series MURDER BOOK and COMEBACK. He's also written for Marvel, BOOM!, IDW and others.

He lives in Vancouver, BC with his wife, their daughter and far too many pets.

You can follow him on twitter at @edbrisson.

SHARI

Shari Chankhamma is from Thailand and has been working as a freelance colorist for about a year now. She has also written and illustrated her own creator-owned titles such as: THE SISTERS' LUCK, THE CLARENCE PRINCIPLE, PAVLOV'S DREAM, and short stories for various anthologies.

She enjoys wasting what little spare time she has on casual games and romance novels.

You can follow her on twitter at @sharihes.

PAUL

Paul Allor is a comic-book writer, editor and letterer who lives in Kokomo, Indiana. He has worked on GI JOE and TEENAGE MUTANT NINJA TURTLES for IDW publishing, as well as writing creator-owned books such as STRANGE NATION and ORC GIRL.

Paul is also on staff at Andy Schmidt's Comics Experience, where he teaches a class on comics production and offers professional script critiques to workshop members. You can follow him on Twitter at @PaulAllor